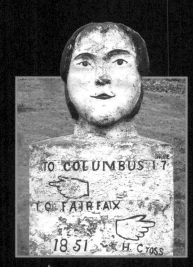

Weird Indiana

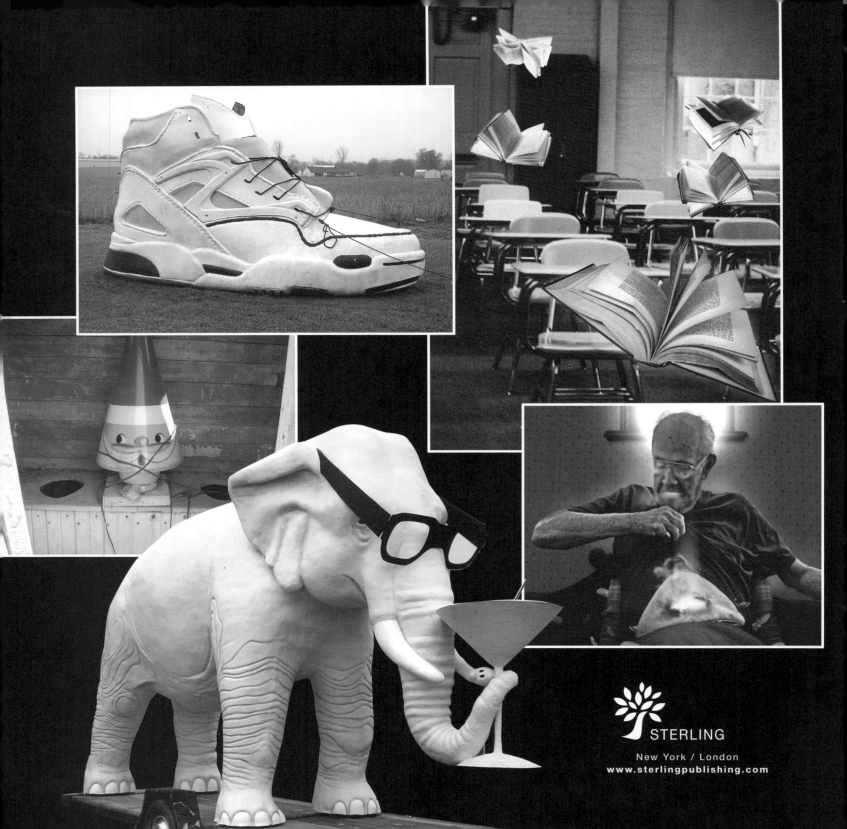

STERLING

New York / London
www.sterlingpublishing.com

Weird Indiana

Your Travel Guide to Indiana's Local Legends and Best Kept Secrets

by MARK MARIMEN, JAMES A. WILLIS, and TROY TAYLOR

Mark Sceurman and Mark Moran, Executive Editors

Baby Ruth
Age 19
weight 702 lbs.

WEiRD INDiANA

STERLING and the distinctive Sterling logo are registered trademarks of Sterling Publishing Co., Inc.

Photography and illustration credits are found on page 253 and constitute an extension of this copyright page.

Library of Congress Cataloging-in-Publication Data Available

10 9 8 7 6 5 4 3 2 1

Published by Sterling Publishing Co., Inc.
387 Park Avenue South, New York, NY 10016

© 2008 by Mark Sceurman and Mark Moran

Distributed in Canada by Sterling Publishing
c/o Canadian Manda Group, 165 Dufferin Street
Toronto, Ontario, Canada M6K 3H6

Distributed in the United Kingdom by GMC Distribution Services
Castle Place, 166 High Street, Lewes, East Sussex, England BN7 1XU

Distributed in Australia by Capricorn Link (Australia) Pty. Ltd.
P.O. Box 704, Windsor, NSW 2756, Australia

Manufactured in China. All rights reserved.

Sterling ISBN 13: 978-1-4027-5452-4
Sterling ISBN 10: 1-4027-5452-3

For information about custom editions, special sales, premium and corporate purchases, please contact Sterling Special Sales Department at 800-805-5489 or specialsales@sterlingpublishing.com.

Design: Richard J. Berenson
    Berenson Design & Books, LLC, New York, NY

CONTENTS

A Note from the Marks

Our weird journey began a long, long time ago in a far-off land called New Jersey. Once a year or so, we'd compile a homespun newsletter called *Weird N.J.,* then pass it on to our friends. The pamphlet was a collection of odd news clippings, bizarre facts, little-known historical anecdotes, and anomalous encounters from our home state. The newsletter also included the kinds of localized legends that were often whispered around a particular town but seldom heard outside the boundaries of the community where they originated.

We had started *Weird N.J.* on the simple theory that every town in the state had at least one good tale to tell. The publication soon became a full-fledged magazine, and we made the decision to actually do our own investigating to see if we could track down where all of these seemingly unbelievable stories were coming from. Was there, we wondered, any factual basis for the fantastic local legends people were telling us about? Armed with not much more than a camera and a notepad, we set off on a mystical journey of discovery. Much to our surprise and amazement, a lot of what we had initially presumed to be nothing more than urban legends turned out to be real—or at least to contain a grain of truth, which had sparked the lore to begin with.

After a dozen years of documenting the bizarre, we were asked to write a book about our adventures, and so *Weird N.J.: Your Travel Guide to New Jersey's Local Legends and Best Kept Secrets* was published in 2003. Soon people from all over the country began writing to us, telling us strange tales from their home state. As it turned out, what we had perceived to be something of very local interest was actually just a small part of a larger and more universal phenomenon.

After *Weird N.J.,* we wrote *Weird U.S.,* in which we documented the local legends and strangest stories from all over the country. We set out in search of weirdness wherever it might be found in the fifty states. And indeed, we found plenty of it!

After *Weird U.S.* was published, we came to the conclusion that this country had more great tales than could be contained in just one book. Everywhere we looked, we found unwritten folklore, creepy cemeteries, cursed locations, and outlandish roadside oddities. We wanted to document it all in a series of books, each focusing on the peculiarities of a particular state.

author of *Weird Ohio*. Jim is best known for his writings on The Ghosts of Ohio, and we found him to be quite a gifted storyteller in all manner of the strange. His contributions to chapters such as "Roadside Oddities" and "Personalized Properties" give a rarely seen side of his talent—a wickedly keen sense of humor.

The third and final author we recruited for this project was Troy Taylor, a longtime *Weird U.S.* compatriot and kindred spirit in weirdness, who is perhaps the most prolific chronicler of American hauntings to ever put pen to paper. With our team of one native Hoosier and authors storming in from Ohio and Illinois, we were prepared to cover a lot of weird territory!

Mark, Jim, and Troy all have what we refer to as the Weird Eye, which requires one to see the world in a different way, with a renewed sense of wonder. And once you have it, there is no going back—you'll never see things the same way again. All of a sudden you begin noticing your everyday surroundings as if for the first time. And you begin to ask yourself, "What the heck is that thing all about, anyway?" and "Doesn't anybody else think that's kind of weird?"

So come with us now and let Mark, Jim, and Troy take you on a tour of the Hoosier State, with all of its haunting anomalies, strange sites, and unique characters. It is a state of mind we like to call *Weird Indiana*.

–Mark Sceurman and Mark Moran

One state we thought we might have trouble compiling a *Weird* book on was Indiana. We'd traversed the state several times in our research journeys, and we began to develop the impression that Indiana was far too flat and wholesome a place to harbor enough oddities to fill a book. But boy were we wrong! After reading the works of Mark Marimen, we found that the state actually had a very rich and colorful weird side to it. Just goes to show, you can never really sum up a state by what you see on its surface. Mark Marimen, a true authority on Indiana ghosts if ever there was one, was the first author we contacted to work with us, and to our delight he jumped at the opportunity.

Then we set out to assemble a team of investigators to work with Mark to travel around the state and dig into all its mysteries, both past and present, wherever they were to be found. The second author we invited to come aboard for this weird ride was Jim Willis, co-

Introduction

indiana has long garnered the reputation as an utterly normal, conventional, "white bread," midwestern state. From the industrial region of the northwest to the seemingly endless panorama of cornfields through the central section of the state to the rolling hills in the south, there is little in our geography to suggest the exotic or remarkable. When driving through the barren cornfields of central Indiana in January, it would be hard to imagine a less romantic landscape this side of the craters of the moon, yet perhaps this accounts for the pragmatic nature of its residents. Indeed, born of practical farming settlers and hardscrabble immigrants in search of a better life, the Hoosier State seems to have instilled its inhabitants with a matter-of-fact nature that would seem to leave little room for whimsy or mystery.

However, when one scratches this thin veneer of prosaic rationality there lies beneath a darker, more mysterious realm. For under the no-nonsense façade of farm fields, small towns, and urban blight, the state of Indiana is replete with ghostly tales. The Hoosier State plays host to strange stories of the restless dead and a legion of things that go bump (not to mention screech and groan) in the night. Theirs is a dim and often overlooked part of Indiana history and culture, yet they are as much a part of that culture as the smoke from steel mills or the harvest moon setting over a cornfield. Some are legends older than the state itself, while others are whispered stories of strange occurrences from our not so distant past. Whatever their history, these stories hint that there may be much more to Indiana than meets the eye.

For the past ten years, it has been my privilege to research and chronicle some of these tales. Time and again I have said that I do not consider myself a writer or even a storyteller, but a story reteller. It all began long ago when I talked about the idea of a book on Indiana ghost stories to a professor of folklore and was told, "Try as hard as you want, but you will never find enough ghost stories in Indiana to make a book." I have always been a sucker for a challenge, especially when someone informs me that it cannot be done, and so I decided to take on the task.

Now, ten years and six books later, I realize I have barely scratched the surface. Today I know what I suspected ten years ago—there are more tales in Indiana than I could retell in a lifetime. There truly is more to Indiana than meets the eye. Enjoy the tall tales, mysterious happenings, and odd history from our state. Trust me, it is worth the tour.*–Mark Marimen*

For over eight years now, I have been driving from Columbus, Ohio, to Indianapolis, Indiana, on business—a three-hour journey that takes me along a pretty bland stretch of I-70. For most people the ride gives the impression that there's nothing out there. But I knew better. And each time I found myself crossing under the I-70 arch and into Indiana, my Weird Eye would start twitching. It was letting me know that somewhere out there, lurking behind the cornfields, were giant cow statues, homemade roller coasters, and haunted bridges. I couldn't see them from the highway, but they were out there, daring me to come find them. So when Mark and Mark approached me to help write *Weird Indiana*, I jumped at the chance.

Michael Jackson was born in Indiana. Johnny Appleseed died here. So you could make the claim that Indiana's got their weirdness covered from the cradle to the grave. Somewhere between all the being born and dying lies a whole mess of weirdness too. For instance, leave it to an Indianan to celebrate the state's being named the limestone capital of the world by attempting to open a theme park dedicated to enormous objects built out of the sedimentary rock. And who else but Indianans would, in a stroke of genius, officially name a creek Nameless Creek? Their roads are weird too. While locals think nothing of directions that tell them to head south on W 300 N until it intersects with E 965 S, the rest of us drive around scratching our heads for hours.

After wrapping up my last story, I made my way back to Ohio. Just as I crossed over the Indiana state line, I swore I heard a strange bansheelike cry coming from somewhere behind my car. It was as if the very essence of the whole state of Indiana was calling me back to uncover even more of its legends and safely guarded secrets.–*Jim Willis*

Growing up in Illinois, I felt a closer kinship with Indiana than with any other state. Indiana was the other state, besides Illinois, that everyone claimed was nothing but cornfields. Of course, as we all know, this statement couldn't be further from the truth!

With my affection toward all things Hoosier in mind, I was thrilled to be asked to take part in another project from the twisted minds of Mark Moran and Mark Sceurman, and with Mark Marimen and Jim Willis. I then set out to explore the history, strange mysteries, spooky abandoned spots, and downright weirdness that make up the state of Indiana.

My journeys would take me from abandoned places to lakes with giant turtles and sea serpents. I hunted for phantom panthers, searched for deserted health spas, bottomless ponds, vanished towns, ghost lights, gravity hills, and more. Indiana is far more than just cornfields—it's a weird traveler's paradise!

I hope you enjoy coming along on our weird journey through Indiana's cities, small towns, and forests and over our hills and down our creepy back roads. Just be sure to keep your headlights on and your doors locked—you never know who, or what, may be waiting around the next bend in the road!–*Troy Taylor*

Local Legends and Lore

Hidden among the cornfields and forests of the state of Indiana are mysterious places that give rise to strange tales. Whether or not these eerie stories are really true will probably never be known. But almost every legend, no matter how bizarre it might seem, has a kernel of truth at its heart.

The tales in the pages that follow are what we at *Weird Indiana* like to refer to as local legends. These stories are different from the stuff of "urban legend," which so many of us are familiar with. These are not myths passed on by "friends of friends." Unlike that kind of vague yarn, Indiana's local legends spring from a particular location, person, or thing, be it James Dean's cursed Porsche, a deadly homemade guillotine, or even the infamous Bloody Mary.

Shades of Death State Park

For most Hoosiers, Shades State Park awakens images of lush green forests that cast dark shadows, and gorges and ravines so deep that even the brightest sunshine is unable to penetrate them. Most people assume that these natural wonders account for the name of this beautiful park, but weird travelers know different. They know that the park's original name was Shades of Death, and that this creepy name came not from forests, rocks, and valleys in shadow, but rather from a dark and blood-soaked history!

Shades State Park, near Waveland, is a nature lover's paradise. Its sandstone cliffs, rugged ravines, and winding trails make an awesome backdrop for a journey into the great outdoors. Thousands travel here to take in the scenery and hike its paths. Long before these outdoor enthusiasts came here, and even long before the first settlers arrived, Native Americans lived in the forests along the Sugar Creek. A large village of the Piankeshaw tribe, an offshoot of the Miami Indians, was once located in the natural stronghold of the cliffs and ravines.

According to some legends, the park came by its unusual name, Shades of Death, because of a bloody battle that took place between the Miami Indians and another, unnamed, tribe. During the battle, more than six hundred warriors fought hand to hand for hours among the trees and rocks. At the battle's end, only twelve men remained standing—just seven from the winning tribe. This horrific tale was still told years later, convincing the settlers to give the area its grim name.

This is one version of the story. Another legend, however, points to a different source—a terrible murder that occurred many years later.

The first settlers came to this area in the late 1820s, after the Miami tribe had ceded the land to the federal government. The shallow soil and rocky terrain along Sugar Creek offered little enticement to farmers, so the forested land remained largely uninhabited for years. In the mid-1800s, developers turned it into a health resort and recreation area. A forty-room inn was built then, but that was eventually torn down because of fire damage.

Joseph W. Frisz owned the property until the 1930s, and he protected its dense forests and natural outcroppings. Thanks, in part, to a public subscription campaign, his heirs helped to turn it into a state park in 1947. It had already acquired the name Shades of Death by then, which was seen as unsavory, so the name was cut to Shades.

In 1919, a newspaper reporter from Indianapolis, named Mary H. Krout, stumbled onto the real story behind Shades of Death. It was not the dark forest of trees and ominous canyons, or even the catastrophic Indian battle, that had earned the region its moniker. It was a blood-curdling axe murder that occurred when a woman could no longer tolerate the abuse that she was suffering at the hands of her husband.

According to the legend, the murderess was the young wife of a settler who came to the area and built a house in the forest. The man was a drunkard who beat his wife unmercifully. One night, she turned the tables on her abusive spouse. After he passed out from drinking a full bottle of whiskey, she took the axe, which her husband had often threatened to use to kill her, and she struck him in the head with it.

When neighbors discovered the body the following day, the young wife told her story, and they allowed her to go free. The men buried the husband's body somewhere in the woods, and the justifiable homicide remained a closely guarded secret for several years. When people did start to talk about it, they were inspired to give the woods its macabre name—Shades of Death.

Bloody Mary Whales

The story of Bloody Mary, a ghost who appears in a mirror when summoned, has been told many times in countless ways. Depending on the version you hear, its leading character is known by any number of names, including Mary Worth, Mary Johnson, and Mary Lou. But in Indiana, she is known as Mary Whales. According to some, she was a real person who lived—and died—in Lake County.

Local legend has it that the Whales family was well known in the region during the years before the Civil War, although not for good reasons. Joseph Whales was said to be a notorious slave-catcher, preying on free blacks and those who fled from slavery in the southern states. Many of the escapees came through Indiana via the Underground Railroad, hiding in homes, barns, and other buildings during the day and using back roads and forest trails to keep moving north once darkness fell. Often, however, they ended up in the clutches of Joseph Whales and his henchmen. The fugitives were allegedly kept chained in the basement of Whales's farmhouse until they could be sold back into slavery.

Whales's wife, Virginia, was said to be a docile woman who lived in great fear of her husband. She evidently had nothing to fear, though, for the only thing in the world that Joseph loved more than money was his wife. When Virginia died giving birth to Mary, Whales was grief-stricken. Severely depressed, he allowed both his farm and his slave-catching business to go to pieces. His fields became overrun with weeds, his home and barns fell into disrepair, and several slaves he had captured managed to escape after being left to starve to death in the cellar.

Whales hated his daughter because she had caused his wife's death, but he kept little Mary alive because she was the only living link to his beloved Virginia. He fed and clothed the child, and after recovering his senses, managed to eke out a living from his farm after the Civil War. Residents of the small towns in the area largely avoided the Whales farm. Joseph had a reputation as an unfriendly man, and he never spoke to anyone when he came into town for supplies. The women did talk about his pretty little girl, though, who was often seen seated next to her unkempt and unshaven father when he came to town in his wagon. The little girl's hair was long and tangled, and her dress was always filthy. She did not go to school with the other children, and throughout her life, no one ever heard her speak.

As Mary grew older, she became even more beautiful, increasingly resembling her mother. In the evenings, Mary sat by the fire and sewed, or read from her books while her father stared at her with hate in his eyes. His drinking got worse and his loathing of the young woman grew stronger as time passed. Finally, one night, he could stand it no more.

While Mary was sleeping, Whales entered her room with a carving knife in his hands and liquor on his breath. He looked down at the young woman who had "killed" his beloved wife—and began slashing at her, over and over again. Mary screamed and thrashed about, but her father had no mercy. When the girl stopped moving, he left her lying there and stumbled out of her bedroom.

The morning light brought clarity to Joseph Whales's whiskey-soaked brain, and he entered his daughter's room to see what he had done to her. But even her bloody body could not erase the anger that he felt toward her. He shed no tears as he carried her down into the cellar and buried her body under the earthen floor. No stone was used to mark her grave. He covered her still form with dirt and tried to forget that she had ever existed.

In this, Joseph Whales was not successful. The stories say that the restless spirit of his daughter hounded him day and night. This once quiet and demure young woman became a vengeful specter, haunting the farmhouse and plaguing her murderous father.

Eventually, Whales hanged himself in the barn. His body was discovered weeks later by neighbors who tried to return cattle that had wandered away. When they searched the house, they found the hastily buried, decomposed body of Mary Whales in the cellar. They also discovered a scrawled suicide note on the kitchen table with an account of the crime that Whales had carried out. And the legend of Bloody Mary was born.

In the years that followed, children in the region breathlessly whispered about Joseph Whales's heinous act, Mary's mutilated body, and her spirit's appetite for vengeance. If you called on her, the stories claimed, she would return from the grave and slash your face to look like her own.

But is there any truth to the story? According to some Lake County residents, there most certainly is!

As time passed, the Whales farmhouse became dilapidated and was known as the local "haunted house." Stories circulated that Mary's ghost lingered there, and those who dared to trespass on the property sometimes found mysterious scratches on their faces and arms—a warning from Mary to leave. One night in the 1940s, the house burned to the ground. Authorities blamed it on teenagers, but rumors persisted that Mary had destroyed it.

Nearly a decade later, a local farmer purchased the Whales property with the intention of building a new home for his family on the stone foundation of the old house. But the project was tainted with bad luck from the start. The new house had problems with the floors, the roof, and the electrical system, which caused a fire one night that almost cost the family their lives. Expensive repairs were made, but the bad luck continued. One of the children was seriously injured in an automobile accident and then the farmer and his wife went through a nasty divorce.

The fate of the house was in limbo. No one was interested in living there, and it was finally torn down in the mid-1980s. The land it sat on is now farmland once again.

With the house gone, was the ghost of Mary Whales finally set free? Not according to local lore. After the discovery of her body in the cellar of the house, Mary was allegedly buried in an unmarked grave in a nearby cemetery, a lonely graveyard that soon gained a reputation for being haunted. Visitors claimed that the scratches and cuts suffered by trespassers at Mary's house also began to plague those visiting the cemetery. Curiosity seekers maintained that after the Whales house burned to the ground, Mary's ghost began attacking those who came to the cemetery instead. Some claim that she still haunts the place today.

But, of course, if you're looking for the spirit of Bloody Mary, you need look no further than your bathroom mirror. Whether you are in northwest Indiana or anywhere else, all you have to do is turn down the lights and call her name:

Bloody Mary.
Bloody Mary.
Bloody Mary.

Just don't hold us responsible if she actually shows up!

Mary Haunts Vernon Too

There is a little town called Vernon in southern Indiana with an awesome Bloody Mary story. According to the legend, Bloody Mary was a witch who was buried in a local cemetery. If you curse over her grave, you will bleed before leaving the cemetery.

My friends and I used to frequent the cemetery in the 1980s, and the brave ones would curse over her grave. More often than not, they would end up bleeding before we left the cemetery, either from getting stuck by a briar, falling down, or in one case a girl fell from the back of a moving pick-up truck while leaving the cemetery and her leg was run over.

The last few times we went, we were unable to locate Mary's actual grave because her tombstone had been moved or stolen. There is also a footpath that leads from the cemetery down to the Muskatatuk River. Along the path are the remnants of an old mill. Not much of the mill remains, but I always heard stories that somehow Mary had something to do with the mill.—*Sue Jordan*

Doc Johnson's All Torn Up

My husband tells a story from his hometown, Sandborn. It's a small town on State Hwy 67, south of Indianapolis. Supposedly, long before our time, there was a doctor who had an office in Sandborn, but he lived just outside of town. Old Doc Johnson never failed to come into his office, come hell or high water as they say. So there was a concern when he didn't make it into the office one day, or the next, either.

After the second day, some folks from town went to check on him, and they found a scene straight from a gore movie. He and his wife were in pieces strewn all over the yard, hanging from the trees, etc. Some say there is no way it was done by a human. The tale is that the doc and his wife were torn apart by banshees. Don't know how I feel about that theory, but I do know when you drive out to where his home used to stand, you notice the complete lack of sound. Not one animal is in sight or making noises. No birds, dogs, nothing!

There is part of an old riverbed that runs through the property and it is completely devoid of any type of fish or aquatic animal. Supposedly a farmer who farms the land there had his tractor start up and proceed to ditch itself in the old bed . . . all by itself. My husband took me out there for a "thrill" one time and I have to admit the hair stood up on the back of my neck. But the mind can make you feel, see and hear some strange stuff when there has been the hint of a suggestion. Don't you think?—*Angela Grigsby*

The Lafayette Guillotine

The name James Moon still conjures up a strange reaction in the city of Lafayette today, as well as a few nervous chuckles when residents are reminded about who this ill-fated farmer actually was. They may not remember the name, but they always remember the guillotine that he invented—and that he used to sever his own head!

James Moon was only thirty-seven when he decided that his life was no longer worth living. The farmer and self-taught blacksmith had land nine miles west of Lafayette but didn't want to end his life at his secluded farm. He wanted his body to be discovered, and he wanted to make sure that people talked about his suicide for many years to come. In that, he would not be disappointed.

On June 10, 1876, Moon traveled to Lafayette and checked into the Lahr Hotel. One has to wonder what the staff thought of the wooden crates and boxes that he asked to be taken to his room, but no record was ever made of their impressions.

After checking into the hotel, Moon went down to the nearest barbershop, got a leisurely shave, and then looked up a few of his old Civil War army comrades for dinner. He bid his friends good-bye and returned to the hotel. After wishing the desk clerk a pleasant good-night, he retired to his room—and was never seen alive again.

Once he locked his door behind him, Moon began the elaborate preparations for his death. He pried open one of the wooden crates and began to assemble a guillotine of his own design. A framework was fastened to the floor with hinges, and he eased a large, sharp blade into place by pulling on a double cord that was fastened to a bracket and then attached to the woodwork at the side of a window across the room. The shining blade was locked into position several feet above the floor. Moon then placed a lighted candle between the two cords holding the blade.

Moon had also brought a soapbox with him, which he placed on its side. The soapbox contained cotton that had been saturated with chloroform, designed to knock him out so that he wouldn't feel any pain as his life was ending. When the candle burned down to the proper point, the flame would burn through the cords. Once they were cut, the blade would fall, severing Moon's head from his body.

Slowly and carefully, Moon made all the final preparations and then placed his head inside the fume-filled box and lost consciousness. He never woke up again.

At some point in the night, a downstairs guest complained of a horrible sound overhead—and what looked to be an ax blade protruding from the ceiling of his room! Horrified staff members unlocked the door of room 41 and found a ghastly and blood-soaked scene.

James Moon had succeeded in his quest for death and had created a legend in the city of Lafayette. He had a morbid bent to his nature, but obviously had a love of black humor as well. Stamped on the blade of his homemade guillotine was a simple message that must have had him chuckling when he inscribed the words: "For sale or for let."

Once he locked his door behind him, Moon began the elaborate preparations for his death.

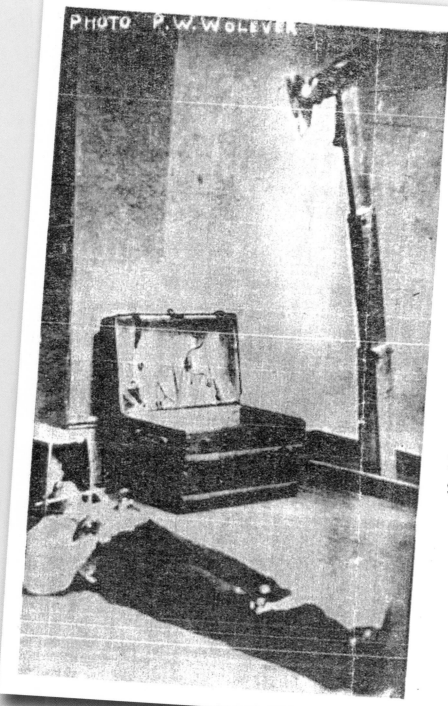

PHOTO P.W. WOLEVER

MOON'S MACHINE — Here's how James Moon, a Tippecanoe County farmer, took his life in classic style back in 1876. The man lying on the floor in the position authorities found Moon is an assistant of P. W. Wolever, a Lafayette photographer, who was on the scene soon after the suicide was discovered. A candle severed a cord holding the huge axe aloft, sending it downward on its deadly mission. The photograph is from the collection of George W. Wolever, 1314 S. 12th St., grandson of the photographer.

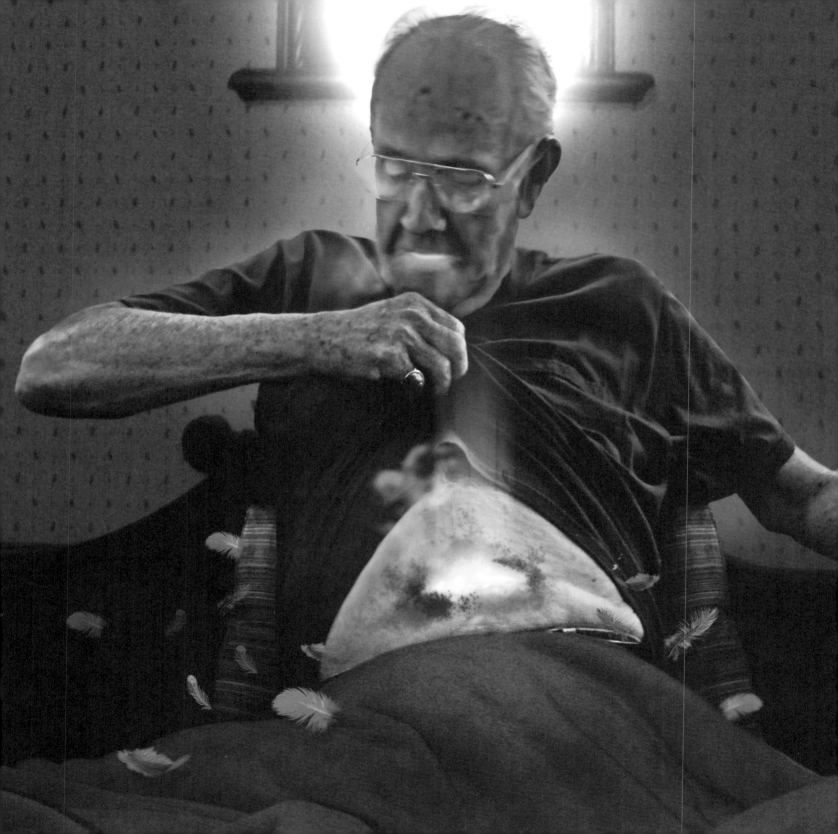

The Meteor That Hit (Or Didn't Hit) Leonidas Grover

One of the weirdest stories in Indiana history came about as a result of a hoax. The story of a homicidal meteor was so widely believed that it appeared in newspapers, official state records, and even a scientific study about projectiles from space. It began as a simple practical joke but took on a life of its own, involving army officers, newspaper reporters, and respected scientists. So how did this innocent joke evolve into such a scandal?

It all began with a man named Leonidas Grover, who never really existed. His strange story appeared as an article in the *Indianapolis Journal* on January 16, 1879. According to the story, the elderly Grover went to sleep one night in his home in Covington and never woke up. At some point in the night, a twenty-pound meteor tore through the roof of his house, passed through Grover's body and bed like a cannonball, and came to rest five feet beneath the earth of the cellar. His daughter and her husband, with whom Grover lived, discovered his body—with a bloody, jagged hole through the center of his chest—the following morning.

At some point in the night, a twenty-pound meteor tore through the roof of his house and passed through Grover's body and bed like a cannonball.

This tall tale, investigation later showed, was slipped onto the wire desk at the *Journal* as a practical joke. The identity of the culprit was never discovered, but he was responsible for a hoax that would endure for years. Other newspapers picked up the odd story, and Grover's grim fate was widely publicized.

Among the readers of the story was Edward T. Cox, who was then Indiana's state geologist. He was fascinated by the odd occurrence and felt that the deadly meteor ought to be recovered. He convinced his neighbor, army major John J. Palmer, to travel to Covington and retrieve the killer stone for scientific study.

When Major Palmer arrived, he quickly learned that there was no Leonidas Grover and no meteor. Cursing his own foolishness, Palmer was contemplating sending a fiery telegram to Cox when he happened to see an oblong-shaped rock on the ground. Since Cox had sent him on a wild goose chase, he began plotting a hoax of his own.

Palmer hurried to a nearby drugstore and bought a bottle of red ink, with which he painted the rock. Then, he heated the rock in a fire until it turned a convincing shade of black. Palmer then headed back to Indianapolis, seeking revenge.

Adding details as he went along, Palmer quickly spread the meteor mishap story, and newspapers picked up the tale. Sightseers became so numerous that Palmer gladly accepted an offer from a friend named Joe Perry to exhibit the "meteor" in his drugstore in downtown Indianapolis. After a while, word leaked out that the story was a hoax, but by then it couldn't be stopped.

In 1880, a year after the tale was first foisted on an unsuspecting public, John Collett, who succeeded Cox as the state geologist, wrote a letter to Major Palmer asking him to produce the infamous meteor. People had been hounding Collett about the rock, and he felt that it should be exhibited in the state museum.

Palmer, still unable (or unwilling) to admit that the whole thing had been a joke, retrieved the stone from Joe Perry's store and turned it over to the state of Indiana. It was proudly displayed at the museum for years, but it later disappeared after Collett left office.

The case of the murderous meteor became known as one of Indiana's most famous hoaxes, and the only one officially endorsed by the state for decades!

Death Comes to the Big Top

Based on a two-hundred-acre farm in Peru, the Hagenbeck-Wallace Circus traveled across the nation and rose to be one of the leading traveling shows of its day in the early twentieth century. By 1918, it could boast of a show featuring "60 aerialists, 60 acrobats, 60 riders and 50 clowns." All told, the circus consisted of twenty-two tents, one thousand employees, and a payroll of $7,500 a day.

On the night of June 21, 1918, the Hagenbeck-Wallace Circus was finishing up two shows in Michigan City. The next day it was scheduled to appear in Hammond for one show before taking a well-deserved day off on Sunday. At about nine p.m., the first section of the circus, consisting of all the animals and about half of the performers, left the Michigan City station bound for Hammond. By two a.m., the tents had been torn down and the second section of the circus prepared to depart.

When conductor J. W. Johnson fired the engine of his locomotive, pulling the second section of the circus train out of the Michigan City depot, his orders were simple and direct. They called for his train to go via the Michigan City tracks to Ivanhoe, a small station between Gary and Hammond, then switch onto the Michigan Central tracks and from there proceed into Hammond. Once in Hammond, he would direct the locomotive to a side rail that would take them to the lot where the circus would play.

The first hour of the trip was uneventful. However, just as the train neared the Michigan Central tracks, the fireman behind Johnson relayed the message that the brakeman in the caboose had seen a small fire on one of the cars—a condition called a hotbox, which was fairly common and usually manageable. No doubt Johnson was more annoyed than alarmed by the report.

Somewhat reluctantly, Johnson began to slow his train to a stop. By the time it ground to a halt, the bulk of the train had turned off onto the Michigan Central tracks, with only the last five cars still resting on the main line. Still, this hardly represented a danger, since the signals behind would warn any oncoming train of their presence. Had the fates been kinder that night, this would have been nothing more than a routine stop on a routine journey.

However, on this night, the fates were anything but kind. Coming in fast and hard behind the Hagenbeck-

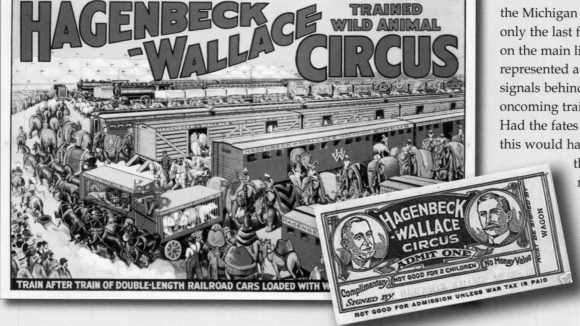

TRAIN AFTER TRAIN OF DOUBLE-LENGTH RAILROAD CARS LOADED WITH W

Wallace train was another train. Engine 8485 was pulling an empty troop train on its way to Chicago to pick up a load of soldiers destined for the front lines of France—and it seemed to be traveling extraordinarily fast.

The fireman in the Hagenbeck-Wallace coal car noted that the steam coming from the other train's smokestack didn't sound the way it should: Instead of the gentle series of puffs it normally emitted, the sound was a constant harsh shrill. From years of experience, the fireman knew what that meant. The engine was running at full throttle, in violation of the speed ordinance on that section of the rail line. As he later testified, he was further alarmed when he saw that the engineer was ignoring all warning lights as the train approached the Ivanhoe station. As he would remark years later, "I saw him pass those lights and wondered what he was about—I wondered what in the world he was doing."

Had the fireman in question been able to get a glimpse into the cab of the engine, he would have readily understood what was happening. In the gentle glow of the control lights, he would have seen the engineer, Alonzo Sargent, slumped over—fast asleep as his train headed toward disaster.

Engine 8485 slammed into the rear section of the Hagenbeck-Wallace Circus train at approximately thirty-five miles per hour. The force of the collision sent the engine careening at least four hundred feet, through the caboose and the last five sleeping cars of the train, before stopping. As neighbor Mrs. Bert Moser described the sound for the *Chicago Tribune* the next day, "There was a crash, a roar and a long drawn out sound, as if a million bricks were crashing onto a tin roof. Then absolute silence."

In the moments after Engine 8485 ground to a halt, first a spark and a small plume of flame shot from within the depths of the wreckage. Within moments, the night

sky of northern Indiana was lit up by bright flames, as the wreck turned into a fiery inferno. Most of those trapped and injured in the wreckage never stood a chance. Eighty-six people died that night, many of them incinerated beyond recognition. Indeed, records from the time reflect that nearly half of the remains later recovered could not be identified.

Amazingly, one of the few survivors was Alonzo Sargent himself, the engineer of the troop train. As he stood and stared in disbelief at the carnage before him, he was approached by the man who had served as his fireman on the engine. As the fireman later testified, "I asked him what had happened and he stared at me for a moment and then said, 'I was dozing—otherwise asleep.'"

Another visitor to the site that early morning was Gary mayor William Hodges. As he later described the scene to reporters:

It was one of the worst wrecks I have ever witnessed.
The injured were lying in many different places.
Bodies of the dead were strewn along the tracks.
The cars were in flames. We saw several bodies in

"It was one of the worst wrecks I have ever witnessed. The injured were lying in many different places. Bodies of the dead were strewn along the tracks. The cars were in flames."

the ruins. Someone said that there were twenty-five bodies in the remains of one car. Most of these were women.

One man found the body of his wife in the weeds. He tried to comfort her but when he learned that she had been killed, his consciousness seemed to collapse. Rescuers shortly carried him to the relief train.

Still, amazingly, the old show business adage, "The show must go on," prevailed. Against all odds, the Hagenbeck-Wallace Circus headed out to fulfill its commitments. The circus left behind many of its performers and stagehands recuperating in area hospitals, and many more in morgues. On June 26, the unidentified and those without family were buried in a mass plot at Woodlawn Cemetery, just outside of Chicago, in a section known as Showman's Rest.

Interestingly, over the years, a strange, unearthly story about the mass grave began to circulate in the area around Woodlawn Cemetery. In the early 1970s, passersby began to report the sound of wild animals roaring from within the precincts of the cemetery grounds, particularly late at night. Rumors spread that a contingent of the circus animals had been killed in the train wreck and had been buried with their handlers in the mass grave. Those cries, the story goes, were the anguished sounds of the ghosts of those unfortunate circus animals. In time, these tales began to be accepted as fact and the reports made their way into the media and eventually into the collective folklore of Chicago.

Just a few miles from Woodlawn Cemetery, across the Indiana border at the accident site, other bizarre tales have been told since that fateful night. These are tales that have caused some to doubt their very sanity: Rail workers and locals have told of seeing a wreck at the site, which turns out to be merely a phantom image; of encountering ghostly specters who appear to be on fire; or of hearing the ghoulish wailing and moaning of those dying a tragic death, but seeing nothing there.

Who knows what lies in the unearthly darkness by the side of the railway junction just outside what was once the station at Ivanhoe? Perhaps it is nothing more than bad memories of a tragic event. However, there might be something more: dreadful remnants of a terrible night when death itself rode the rails and found its way into the realm of Indiana ghostlore.

Phantom Wreck Still Smolders at Night

My dad worked for the railroad for many years as a brakeman, and at his retirement party a couple of his old buddies started talking about the old days. They cussed and discussed some of the foremen they had known, and then they started talking about the old wreck. One of the guys got real serious and said that he had once defied an order to go out and inspect the section of rail where the wreck had happened. It seems that an engineer had radioed in that he had seen strange lights out there late one night and had seen some wreckage by the side of the track, and this guy, who was working the late shift, had been ordered to go out there and check it.

He got there and it was dark and unnaturally quiet, and he shined his flashlight around a bit but didn't see anything. He said he was about to go back to his truck when suddenly he was overwhelmed by the awful smell of smoke. He said it smelled like a barbeque gone very wrong—it was so thick he was choking on it. At the same time, he said he was hit with  this unexplainable sense of sadness—for no reason, he was ready to cry. That's when he got out of there, went back to the shop, and said there was nothing out there to be seen.

The next night his supervisor came to him and said that another train engineer had radioed in again—this time seeing smoke on that stretch of rail, and he was supposed to go out and make sure no kids were setting fire to the cross ties, as they sometimes did. However, remembering his experience the night before, my dad's friend looked at the supervisor and told him he would not be going out there again at night. The supervisor made it a direct order, and this guy told the supervisor to write him up or go to hell—either one, but he was not going out there again. I guess he got the write-up, but he swore that for the next 26 years he never went out to that part of the railroad at night again.—*Bobby Spencer, Hammond*

From Cradle to Grave: James Dean and His Cursed Car

He made just three movies during his short life, but the actor James Dean is a legend. His untimely death in a car accident in 1955, at the age of twenty-four, would enshrine Dean as an American icon, but he has special meaning to Indiana, since he spent most of his life living in its small towns, including Fairmount. That's the location of several of his childhood homes, his high school and church, a shop where he bought his first motorcycle, and the funeral home that would eventually lay out his mortal remains. You can find maps of many of these places online, but along with Dean's grave in Park Cemetery there are a few other places nearby that let you know a legend lived (and was buried) among them.

One is Dean's first home, at the Seven Gables apartment complex. It was located at the corner of McClure and Fourth streets in Marion but has long since been demolished to make way for a parking lot. Today, its location is noted by a small, carved rock, sitting on the corner, and a bronze-colored star, bearing James Dean's name, embedded in the sidewalk.

Another is the James Dean Memorial Park, on Main Street in Fairmount. Dedicated in 1995, the park contains a pedestal monument on which sits a bust of Dean. It was sculpted by Kenneth Kendall, whom Dean had approached in early 1955 about doing a sculpture of him. Kendall put the idea on the back burner until he heard about Dean's death. He began the Dean sculpture that evening but didn't have it cast until 1984. Eleven years later it was included in the new park to commemorate the fortieth anniversary of Dean's death.

The Fairmount Historical Museum on East Washington Street also has many Dean artifacts, including his first motorcycle. It's open from March to November.

The Adventures of James Dean's Headstone
Visitors to Dean's grave at Park Cemetery leave behind mementos, including cigarettes (Winstons being a favorite). It's not uncommon to find his headstone covered with lipstick kisses left behind by his adoring fans. They aren't, however, kissing Dean's original headstone, which had a bad year in 1983: stolen in April, recovered that May, and then stolen again for good in August. The stone that sits there today is a replica of the original.

James Dean and the Curse of the Spyder
On September 21, 1955, Dean traded the car he owned then for a Porsche 550 Spyder, one of only ninety that were ever made. Dean, an avid race car driver, was planning on

James Dean's boyhood home in Fairmount

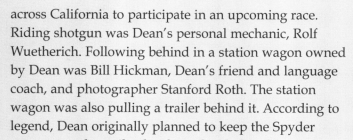

across California to participate in an upcoming race. Riding shotgun was Dean's personal mechanic, Rolf Wuetherich. Following behind in a station wagon owned by Dean was Bill Hickman, Dean's friend and language coach, and photographer Stanford Roth. The station wagon was also pulling a trailer behind it. According to legend, Dean originally planned to keep the Spyder on the trailer, but later decided to drive it so he could get used to handling it. That decision would prove to be fatal.

Dean and his entourage were heading west on U.S. Highway 46 (later renamed California State Route 466) near Cholame, California, when twenty-three-year-old college student Donald Turnupseed, driving a 1950 Ford Tudor, attempted to make a left-hand turn in front of Dean's approaching car. Police later concluded that since the silver Spyder rode so close to the ground and the color of the car blended with the twilight sky, Turnupseed never even saw Dean's vehicle coming. The result was that the two cars crashed head-on into each other. Upon impact, Wuetherich was thrown from the Spyder, which probably saved his life. Dean was transported to Paso Robles War Memorial Hospital, where he was officially pronounced dead at 5:59 p.m. Turnupseed was treated for facial cuts and bruises. He was not ticketed for the accident.

Almost immediately, rumors about Dean's car (and, in some instances, Dean himself) being cursed began to spread like wildfire. The following is a list of events that have been attributed to the curse of James Dean's car. Some events have been verified, while others are just weird

racing the Spyder, so he hired legendary car customizer George Barris—who would later design the famous Batmobile for the 1960s TV show—to paint 130 on the Porsche. Barris also put the car's name across the back: Little Bastard.

Legend has it that several of Dean's close friends, including actor Alec "Obi-Wan Kenobi" Guinness, warned him about bad vibes from the car, including fears of Dean's being killed in it. But Dean was not superstitious and shrugged off the warnings.

On September 30, 1955, Dean was driving the Spyder

(and vague) enough to keep you guessing as to whether they really took place. But all of them combine to create the twisted legend that is James Dean's Cursed Car.

☠ At the scene of the accident, a young man attempted to take the Spyder's steering wheel as a souvenir and ended up slicing his entire arm open in the process. While the crushed remains of the Spyder were waiting to be towed away, several ghoul-like individuals attempted to rip off blood-soaked pieces of the car's upholstery. All were said to have been seriously injured in accidents shortly afterward.

☠ Having taken a liking to Dean's car when he first saw it, George Barris believed the wreck could be salvaged for parts, so he plunked down $2,500 for the

wreakage. As it was being delivered to Barris's garage, the car fell off the trailer and onto a mechanic's leg, breaking his leg instantly.

☠ The first items Barris allegedly sold off from the wreckage were two tires, which were bought by a young man. According to legend, within days of being placed on the man's car, both tires blew out, at the exact same time, sending the car and its occupant crashing off the road into a ditch.

☠ Things really started getting weird with the cursed car legend when Troy McHenry, a physician and avid race car driver, reportedly purchased the engine. The drivetrain from the Spyder was said to have been sold to William Eschrid, another physician/amateur race car driver. The strange twists continued when both men added Dean's parts to their own cars and raced the cars together for the first time on October 2, 1956, at California's Pomona Fairgrounds. Although it is still debated whether or not McHenry did indeed have Dean's engine in his car, what is known is that, during the race, his car suddenly veered off the track and slammed headfirst into a tree. McHenry was killed on impact. As for Eschrid, he is said to have barely escaped with his life when his car spun out of control and rolled over.

Those last two accidents seemed a little too coincidental for Barris, who reportedly began to believe in the curse. As a result, he decided to stop selling parts and quietly put Dean's car into storage. But curses don't like to lie low for long. So when the California Highway Patrol persuaded Barris to lend them the remains of the Spyder to be featured in a traveling exhibit on highway safety, the curse saw an opportunity. It took a while for it to get back in the swing of things, though, and the first few appearances of the vehicle went off without a hitch. But then, according to legend, the curse came back with a vengeance.

☠ First, the garage in Fresno, California, where the Little Bastard was being stored, along with other classic cars, reportedly caught fire, destroying everything inside—except Dean's car, which escaped with only minor paint damage.

☠ During an appearance at a Sacramento high school, the car fell off its raised pedestal, seriously injuring a student. And—wouldn't you know it—this mishap is said to have taken place on the anniversary of Dean's death.

☠ Yet another fatal freak accident happened when the car was being hauled on a flatbed truck to an appearance in Salinas. Driver George Barhuis is said to have lost control of the flatbed and crashed, ejecting himself in the process. Somehow, the Spyder not only managed to fall off the flatbed, but also crashed down on top of Barhuis, killing him.

☠ In 1958, the cursed car was being put on display throughout Oregon. While the car was sitting peacefully on the back of a truck parked on a hill, the truck's brakes suddenly gave way, sending it crashing into another vehicle.

So what became of Dean's cursed Spyder? Plain and simple, no one knows for sure. Sometime in 1960 the car had just finished being shown at an exhibit in Miami, Florida. It was crated up and placed on a train (although some reports say that the car was loaded onto a truck) headed for Los Angeles. But when the train arrived, the Spyder was no longer on board, with no sign as to what happened. It was as if, as the old-timers say, "that Little Bastard just up and vanished."

To this day, no one has ever come forward and admitted that they have the car's remains or even that they know what happened to it. Even the $1 million offer by the Volo Auto Museum in Illinois for the car's return—"No questions asked"—in 2005 went unanswered, leading many to believe it's been lost for good. But we're dealing with the legend of a Hollywood icon's cursed car here, so that's not good enough. Let's say that maybe, just maybe, Dean's Spyder is still out there, waiting patiently for some unsuspecting victim to come along and resurrect the curse once again.

House of Blue Lights

When Charles and Mary Test decided to give their newborn son the name Skiles, it's a pretty safe bet they wanted him to do something unique with his life. Little did they know that Skiles would give the state of Indiana one of its most enduring legends: the House of Blue Lights.

Skiles E. Test was born on October 16, 1889, and wasted little time making a name for himself in the Indianapolis business world. By the time Test reached his twenties, he was already a millionaire. In addition to his successful business, Test Realty Corporation, he was also the president of the Indianapolis Motor Inns. He would also become a long-serving member on the board of the Indianapolis Transit System.

Test may have been a businessman by trade, but in his spare time he was something of an amateur inventor and even dabbled in architecture. In 1913, he married and moved to a small farm on an enormous tract of wooded land in northeast Marion County. His new land would serve as the blank canvas on which Test created some of his most remarkable works. He had already become known as something of an eccentric in the Indianapolis community, and some of what he created would do nothing to downplay that label.

One of the first structures to raise eyebrows was the swimming pool. Sure, the forty-by-eighty pool was large, but it was the bathhouse more than anything that blew people's minds. For one thing, Test decided his bathhouse needed several stories and even a full basement. When he added high dives to the top level of the bathhouse, he felt that bathers needed a convenient way to reach them. So he built an elevator to take them from ground level. As an added bonus, he installed a motorized surfboard in the pool just in case any of his guests wanted to try to learn to surf. And to make sure that the pool was ready any time

he wanted to use it, Test installed solar panels, something unheard of at the time, to keep the pool heated year-round.

Perhaps one of the most amazing things Test created on the property was his own power plant. Legend has it that he decided to build it after an argument with the Indianapolis Power Company. He was also something of an animal lover and kept dozens of cats and dogs on his property. This is not something out of the ordinary on a farm. What was odd was that Test also created a pet cemetery where he buried his animals when they passed away, each animal with its own casket and headstone.

Every holiday Test would decorate the farmhouse and many of the trees on the property with lights. For Christmas he chose blue lights. One Christmas the blue lights went up as usual and never came down. Most people thought Test had simply gotten lazy in his old age, but some claimed the lights remained up for a more bizarre reason.

It was said that one night Test's wife died in a tragic accident in the house. The grief-stricken Test could not bear to be apart from her and decided to place her in a glass coffin in the living room. Legend has it that Test then placed blue lights all around the coffin and outside the house. The reason why he chose blue lights is open to debate. Some say it was because blue was his wife's favorite color, while others contend he believed the color blue attracted spirits. Whatever the reason, the legend of the House of Blue Lights was born.

For years, visiting the House of Blue Lights was something of a rite of passage for Indianapolis area teens. Beginning in the 1950s, carloads of kids would drive to the property and dare each other to go up to the house and ring the doorbell. Most never made it to the front door. But a few who did swore that as they approached the house, they could see the body of a woman encased in a glass coffin surrounded by dozens of blue lights. Test eventually had the property enclosed behind a giant fence to discourage the light seekers, but it didn't work. It was not uncommon to drive past the property at night and see kids hanging on the fence, attempting to catch a glimpse of the blue lights twinkling in the distance and of the alleged glass casket.

The Treasure Hunt

Test died on March 19, 1964, and his body was laid to rest in Crown Hill Cemetery. After the funeral, a three-day public auction was held to liquidate the many items found on his property. On the first day of the auction, thousands of people lined up waiting to get inside. Over the course of the entire auction, close to 50,000 people wandered across the property. Sure, there were those interested in finding some good deals on some cool stuff. But most were intent on finding out once and for all if Mrs. Test was indeed lying in a glass coffin somewhere in the house.

She wasn't. In fact, not a single human-size coffin, glass or otherwise, was ever found. And what became of the blue lights themselves remains a mystery, as no one is sure who purchased them.

Upon his death, Test had wanted his property to be turned into a Boy Scout camp. But Test's final wishes were not to be honored. Eventually the eighty acres, including the spot where the infamous House of Blue Lights stood, would become property of the Indianapolis State Park system. By 1978, despite a public outcry, the House of Blue Lights and all its outbuildings had been bulldozed to make way for what would become the Skiles Test Nature Park. You would think that would be where the story ends . . . but it's not.

Although the House of Blue Lights has been gone for almost thirty years, we all know that great legends never die. Perhaps that's why to this day, people driving past the Skiles park at night have reported seeing strange glowing blue lights dancing among the trees. Presently, the nature park is working on building more trails, including some that will bring park visitors even closer to the spot where the House of Blue Lights once stood. So there's no telling exactly what a late-night hiker might encounter.

Ancient and Unexplained

This chapter is about lots of things in Indiana that are either really old, unexplained, or both. While we know that could probably include your great-aunt Myrtle, we're trying to keep it less personal here.

Which is why we'll start by asking, "Who can't get enough mounds?" (the earthen kind, not the candy bar). Certainly not the people of the Hoosier State! Indiana's got a slew of ancient mounds, built by ancestors of Native American tribes who mysteriously disappeared. These early architectural wonders are designed to be burial sites, astronomy labs, and maybe even early versions of Google Earth.

We'll take you to a dark place where phenomena called spook lights have been known to make their appearance. And we've got the buzz on the annoying Kokomo hum.

"What," you say, "no Indiana UFOs?" Nope, not as far as we know. Why they've bypassed Indiana is a question for the ages, and we ask you to consider it among the

Ancient Angel Mounds

For thousands of years, a succession of Native American cultures made their home along what is now the Ohio River, in southwestern Indiana. From about A.D. 900 to 1500, the Mississippian culture of the Mound Builders was dominant in southwestern Indiana. According to best estimates, a community of thousands of people lived along the Ohio near the point where Indiana, Illinois, and Kentucky meet, at a site that has since been dubbed Angel Mounds, after the giant earthen mounds the community built and lived among. But these people are long gone. Early explorers of the region found only scattered settlements that had been abandoned by the cultures that once lived there. The Mound Builders had mysteriously disappeared, leaving behind much debate as to who they were and why they left.

Who built the mounds? Opinions among the early American colonists were divided into two main schools of thought. The first held that ancestors of the Native Americans created the mounds. The second maintained that they were built either by Old World visitors or by some mystical cataclysmic civilization (like Atlantis). The reasoning behind this line of thinking was twofold. Evidence of an ancient lost civilization in the Midwest would show that the United States had a long and honorable heritage and was not just home to an upstart band of revolutionaries. This belief also justified the greed and racism of those who profited from taking the land from Native Americans. If they could establish that the ancient civilization responsible for the mounds was really founded by whites, who were then brought down by the "red savages," it meant the Indians had no legal right to the land they had "taken" and could easily be removed from it.

This assertion was debunked in 1894 by authors Cyrus Thomas and William H. Holmes, who completed an exhaustive study for the Bureau of American Ethnology. They discovered that several tribes in the Southeast, like the Creek Indians, were still building mounds. They also found that early European explorers had noted the mounds. They compared artifacts from the mounds with objects made by Native Americans of the time and found them quite similar. They also proved that many ancient and contemporary Native American groups practiced corn agriculture, as did the Mound Builders.

Death and Astronomy

Whatever debates and mysteries surround the ancient mounds, there is no question that they were used for burials. Prehistoric people in the region began burying their dead on high bluffs about six thousand years ago, often covering the burial grounds with a mound of earth that was visible from the floodplains below. The Mound Builders may have believed that the spirits of their ancestors needed to look down from a position where they could influence the living and, to make up for the general flatness of the midwestern landscape, simply constructed their own lofty perches for the dead.

Starting around A.D. 1400, something changed the Mound Builders' civilization so much that they abandoned their city, and within a few years, it was vacant.

Starting around A.D. 1400, something changed the Mound Builders' civilization so much that they abandoned their city, and within a few years, it was vacant. The mounds bore no signs of life when they were first seen by explorers. The people had long since disappeared. Some archaeologists believe the last survivors of the Mound Builders became the Natchez Indians of the lower Mississippi Valley. These Indians were known for being devout worshippers of the sun, which was something also ascribed to the Indians of southwestern Indiana.

Many believe the residents of Angel Mounds moved south, perhaps because of climate changes. Temperatures in the Midwest became increasingly colder around 1250, possibly shortening the growing season. Changing rain patterns, leading to floods and drought, may have made the situation worse. Warfare may have broken out among rival groups, decimating the population.

Or the reasons may be even darker. . . .

There's a new cult in town

Around 1500, a religious movement dubbed the Death Cult seized the Midwest. A new type of grotesque artwork became prevalent, portraying winged beasts, skulls, and weird faces. The rituals practiced are unknown, but scholars have imagined them to be quite dark. Some have even hinted at human sacrifice and cannibalism.

According to legend, a bearded and robed god originally visited the Mound Builders and inspired them to love one another, live in harmony with the land, and build the great earthworks. But during the Death Cult period, they degenerated into human sacrifice and warfare. The possible survivors of the Mound Builders, the Natchez, were described by the French as being the "most civilized of the native tribes," but their tribal traditions sometimes had dark elements to them. Reports describe the death of a chieftain that touched off a religious orgy including ritual human sacrifice.

Are the Death Cult legends true? Had the Mound Builders destroyed one another in such a way that the remaining members of the society abandoned their mighty cities? One thing is sure—we will never really know. No matter how many theories are put forth, ideas created, or excavations carried out, the people of Angel Mounds will always remain the state's greatest ancient mystery.

For a small admission fee, you too can experience the mysterious Angel Mounds. The site is open Tuesday through Saturday from nine a.m. to five p.m., and on Sundays from one p.m. to five p.m. It's closed on Mondays.

More Mounds in Anderson

Not many of the drivers speeding along I-69 in Anderson realize that just a stone's throw away lie ten earthworks that have been around for thousands of years. These mounds were believed to have been built by the Adena-Hopewell Indians around 150 B.C. There is still confusion as to their exact use. Unlike the Angel Mounds, they were not used for burials. Some believe they were involved in religious ceremonies, while others think they were a calendar of sorts. Those who subscribe to the calendar theory note that when combined, the mounds can be used to track the sun, moon, all the visible planets, and close to one hundred of the brightest stars in the sky!

The centerpiece of the mounds is the Great Mound, a circular enclosure that is close to a quarter of a mile in diameter, which makes it the largest of its kind in Indiana.

Though now safely protected within Mounds State Park, the structures weren't always so respected and revered. At the beginning of the nineteenth century, the Bronnenberg family purchased over six hundred acres in the area, including all the mounds. They operated a farm on the property, and their house still stands in the state park. Things

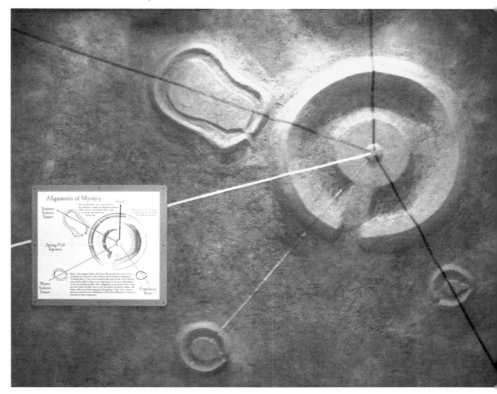

got a little weird in 1897 when the Bronnenbergs sold large portions of their land (including the mounds) to the Indiana Union Traction Company, which promptly opened up a mini–amusement park in the area. The park featured a skating rink, dance halls, boat rides, a roller coaster, and a carousel, which was placed right on top of the Great Mound.

When the Depression hit, the amusement park folded and sat abandoned until the Madison County Historical Society purchased the property and then donated it to the state of Indiana. In 1930, the area officially became Mounds State Park and was opened to the public so that everyone could come and marvel at these wonderfully weird mounds.

The Legend of Moody's Light

In the utter darkness of an Indiana night, it appears—a light that pierces the blackness cloaking the rural countryside all around. The light generally emerges as a soft glow, changing as it moves through the fields and along a nearby road, between the towns of Rensselaer and Francesville. At times, it is a dull yellow, as from a lantern; yet at other times, its hue changes to a brilliant orange or red. It will seem to hover in the inky blackness, then move forward at a bobbing lope, only to zoom ahead before suddenly stopping short. Sometimes it even seems to separate into several balls of light.

The presence of this mysterious glow, known as Moody's Light, has been noted for nearly a century, and the tales surrounding it have been handed down for generations. It is well documented that it tends to be seen along a narrow stretch of Division Road that has long been known as Moody Road.

But its origins are more obscure. Over the years, many tales have been spun to explain its presence; most are dark and macabre, and none truly verifiable by historical records.

Many stories have a decapitation theme. One tale tells of a man who was attacked by bandits as he rode home along the road late one night. The bandits pulled him from his horse, and during the ensuing struggle, the man's head was severed. A different story involves a farmhand, also traveling the road at night, who was thrown from his wagon and decapitated by a wagon wheel. In both cases, the head was never found. The strange light is from the lantern the dead man's ghost carries as he searches for his head. And if you point out that a headless ghostly body would search more efficiently for its missing noggin by feeling around for it, as opposed to lighting a lantern, well, you probably also like to tell kids that Santa Claus isn't real.

Still another take on the headless theme involves two brothers who were riding in their farm wagon when they got into an accident in which one brother was decapitated. As in the versions above, said head was never found, but here the light is from the lantern being used by the ghost of the other brother as he searches for his dead sibling's head. In this story, the accident occurred in the summer, which some witnesses say is the best time of the year to see the light as it passes through the cornfields.

But the most common tales involve a farmer named Moody, whose land is said to have been near the road that now bears his name. Again the stories vary, but all agree that a tragedy struck this man and his family—a tragedy with supernatural repercussions.

In one story, Moody lived with his wife and two daughters in a farmhouse just off the road and farmed the large tract of land that surrounded their house. One evening he arrived home to find a scene of almost unimaginable horror. Blood was streaked across the floor and walls of the kitchen, and furniture in the living room was overturned as if a life-and-death struggle had taken place there.

Venturing upstairs, he found the lifeless bodies of his daughters in one of the bedrooms. Rushing downstairs and into the yard, he found the corpse of his wife. All had been savagely stabbed. Horrified, Moody ran to a neighbor's house for help.

Authorities conducted a thorough investigation, but found no clues to indicate who might have perpetrated the horrible crime. The bodies of Moody's wife and daughters were quietly buried at a small country cemetery nearby, and as time passed, the community recovered from its collective shock over the horrible murders. Life resumed its normal course.

Except for farmer Moody. As the days and months

passed, it became apparent that shock and grief had unhinged his mind. Late at night neighbors began to notice the light of a lantern bobbing through the fields and along the road in front of the Moody farm. It seemed the farmer was out searching for the killers of his family. Gradually, Moody withdrew to his farm completely and was seen only during these nighttime rambles through the countryside. Perhaps they somehow helped ease the pain of his grief and quieted the demons in his heart.

In the end, whatever solace Moody found in his nocturnal walks was not enough. One early morning a few years after the murders, a neighboring farmer traveling down the road by the farm found Moody's body swinging from an overhanging tree. Unable to cope with the loneliness of his life and the grief over what he had lost, he chose to join his family in death.

Under normal circumstances, that might be the end of this tragic story. However, shortly after Moody had been laid to rest, local farmers reported seeing the soft light of a lantern floating through the fields around Moody Road late at night. When approached, the light moved in a different direction or simply vanished into the darkness. Some thought it was the ill-fated farmer, still searching for those who had brought tragedy to his family.

Eventually, the legend of Moody's Light leaked into the surrounding community, and over time, many people have come to witness the phenomenon. A trip to see Moody's Light is an annual tradition for students at nearby St. Joseph's College. More than a few people have managed to catch the mysterious ball of light from a distance on film and video, yet no one has ever come close enough to determine its true nature or cause. Some have suggested that the source is swamp gas, which sometimes incandesces with an eerie light. However, swamp gas appears in marshy areas, which don't exist in the immediate vicinity of Moody Road.

Others have suggested ball lightning, which is a natural electrical charge from the earth that sometimes accumulates and flashes with a strange light, but Moody's Light appears for longer durations and in a wider variety of temperatures and wind conditions than ball lightning.

Perhaps no explanation for Moody's Light will ever be found. Regardless, it regularly appears out of the darkness, quietly making its way along the cornfields and the gravel shoulder of the road. Whether it is caused by a ghost looking to get "a head," the spirit of a tragic farmer still searching for his family's killers, or some other, more prosaic occurrence, for the legion of Hoosiers who have seen it, it will always be a wondrous mystery. And, perhaps, that is the way it should remain.

Weird Experiences with the Moody Light

Some claim that the Moody Light can be summoned on command, so *Weird Indiana* went in search of it, excited at the prospect of seeing this strange occurrence and more than ready to chase it. Having hunted for scores of Crybaby Bridges, haunted railroad tracks, and other spook lights over the years, we were also prepared for failure. We embarked upon our search one warm July night, with a beautiful clear sky overhead. We had a long list of things the light was supposed to do, what it would look like, and what might happen when we got to the site where it was normally seen. And if the light decided to chase us (as some of our contacts told us that it might), we all knew that we planned to go quickly in the opposite direction!

We followed the directions that we'd been given and ended up at a three-way intersection, heading south. We flashed our headlights three times and then drove about a mile and a half down the lane (the locals call it Moody Road) until we found this tree stump that we were supposed to be looking for. It was not easy to find in the dark, but we managed to track it down. When we found it, we turned the car around, parked, and flashed our lights three more times before shutting them off. Then we waited for the light to cross the road.

As we peered out through the windshield, we saw an orange-and-red light that looked like a traffic light appear in the distance. It seemed to come and go, and it never got any closer to us. It was almost like someone flipped a switch and it came on, and then they switched it off again. We had been told to expect the light to move side to side, back and forth, and even come right at us across the cornfields. Unfortunately, it didn't do any of these things,

but we couldn't explain what was causing it to appear either.

Some have suggested that the light is nothing more than reflections from cars passing along Highway 49, which is two miles directly to the north. That's not what it seemed like to us, but we did try to get a better look. We drove all the way down to the end of the road, but the light still seemed pretty far away. We had run out of road at this point, and we had run out of theories too. Whatever causes the Moody Light, be it headless ghosts or less-than-mysterious automobile lights, it remains an enduring Indiana enigma.

Setting the Moody

I guess you could say, "I saw the light." As a matter of fact, I have seen it several times.

I grew up in Lowell and went to high school there. A science teacher told us about Moody's Light. He said that it was just a natural phenomena, but we weren't too sure he was right, so a group of friends and I went out there one weekend night. We parked our car on the road, flashed our headlights three times, which was supposed to call out the spirits, and then just waited.

Within five minutes, a speck of yellow light appeared in the distance, moving toward us. It kind of bobbed up and down as it went along, and when it got closer we could see it was in the shape of some sort of orb. One of the kids let out a yell, and we drove out of there fast.

Since then, I have been there at least a half dozen times, and only once or twice have I been disappointed. Most of the time it appears as a soft, orangish glow, but sometimes it has turned color, and at least once it seemed to have split into a couple of balls of light. We have never tried to chase it, and usually when it gets within a couple of hundred yards of the car it simply vanishes. I have read all of the so-called explanations for the light, but all I know is that it is very real, and a great many people around here can attest to that fact.—*Sarah P.*

1050 North Ghost Lights

Lights used to haunt 1050 North, until it was paved. The lights would appear and then separate before finally rushing off in the woods. Also nearby is an old Erie Lackawanna right-of-way. You can go down there at about 2:00 a.m. and see a light coming down the old railroad bed. I know the light can still be seen as I just witnessed it last night. Thought you should know that strange happenings like this are rife through northwest Indiana.—*Dan H.*

Getting a Head on Spook Light Hill

Near Brazil, off of a gravel road, there are three hills. On some nights, if you go up to the third hill, face towards Highway 59, flash your headlights three times and turn off your vehicle, you will be able to see a dim light moving around.

The story behind this is that years ago when transportation consisted of horse-drawn buggies, a young woman asked her father if she could go on a date with a young man. After much consideration and pleading the father told her she could but she had to be home before it became dark. While the young lady was on her date, she was having a great time and before long it started to get dark. Knowing her father would be upset if she didn't arrive home soon, she took a shortcut that goes through the creek. However, her horse got spooked and took off, and the wheel of the buggy broke and she flew off, becoming decapitated in the process.

The light that you can sometimes see is supposed to be her father with a lantern roaming around in search of his daughter's head.—*Joetta*

Indiana Poltergeists

Of all the varied species of the undead, perhaps the most mysterious and bizarre is the poltergeist. Taken from the German and meaning "noisy ghost," poltergeist activity includes strange noises, the seemingly inexplicable movement of objects (often in the plain sight of witnesses), foul odors, and even spontaneous fires. Those unlucky enough to be present at the time of such incidents report being shoved, slapped, or even choked by unseen hands.

Poltergeist cases have been reported for centuries all around the world, and Indiana has hosted several of its own such incidents. One, in 1977 in Kokomo, caused a brief sensation when police were called numerous times to a home on a quiet street. The family living there reported the sound of loud bangs and explosions coming out of thin air, foul odors, and furniture being moved by unseen hands. Fire officials, state and local police, and legions of private contractors came to examine the home, yet no explanation was found for the events.

Two other Indiana cases provide a detailed and fascinating look into the world of the poltergeist, and we've included both here. Whether the cause is ghosts, psychokinesis, or pranksters, we leave to you to decide.

A Poltergeist Knocks in Indianapolis

Throughout the history of paranormal research, poltergeists have commonly been blamed for any violent or destructive activity in a haunting. Researchers once believed all such activity at a haunted location was the work of spirits or an outside force, but this may not always be so. Another theory points to the cause as a "human agent."

The human agent is a person in the household—frequently an adolescent girl—who is troubled emotionally. It is believed that agents unconsciously manipulate physical objects in the house by psychokinesis (PK), which is the ability to move things by energy generated in the brain. This energy is almost always unconscious, and agents rarely realize that they are the source of the destruction around them. The bursts of PK come and go and usually peak early and then slowly fade away.

The human-agent theory makes for a convenient explanation of poltergeist activity. But what of cases where such events are so bizarre and baffling that they remain unsolved more than four decades later? Such is the case with activity that took place at an Indianapolis home in March 1962.

Before describing what happened, it's worthwhile to take a close look at the family involved. Researchers often point to family relationships when trying to determine the cause of poltergeist outbreaks, and the family in this case was far from a peaceful and contented group.

Renate Beck was a thirty-two-year-old woman who resided in a large two-story house on North Delaware Street. She was divorced from a former U.S. embassy officer whom she had married in her native Vienna. She was well educated and spoke English fluently. She shared the house with her daughter, Linda, thirteen, and her widowed mother, Lina Gemmecke, sixty-one. Investigators described Linda as being shy and uncommunicative; it was Lina Gemmecke who seemed to be the biggest detriment to household tranquillity. She had moved from Germany to Indianapolis in 1959, following the death of her husband. Friends and neighbors later told investigators the family did not get along very well, and noisy and unpleasant fights could often be heard coming from their home.

The family first experienced something odd in the house at about ten p.m. on March 11. A heavy glass beer mug lifted out of the kitchen sink

and fell behind a flowerpot. Both Mrs. Beck and her mother were in the room at the time, but neither of them had been close to the glass. Later there was the sound of a loud crash from upstairs. Because of a number of robberies in the neighborhood, Mrs. Beck first assumed it was a burglar. However, when the family investigated, they found a large piece of crystal lying on the floor about four feet from the bookcase on which it had been sitting. The crystal was broken into pieces. "I don't see how it could have gotten off the bookcase in the first place," Mrs. Beck said, "nor how it landed four feet away."

Although disturbed by the incident, they thought little more about it until a few minutes after eleven p.m., when a heavy glass ashtray hurtled across a downstairs room. Half an hour later another piece of crystal inexplicably shattered. Too unnerved to stay in the house, the family left and checked into a hotel for the rest of the night. Little did they know, however, that the strange events had just begun!

The three women returned home the next day at around one thirty in the afternoon. Nothing had been disturbed while they were away, but within thirty minutes, they again heard the sounds of shattering glass. The women ran from room to room to find bowls, vases, and glassware lying broken and cracked. When Mrs. Gemmecke stood up from a chair where she had been sitting in the kitchen, a coffee cup that had been lying in the sink on the other side of the room suddenly flew and smashed against the wall, just above the chair she had vacated. Bewildered and frightened, the family did what so many others in similar circumstances have done—they called the police.

Sergeant John Mullin was the first officer on the scene. He found three nervous and agitated women in a house littered with broken glass, plates, and assorted objects. He suggested that the damage had been done by the sounds from a "hi-fi stereo" or by a "pellet gun," despite the fact that the house contained only one small record player (unplugged at the time) and intact storm windows that were free from any kind of cracks or holes that bullets would have made.

Another officer, Ray Patton, witnessed the strange events firsthand. Around eight thirty p.m., Mrs. Beck took Patton to her bedroom to show him a smashed mirror that was lying on the floor. She also showed him three matching glasses that had been part of a set of six the day before. The other three had been mysteriously broken, and

for safekeeping, Mrs. Beck had placed the remaining three under a hat on the dresser in her bedroom.

As Patton left the empty room and walked into the hall, one of the glasses that had been hidden under the hat struck him in the back and broke into several pieces. The glass flew with such force that it left him bruised and sore for days afterward. A moment later he heard the sound of more breaking glass. Patton crossed back into the room and found another glass lying broken on the floor. He raised the hat where the three glasses had been and found only one left! The room had been completely empty at the time, and there had been no one else nearby but the officer—a witness that even a skeptic would have to believe was a reliable source.

The police were also baffled by a new angle in the strange case. Bizarre punctures or bites appeared on the hands and arms of Mrs. Beck and her mother. The tiny puncture wounds looked like those made by a bat, according to police records. How could a bat have been flying around a house in Indiana in the middle of the winter? Even debunkers haven't been able to explain this.

The phenomena subsided by March 22, leaving the house a disaster. Aside from the broken objects, feathers had been torn from pillows, pictures had been ripped from their frames, and walls and woodwork were dented from where objects had been violently thrown against them. The three women were left with no answers as they began cleaning up. But the Beck family was not yet out of the news!

On March 26, a call from one of the neighbors brought police back to the Becks'. They arrived to find Mrs. Gemmecke lying on the floor, apparently semiconscious. She revived for a moment, and one of the officers observed her throw a heavy ashtray against a wall and then overturn a piano bench. Naturally, she was immediately under suspicion for causing the other

recent incidents and was arrested for being "disorderly."

Mrs. Beck said her mother was in diabetic shock and needed medical care. The older woman was taken to the hospital and examined, then brought to the city jail for the night. In court the next day, the judge proposed holding her for a mental examination but agreed to dismiss the case if Mrs. Gemmecke returned to Germany within ten days. She agreed and was released into the custody of her daughter.

The newspapers reported that it was Mrs. Gemmecke who had caused the poltergeist activity at the house. They were aided in this conclusion by "research" done by Lieutenant Francis J. Dux of the Indianapolis Police Department. He told the papers he had "tried to get the spirits to come out and play, but they wouldn't." It seems his research consisted of sitting the Becks down in their home for an hour and a half and observing them. When nothing occurred, he concluded the activity happened only when one family member was out of sight and away from the others. Nothing paranormal was involved in the case, he said.

But a family friend disputed the charges against Mrs. Gemmecke. Emil Noseda was a respected Indianapolis businessman, and he and his wife had been on the scene for most of the outbreak. His account of the events differs greatly from those in the newspapers and official reports.

From what he had seen and heard in the house, Noseda said there was no way that Mrs. Gemmeke (or anyone else) could have done all the things that had taken place. He was sure something else was involved—a force that had deliberately broken objects in other parts of the house while all of them were seated together in another room.

One night, he said, a wall lamp was pulled off the wall, and Noseda reattached it with a larger nail. A few minutes later, it came down again, this time breaking, but no one was near it at the time. On another evening, Noseda, his wife, and the Becks were all in the living room when they heard a loud "racket" in the kitchen. They went to see what was going on and found three steak knives lying on the floor in the shape of a cross. The knives were put back in a drawer, and the group returned to the living room. The sounds were repeated a few minutes later, and they again found the knives on the floor and in the shape of a cross. "I have never seen anything like it," Noseda said, "never!"

There are also firsthand reports from Dr. William Roll, an eminent researcher of poltergeist phenomena. He was present in the Beck house between March 16 and March 22. He was impressed with Mrs. Beck's no-nonsense accounting of the events, which he noted were much less dramatic than the newspapers reports. He was also present

for many of the unexplained disturbances and chronicled 110 movements and incidents in all.

To rule out Mrs. Gemmecke as a suspect in the case, he used a more scientific method than had Lieutenant Dux. Dr. Roll enlisted the aid of Dr. David Blumenthal, a clinical psychologist in Indianapolis, who had first brought the case to his attention. The two men divided their time observing individual family members, which became crucial when they began to suspect that a strange knocking sound might have been the work of Mrs. Gemmecke. The sound could have been made by the movement of a large picture above her bed. Late one evening Dr. Roll was in the kitchen with Mrs. Beck, Linda was in bed, and Dr. Blumenthal was in the bedroom, holding onto the hands of Mrs. Gemmecke. A series of knocks came again—and no one present could have caused them!

Dr. Roll detailed the case in his 1972 book *The Poltergeist,* but even this well-known researcher could not find an explanation for what had taken place in the Indianapolis house. Despite his ruling out every natural cause and possible hoax he could think of, the case remains unsolved. It leaves a mark on the map of Indiana as a place where the unexplained made an appearance—if only for a little while.

Odon Fires

The rarest of poltergeist-related reports involve objects that catch fire for no apparent reason. Cases of so-called spontaneous combustion have been reported for centuries around the world, and while many can be explained away as the work of vandals or arsonists, some defy explanation despite careful and thorough investigation. One of the strangest of such cases occurred in the peaceful countryside near Odon in April 1941, in the home of a farmer named William Hackler.

The morning began as usual for the Hacklers. Since that spring had been unseasonably warm, Mr. Hackler rose early to begin his season's planting. Just after eight a.m., as the family was clearing the breakfast table and Mr. Hackler was headed toward the barn, the smell of smoke began to filter down to the main floor from the second floor of the home. The family frantically ran upstairs to search for the source of the smoke, only to discover a blaze in the wall of an upstairs bedroom.

Immediately the local fire department was called; they arrived in short order and extinguished the smoldering blaze. With the fire dead, the firemen left the Hackler farm, no doubt feeling the satisfaction of a job well done and a home spared from imminent destruction. As it turned out, however, this was one job that would not be so easily dispensed with.

Shortly after returning to their station, the firemen received a frantic call to return to the farm. Mrs. Hackler had discovered a second fire, this time in a mattress in an upstairs bedroom. The room was a guest room and rarely occupied; no one had gone in or out of it all morning.

When the fire department arrived, they were shocked to discover the smoky fire burning within the mattress, rather than on the outside. It seemed as though the feathers in the mattress had been set ablaze from the inside, without any cut or tear in the mattress cover. The mattress was dragged outside, cut open, and the flames doused. As one volunteer fireman later told a local paper, "It was like the fire was completely contained in the mattress—there was no way in the world you could set a fire like that."

Before the firemen could return to town once again, more fires were discovered throughout the house, seeming to erupt spontaneously in areas where no one had recently been present. No sooner had one fire been extinguished than another two were found. All told, nine fires were discovered at the farm by eleven a.m.

The number of fires was puzzling, but equally bewildering was their strange locations. A wall calendar suddenly burst into flames and simply disintegrated into ash and smoke. A bedspread was reduced to ashes while neighbors standing in the room at the same time watched in amazement.

One firefighter noticed a thin ribbon of smoke coming from a shelf in the living room. He walked over and picked up a book that seemed to be the source of the smoke. When he opened it, he found that it was burning on the inside! The cover of the book was in perfect condition.

A short time later another fireman, sitting at the kitchen table taking a break from the morning's events, was chagrined to see Mr. Hackler's overalls, hanging on a hook by the back door, start to smoke. Before he could intervene, they erupted into flame before his eyes and were reduced to ashes.

By two p.m., firemen from two adjoining counties had joined in the fight to save the Hackler farm, and by all accounts, they had their hands full. Twenty-eight separate fires were discovered and extinguished. No room was spared, and it was due only to the dedicated work of more than one hundred volunteer firefighters that the house was saved from total destruction.

turn their home into an inferno at will. The next day they moved in with Mrs. Hackler's sister, and a week later Mr. Hackler, with the help of neighbors and friends, tore down the farmhouse. He salvaged the lumber and eventually built another house a few miles away, where they lived for many years, unmolested by what had become known in the area as the "fire poltergeist."

No adequate explanation has ever been offered for the fires at the Hackler farm. At first, suspicion fell on the children of the family, yet the sheer number of fires that erupted so quickly in a home filled with firemen argued against such an assumption. Today faulty electrical wiring might be pointed to as a possible cause for the fire in the wall, yet at the time, the Hackler farm had not been wired for electricity. And faulty wiring wouldn't explain the fire in the mattress or in the book.

An hour later the fires ceased as suddenly and mysteriously as they had begun. Peace returned to the Hackler farm, and the firemen wearily returned to their homes, still perplexed by the day's events.

The Hacklers had had enough. They moved their beds to the backyard and spent the next night sleeping under the stars, reasoning it was better to suffer the chill of the night air than risk a return of the strange force that might

Today the former site of the fiery farmhouse lies peaceful and quiet. Looking at the pastoral field, it is hard to imagine that it was once the site of seven hours of terror and seemingly supernatural events that still defy explanation. For the moment, at least, the "fire poltergeist" of Odon is quiet. One can only hope that it will remain that way.

Things That Make You Go Hmmm in Kokomo

People in Kokomo are sick and tired of feeling sick and tired. For years, they have battled everything from headaches and nosebleeds to bouts of fatigue and diarrhea. But it's not the latest strain of flu that's responsible for this creeping malaise. Rather, it's a mysterious humming noise that has yet to be fully explained.

The first documented reports of what has become known as the Kokomo Hum date back to 1999. Initial reports described the noise as either a low-pitched hum or a rumbling noise. Some people reported that when they heard the sound, the ground also shook slightly. Mostly, though, it was just an annoying humming noise.

Think tracking down the source of an odd noise being heard throughout a city is easy? Think again. There didn't seem to be any discernible pattern to the hum. People of all ages reported hearing it at all hours of the day and night. Men heard it as often as women did. Some people claimed they heard the noise only in certain locations, like inside their house, while others could hear it no matter where they were in Kokomo. Strangest of all: With over 45,000 people living in the city, only a small percentage reported hearing the noise. Those who could hear it stated that their health began to suffer and that over time they became quite ill.

In 2000, one Kokomo resident took matters into her own hands and hired an acoustic consultancy firm to check her house for any strange noises or vibrations. Oddly enough, a low-frequency noise, at around 60 decibels, was detected in the home. The firm could not locate the source of the hum, but thought a nearby factory might be to blame. Regardless, shortly after the study, the homeowner packed her things and moved to another, presumably hum-free, city in Indiana.

In 2002, amid public outcry, the city of Kokomo announced that it was setting aside $100,000 for a study of the noise and that it was accepting proposals. Over a dozen consultant firms and research groups from all across the United States responded, and in November 2002 the Board of Public Works and Safety for the city of Kokomo officially hired a Massachusetts-based firm, Acentech.

Acentech was asked to determine if the hum actually existed, and if it did, to find its source as well as methods to reduce or eliminate the sound. When all the research was done, the company identified 126 homes and businesses where people reported hearing the hum or being affected by it. After plotting the locations on a map, Acentech began combing the area in an attempt to round up the usual humming suspects.

The company announced its findings in an October 2003 report. Two things were responsible for the hum, they said. The first was a cooling-tower fan located on the roof of the DaimlerChrysler casting plant in downtown Kokomo. A second, fainter noise was detected at Haynes International from an air compressor fan. As a result of the study, both companies took steps to minimize the noise. Haynes International even went so far as to install a muffler on their fan.

So, did the humming stop? It depends on who you ask. City officials are content with Acentech's findings and the subsequent changes DaimlerChrysler and Haynes International made. But some Kokomo residents say the hum is still there, though it now sounds more like expressway traffic off in the distance. These residents believe that more than a couple of industrial fans cause the hum, and they point to other such sounds being reported in the United States and as far away as Scotland, Japan, and Scandinavia. They feel more research is necessary and that the humming in Kokomo will continue until the real source is identified . . . or until it finally learns the words.

Buried Alive—Almost!

Sad news spread throughout the community around Penville that George Wellington had died. Most people believed the news and, at times, so did George Wellington. He was not a victim of the Grim Reaper, however. Instead, he was the victim of a strange malady that mimicked death—and almost resulted in his premature burial!

At the time of his "death," Wellington was a forty-two-year-old farmer. Well-liked, robust, and healthy, he enjoyed the outdoors, music, and spending time with his wife and his many friends. He and his friends had gathered at his home on the night of June 18, 1868. They laughed and drank late into the night, and Wellington said that he felt more like singing and dancing than sleeping when the party broke up. Nevertheless, he sent the revelers on their way, and he and his wife retired.

When his wife awoke the next morning, she was surprised to find that her husband was still in bed. She tried to wake him but couldn't. Terrified, she realized that he had died some time in the night. A doctor was summoned to the house and made the fatal diagnosis. He attributed the man's death to heart disease and surmised that Wellington had died at about three a.m.

The grief-stricken widow turned her husband's body over to the undertaker. In those days, an undertaker's work was not as invasive as it is now, but the man was perplexed by the pliant and robust condition of Wellington's body. He did not appear to be breathing, but he did not look dead. He seemed to be sleeping.

Cautious, the undertaker called in two more doctors to examine the corpse. They both said that Wellington was dead, but his family postponed the funeral for two days, just to be sure. When it was at last decided that he really was dead, his body was placed in a casket and a funeral service was held.

The body was loaded onto a hearse for the journey to the cemetery, and the mourners followed behind. Suddenly a runaway team of horses appeared, pulling an empty wagon. The hearse and wagon collided and both vehicles overturned. Wellington's casket crashed to the ground.

It took several minutes to get the horses from both vehicles under control. As men went to pick up Wellington's casket, they heard a blood-chilling sound from inside! It was a man's voice: "For God's sake, let me out!"

Friends and funeral attendants helped Wellington from his casket and listened in amazement to his story. He had awakened on the morning of his "death" at around five a.m. but had been unable to move. He said, "I had full use of my ears, but I could not open my eyes." He felt his wife trying to shake him awake, but there was no way that he could communicate with her. He became convinced that he was in a trance that mimicked death. He was terrified when all the doctors pronounced him dead and he realized that he was going to be buried alive!

While he was in his cataleptic state, Wellington could hear everything going on around him. He listened to his family, friends, and neighbors talking about his death during the wake and heard his funeral sermon as it took place. He knew from the sensations that followed that he was being taken out and placed in the hearse. He even heard the oncoming wagon just seconds before the crash that awakened him from his bizarre stupor. Wellington said, "I heard them trying to back the hearse and let the team go by, but they were not quick enough. As the collision came, my eyes opened and my speech was restored, and from that moment on, I was all right."

No one knows what ailment afflicted Wellington, but as far as is known, it never plagued him again. One can imagine, though, that when the time of his actual death eventually came, his family and friends made doubly sure that he was really dead before they buried him!

Santa Claus Statue, Santa Claus, Indiana

DEDICATED
TO THE CHILDREN OF THE WORLD
IN
MEMORY OF AN UNDYING LOVE
DEC 25 1935

Fabled People and Places

There's *a lot more* to Indiana than just cornfields and John Dillinger. There are unusual and unsuspected spots here and people who have made them great—or weird. There are strange places where tragic or mythic events have occurred. They include sites associated with mystical happenings, battling businessmen, and crimes attached to Indiana characters who have become larger than life. Some places we've heard of but have never been able to find, and some we don't believe ever really existed at all.

Keep that in mind if you go in search of these fabled places and people. The highways and back roads of Indiana can be adventurous, puzzling, and sometimes even spooky. We may be proud of Dillinger and the cornfields, but we can't help also feeling a swell of pride at the weirder side of the state.

Wolf Man of Versailles

Warren Zevon made us all familiar with piña colada–drinking werewolves in his song "Werewolves of London." But only from Indiana comes the strange tale of an ex–Civil War soldier who officially joined a wolf pack and became something like a wolf himself.

As the story goes, a man who has come to be known as Silas Shimmerhorn was fighting for the Confederates in the Civil War as part of John Morgan's Raiders. As the band of men neared Versailles in 1863, they were intent on disrupting the Union forces' supply route. But something happened along the way, and for some reason Shimmerhorn broke ranks from the rest of the Raiders and hid out in the woods of Versailles. This would seem to be a simple case of desertion, but then things got weird. The legend says that Shimmerhorn wandered through the woods for a while before finally settling into what has become known as the Bat Cave—a cavelike structure that is now part of Versailles State Park. In the beginning, we can assume that Shimmerhorn used his gun to get his food. But it was only a matter of time before his ammunition ran out. Plus there was the fact that the Union forces, and now the Confederates, would be searching for him, so any gunshots might attract attention. Consequently, Shimmerhorn took to hiding out in the cave during the day and then creeping out under the cover of darkness to raid local farms.

Shimmerhorn also had another, more pressing, problem: the pack of wolves that had moved into the area and were intent on claiming the Bat Cave for their own. We're not sure what type of negotiation skills Shimmerhorn had, but they were obviously pretty darn good, because he and the wolves apparently struck up a deal to join forces and live in the cave together. What's more, legend says that Shimmerhorn became part of the pack and started running and hunting with them. Perhaps that's the reason that local farmers would often come across animal carcasses bearing marks from the teeth of wolves, along with some strange markings and puncture wounds they were unable to identify.

As time went on, locals began seeing a naked man with long, scraggly hair and beard running in their fields at night alongside a pack of wolves. As more and more cattle were killed, the farmers decided to band together and track down these animals, as well as the person that they were now calling the Wolf Man of Versailles.

One story claims that a farmer spotted the pack entering the Bat Cave and ran to tell his neighbors. When all of them were armed, they proceeded to the entrance of the cave, where they were met with the most ferocious snarling they had ever encountered. Their lamps were not bright enough to pierce the darkness of the inner cave, so they had no idea what they were walking into, but the snarling they heard made them aware that, guns or no guns, they were incredibly outnumbered. At that point, the farmers chose to retreat from the cave's entrance.

But they hadn't given up completely. They made the decision not to try entering the cave again as long as the pack was so large. But every time it was spotted running through fields, farmers would open fire. No one ever managed to get a clear shot at the Wolf Man, though. Or maybe it was simply because he still looked too much like a man for someone to be able to take aim and fire at him.

The farmers had no problem shooting the wolves, though, and soon the pack's numbers began to dwindle until they were all but gone. It was then that a few brave souls decided it was time to try to reenter the Bat Cave. This time, there were no growls and snarls coming from the entrance. As the men made their way to the back of the cave, they found it empty except for an old straw bed and a rifle with "SS" engraved on it. That would seem to be the end of this weird story, but it's not, for even today there are reports that the area around the Bat Cave resounds with the howls of wolves late at night. Sometimes people catch a glimpse of a ghostly pack running through the woods. And running along with them is the spectral form of an unkempt man with long hair and a beard.

Mysterious Blue Hole

Located just outside the town of Prairieton is a legendary three-acre lake known as the Blue Hole. It is alleged to be a bottomless body of water, and has an almost equally bottomless capacity for stories of pirates, gangland ghosts, missing children, and even mysterious monsters.

Early Indiana folklore hints that the Blue Hole was a hiding place for Wabash River pirates. Locals claim the pirates buried their treasure nearby, possibly at the bottom of the lake itself, and then devised a series of traps to protect the loot. Thanks to this, no one has been able to find even a single gold coin. Many have died trying, adding to the extensive body count that has been linked to the Blue Hole.

In addition to luckless treasure hunters, years ago a busload of children was said to have plunged into the Blue Hole. As the bus crossed the bridge over the lake, the story goes, the driver lost control. The bus crashed into the water, and neither it nor the children were ever found. Another tale involves a train that derailed as it crossed the same bridge and tumbled into the lake, never to be seen again.

It's the telling and retelling of these tales that has created the persistent rumor that the Blue Hole is bottomless. Prohibition-era gangsters apparently believed this to be true. Six cabins that once stood on the shores of the lake were supposedly used as hideouts by Chicago mobsters. Many believe these men did not come here for the fishing, but instead dumped the bodies of their victims in the shadowy waters.

Further adding to the bottomless rumors is an incident that allegedly occurred in the 1950s. A group of teenage boys went swimming in the Blue Hole, and when they did not return, their worried parents came looking for them. When they reached the lake, they found the boys' clothing on the shore, but no sign of their sons. Word quickly spread that the boys had been sucked into some sort of whirlpool in the bottom of the lake, where they drowned.

In the 1960s, stories began to circulate of a monster that lived in the depths of the Blue Hole. This Hoosier version of the Loch Ness Monster was allegedly sighted many times by weekend partiers and fishermen, and arguments raged as to what it actually was. To some it was a huge water serpent risen from the depths of the lake. To others it was a huge catfish that had grown to the size of a cow.

Curiosity got the better of two Vigo County sheriff's deputies in 1969. They launched an expedition to explore the depths of the Blue Hole and spent most of the day below the surface of the water. They didn't find any sign of a train or a school bus but did feel the pull of an underground stream near the bottom. Could this be the "whirlpool" that is said to have claimed the lives of some of the victims who disappeared into the lake? The deputies didn't know, but they did prove the pool was not bottomless. They estimated the deepest spots at between twenty-two and thirty feet.

Did the deputies solve all the mysteries of the Blue Hole? Most would say no. Beneath the surface of the water, mysteries still lurk and legends still linger.

Corpse in the Closet

John Brown's body may have been moldering in the grave, as the old song goes, but the body of his son, Watson, ended up being stored in an Indiana closet! The story of the cadaver of Watson Brown is one of the weirdest ever told about the pre–Civil War era.

John Brown was an abolitionist with a hatred for slavery so strong that he would do anything to stop it: even kill. Many northern abolitionists viewed him as a hero (if not also a fanatic), but he was seen as a madman and a zealot in the South and feared by everyone who knew him. In 1856, he had been one of the fighters against slavery in "Bloody Kansas," and three years later he devised a plan that he believed would create an army of slaves that would battle to end slavery once and for all. On October 16, 1859, he put his plan into action.

He and fifteen recruits (including his four sons) armed themselves heavily and set out for Harpers Ferry, Virginia, under cover of darkness. They managed to surprise the handful of defenders at the small federal arsenal there and easily took it over. They planned to use the weapons they captured for Brown's slave army, but it all backfired when the first townsperson killed in the raid was a free black man. Instead of being met by masses of escaped slaves eager to join the cause, Brown was met by angry townspeople. These were soon joined by a militia force, and when Brown refused to surrender, they stormed the building and overpowered his

men. Brown was wounded, captured, and turned over to Virginia authorities. Ten of his followers died at Harpers Ferry, including his sons Oliver and Watson.

Brown was tried for treason against the state and conspiracy to incite insurrection, found guilty, and sentenced to hang on December 2, 1859. The sentence was executed, and both his body and the body of his son Oliver were buried. However, for many years, no one knew what happened to the body of his other slain son, Watson. It would turn out that instead of being buried, his body had been preserved in a salt barrel and sent to a medical school at Winchester, Virginia. It remained there in storage for the next three years.

HARPER'S FERRY INSURRECTION—BRINGING THE PRISONERS OUT OF THE ENGINE-HOUSE.—FROM A SKETCH BY OUR SPECIAL ARTIST.

Meanwhile, the Civil War had begun in earnest. When Dr. Jarvis Johnson of the Twenty-seventh Regiment of Indiana Volunteers arrived at Winchester with occupation troops in 1862, he took command of the medical college. He soon learned that he possessed the body of Watson Brown and that southerners wanted it. Johnson refused to turn over the body because he believed it was a symbol of the fight against slavery.

What happened next was described by Johnson in 1882. "I, afterward, in the summer of 1862, shipped the body by express to Franklin, Indiana, that point being the nearest express office to my home, then Morgantown, Indiana, and the said specimen had been in my possession and under my control ever since. And I have no doubt whatsoever but that it is the son of the heroic John Brown."

Johnson kept the body, which was eventually reduced to a skeleton, as a treasured possession. When he and his family moved to Martinsville, they kept the remains in a second-floor closet on a sun porch.

In 1882, Dr. Johnson learned that a monument was being placed in honor of John Brown and his sons at the old Brown family farm. In a newspaper story, he read that Mrs. Brown knew nothing of what had happened to the body of one of her sons, so he quickly wrote to her and told her that Watson's corpse was in his possession.

John Brown Jr. traveled to Martinsville and, with Dr. Johnson and the state geologist, John Collett, authenticated the identity of the skeleton. We can only hope that Johnson removed the remains from his closet before the brother of the dead man arrived.

The younger Brown took the body to North Elba, New York, and it was placed in the family burial ground, bringing to an end one of the longer, weirder journeys ever taken by a corpse.

Camp Chesterfield and the Ghost That Never Was

Here's a ghostly tale without a ghost, only some shrewd Hoosiers. And, to be honest, some gullible ones too. It began when a pair of young sisters, Maggie and Kate Fox, started claiming they could communicate with the deceased. They became celebrities, and their story gave birth to the booming movement of spiritualism. Before her death, Kate Fox admitted that the sisters had made up their supposed communications with the Other Side, and it seemed that spiritualism would be dealt a death blow.

However, the movement survived through the years and even into modern times. One of its best-known centers is located near Indianapolis in the small town of Chesterfield. The first of several large meeting halls was built there in 1891, and since that time the halls at Camp Chesterfield have been used for large public séances.

As the summer session of 1949 began, a new medium—Madam Mimi, as she was called—soon became renowned among the faithful at the camp. Mimi had reached the heights of full-trance mediumship, including the channeling of unearthly voices as well as the production of "apports," or physical objects produced by the spirits. Word of the seemingly extraordinary talents

of this medium soon reached the ears of an Indianapolis newspaper editor named James Sevrin. He found the story interesting enough to send a young reporter, Bob Leazenby, down to Camp Chesterfield to observe the proceedings. No doubt he intended that Leazenby would produce an exposé on the fraudulent practices employed by Mimi and spiritualist mediums in general.

If this was his intention, the editor must have been gravely disappointed. Within two days, the cub reporter was back in his office with an article relating, in glowing terms, the inexplicable phenomena produced by the medium. He had become a believer.

When Madam Mimi, a short, robust woman garbed in a flowing white robe, took the stage, Leazenby reported, she spoke for about twenty minutes, preaching the truth of spirit communication and the wisdom imparted to her from her spirit guides. Next an assistant came on stage and draped a blindfold securely around her head. A bowl was produced containing small slips of paper upon which audience members had written questions. It was stressed by Madam Mimi that the questions had been kept backstage, unread by her or her assistants.

With great dramatic flair, Madam Mimi reached blindly into the bowl before her, retrieved one of the billets, and held it to her forehead. Then, swaying slightly, she read out a question and gave a brief answer. A scream of delight from one of the audience members made it clear that Madam Mimi had correctly adduced both the question asked and the answer sought. Time and again she retrieved slips from the bowl before her, each time apparently reaching the right vibrations with regard to the queries.

Madam Mimi then removed her blindfold and entered the audience. Stopping at the seat of one elderly man, she grasped his arm, closed her eyes, and muttered, "The spirits tell me that you have lost someone near to you . . . a nephew perhaps?" Dumbly, the man shook his head in assent. "Your nephew is here tonight," Madam Mimi intoned. "He says that his passing was difficult. . . . Was he killed in a forest?" "Yes!" the gentleman erupted, "in France!" "Your nephew wants you to know that he is at peace and his mother is here with him," Madam Mimi concluded. "That's right—my sister died last year!" came the reply from the man.

Now Madam Mimi continued up the aisle, stopping at the seat of a young woman. Once again, she grasped the woman's arm and pronounced that an elderly woman named Florence wished to convey her love to her and to say that she should make peace with her sister. At this, the young woman leaped up and hugged the medium, crying, "My mother, my mother!"

Madam Mimi once more climbed to the stage, and the lights were dimmed. A "spirit cabinet" was wheeled out. Several assistants came forward to tie Madam's hands securely together. Next she was placed on a small seat in the cabinet, and her head was tied with a band of cloth to a wooden post at the back of the box. The door to the cabinet was shut and latched.

A few dramatic sounds emanated from the box, perhaps an unearthly trumpet or a beating tom-tom. Then a small aperture at the top of the door was opened, just above the level of the seated medium's head. Slowly at first, a white vaporous substance began to appear through the small opening. Increasing in volume, it billowed forth from the cabinet and stretched out toward the crowd. Someone in the front row gasped, "My God, it's ectoplasm!"

Now from the midst of the white fog there appeared a spectral face. It was that of an Indian maiden, who peered out at the audience for a long moment before melting away, only to be replaced in an instant by the face of a young soldier. This face also disappeared behind the mist, and another face, that of a weathered old man with a long white beard, emerged.

Slowly the white cloud emanating from the cabinet began to dissipate, some of it seeming to withdraw backward into the box. The door was then opened, and Madam Mimi, clearly exhausted from her ordeal, was untied and helped out.

Back home in Indianapolis, the young reporter waited in expectant silence as Mr. Sevrin read the article he had written. When the wizened old editor finally looked up, his eyes seemed to twinkle with an odd mirth. "This is certainly an interesting story," the editor began, "and worth some investigation. However, before we print this story, I think we need to go back to see Madam Mimi. I even have a friend who might be interested in coming too."

The next week Sevrin accompanied Leazenby and met up with two gentlemen in a restaurant just a few miles from Camp Chesterfield. The older man, who sported a graying goatee beneath a hawk nose and dark eyes, introduced himself as Wayne Wirtz. His companion, a small studious-looking young man, he introduced as Sam Nesbitt.

As the four sat and talked, Leazenby eagerly gave an account of what he had seen on his trip to Camp Chesterfield. He was puzzled to see his two new companions taking careful notes and sharing knowing glances at each other across the table. An hour later the four found themselves seated in the large hall on the grounds of Camp Chesterfield waiting for Madam Mimi to appear.

The performance was a repeat of what the young reporter had seen previously, complete with floating ectoplasm and grateful audience members. After it ended, Mr. Wirtz and Mr. Nesbitt spoke together for a moment and then suggested that the four meet at the restaurant in an hour. They then excused themselves, saying that they had some "business to attend to."

When the four met later, young Bob Leazenby was eager to hear if Madam Mimi had made believers of his companions. Mr. Wirtz was the first to respond. "Oh, she made me a believer all right," he said. "I believe that she is a total fraud—and not a very good one either." "How can you be so sure?" gasped the reporter. "Because," the older man responded, "we can do everything that she can—and better too!"

At this point, Mr. Sevrin interrupted. "Bob," he said, "perhaps I should tell you a little more about my friends here." The pair, he revealed, were professional magicians, both members in good standing of the Hammond Mystics, one of the oldest and most respected magicians' clubs in Indiana. Magicians were sworn enemies of spiritualists—no less a personage than Harry Houdini had mounted a one-man war to expose them as frauds. Magicians everywhere considered it their duty to discredit those who preyed upon people's grief and vulnerability.

Patiently, Wirtz and Nesbitt then began to explain the methods the medium had used to sham the audience. Blindfolds, they explained, could be gimmicked to give the medium a clear view of questions written on paper. All the medium need do was make her answers vague, and an impressive display of "psychic reading" was accomplished.

With regard to the impromptu readings given members of the audience, Nesbitt noted that it was common practice for mediums to put "plants" in the audience prior to a séance to talk to audience members. With a few innocent questions, these allies were able to pick up information that, when relayed to the medium, would provide her with seemingly supernatural knowledge.

Finally the two conjurers said that the "spirit cabinet" was an old magicians' trick. It was easy to appear to tie the hands of a person, while in reality allowing them easy escape from their bonds. The medium could then produce endless effects with the aid of musical instruments and other paraphernalia hidden in the closet. The so-called ectoplasm was nothing more than smoke and gauze, unrolled so as to look, from a distance, like a white vapor. A mask behind such a fog would reveal a ghostly face of startling appearance.

Crestfallen and disillusioned, Leazenby remarked that now there was nothing to do but go back and write another story revealing Madam Mimi as a fraud. However, at this, one of the magicians replied, "Not so fast young man. The fun is just beginning."

The pair then revealed that they had arranged for a private séance with the medium. The time was set for the next evening, prior to the scheduled public performance. "Be there tomorrow night at six," Wayne Wirtz directed.

The next evening the four met outside the hall and were ushered into a dark room with heavy curtains cloaking each side. There was a large round table; in its center sat a smoldering bronze brazier. In due course, Madam Mimi entered, resplendent in her flowing white gown. She instructed the four men to sit with her at the table and to join hands in silence.

As the men took their seats, the medium explained that she was about to go into a trance, and that they were to remain absolutely still and silent. With these words, she lowered her head and shut her eyes in an attitude of rapt concentration.

After some moments, Madam Mimi began to roll her head back and forth, murmuring, "I feel the presence of spirits. . . . Are you here?" Suddenly a knock was heard

coming from the table. Next the sound of a spectral bell rang through the air. Madam Mimi adjured the spirits to make themselves known.

The table began to tip slightly on one end as though lifted by a powerful hand. "The spirits are strong this night," intoned Madam Mimi. "With whom do you wish to speak?"

She never received her answer. Abruptly, the table, which had tipped just moments before, lifted completely off the floor, levitating sideways in a long arc before landing back on the floor with a dull thud. Then a series of knocks erupted from the table, until all present recognized the familiar cadence of *Shave and a haircut, two bits.* Suddenly the sound of a bell again filled the room, this time ringing frantically. "Sounds like it's dinner time!" whispered Mr. Wirtz.

Madam Mimi's eyes snapped open, and her head jerked forward. At that moment, the fire in the brazier erupted in a geyser of flames that shot three feet upward, sending sparks flying across the table. The brightness of the blaze blinded the Madam, who reared back in fear.

It took a moment for the medium to regain her sight. Through the darkness of the room, she could see the figures of the four men seated before her. Behind them, she beheld a number of faces peering down at her. Between them, in luminous letters across the dark air were the words "Madam Mimi—FAKE!"

More loud knocking and the frantic clanging of the unseen bell echoed through the room. The table was lifted a foot from the floor despite the fact that those present still sat serenely in their seats, their hands joined on the elevated table.

Perhaps a braver mystic might have stayed and attempted to recapture the situation. Madam Mimi, however, opted for a quick escape. In a voice choked with fear, she uttered, "I don't know what the hell is

going on here, but this ain't part of the act!" She ran from the room, and the two magicians erupted in convulsive laughter.

Finding the light switch, Mr. Sevrin illuminated the room, revealing the masks and slate board painted with luminous letters that the magicians had used during the séance. "I'm just sorry the Madam left so soon," said the younger magician. "We were just getting warmed up." The two magicians did not reveal the secrets behind the other strange happenings they had engineered, the wildly levitating table, the blazing geyser, and syncopated knocking. Some illusionist mystery must be preserved. One thing is certain though. They were a product of this world and none other.

Madam Mimi did not appear for her public séance that night. Indeed, the esteemed medium packed her bags and was never seen in Indiana again. The magicians returned to Hammond with their effects, another notch in their belts. Newspapermen Sevrin and Leazenby returned to Indianapolis to write their story, which ran on the front page the next week.

Camp Chesterfield continues to thrive and vehemently disavows the presence of Madam Mimi on the campus, as well as the visit of magicians Wirtz and Nesbitt. While the camp does not deny the existence of fraudulent mediums, it still considers most mediums to be genuine, and it staunchly defends the truth of the doctrines they promote.

But if you ask a member of the magical arts community in Hammond about the validity of the phenomena they produce, chances are he will smile and ask you to sit for a while to hear a story. Then, perhaps with a smirk, he will tell you the greatest ghost story that never was.

Wolf Lake: Gangland Graveyard

Few can deny the haunting quality to the ancient woods and swamps around the William W. Powers Conservation Area, better known as Wolf Lake. This area of grasslands, swamps, and forest straddles the border of Indiana and Illinois south of Chicago. It is perhaps the most notorious spot in the region, and with very good reason.

In addition to the drowning of many young children in the cold waters of the lake, bodies have been discovered in the wild, swampy lands surrounding it. Over the years, police officers from both Hammond, Indiana, and Chicago have been seen tramping through the woods, searching for evidence of one crime or another. Is it any wonder that

stories of restless spirits and lonesome ghosts surround this eerie place?

During Prohibition, the most talked-about "one way ride" to Wolf Lake involved Al Capone's gunmen John Scalise and Albert Anselmi, and Unione Siciliana president Joseph "Hop Toed" Guinta. Their bullet-riddled bodies were found on May 8, 1929, inside a car that had been dumped into a ditch along an undeveloped piece of Wolf Lake property, just across the Indiana border. Who killed them remains a mystery. Some believe that Al Capone took the men out himself. It was said that he might have feared they were plotting to move against him.

In 1935, Wolf Lake became a dumping ground for

"Wrigleyville Torso Murder" victim Ervin Lang. Ervin's mother-in-law, Blanche Dunkel, hated him because he had spurned her advances after her daughter's death. Blanche recruited her friend, former stripper Evelyn White, to actually carry out the crime. It was Evelyn who drugged and then strangled the unfortunate Lang.

The next morning her estranged husband dismembered the body and shoved the torso into a large trunk, which they then drove to Wolf Lake. (Ervin's legs were left in a roadside ditch near Munster.) They dumped the trunk into one of the many swampy areas nearby, never expecting it to be found. But someone stumbled across it just four days later. Blanche and Evelyn were both later convicted and sentenced to prison.

The most famous crime tied to Wolf Lake is the abduction and thrill killing of fourteen-year-old Bobby Franks by Nathan Leopold and Richard Loeb in May 1924. This is one of the saddest and most inexplicable of crimes. Bobby was kidnapped from the fashionable Kenwood section on Chicago's South Side and murdered by the two young men, merely for the thrill of carrying out the "perfect crime." Within twenty-four hours, the body of the young boy—and a pair of eyeglasses that Leopold dropped at the scene—were discovered. Loeb and Leopold had stuffed the body into a culvert underneath some railroad tracks near 121st Street.

The killers were soon in custody, and detectives and prosecutors quickly unraveled their perfect crime.

The spot where Bobby's body was discovered is hard to find today, but not impossible. The railroad tracks that once crossed the area have been replaced with an asphalt bike trail. The culvert was destroyed many years ago, but those who grew up in the area remember where it once was and can take you to the place where Bobby was discovered. It is a grim, silent, and desperate spot that could be haunted in its own right.

In the late 1990s, Wolf Lake was also the dumping ground for at least three victims of serial killer Andrew Urdiales. A Marine who had been honorably discharged in 1996, Urdiales had returned to the southeast side of Chicago to live with his parents, where he got a job as a security guard. Restless and unable to sleep, he sought psychiatric help from a Chicago veterans hospital. In April 1996, a psychologist there urged him to "become more open about expressing his anger." Urdiales probably didn't mention his history as a serial killer–rapist in California at that time.

So Urdiales set about finding ways to express his anger in the Chicago/Indiana area. Between April and August of that year, he assaulted and murdered three young women; then he finished each off at Wolf Lake, to which he was strangely drawn. Perhaps its nefarious past appealed to him, or maybe it was the many secluded, marshy places surrounding it: perfect spots for dumping bodies. He'd later tell detectives that after he killed the third woman, Wolf Lake just "seemed like the right way to drive."

DEDICATED
TO THE CHILDREN OF THE WORLD
IN
MEMORY OF AN UNDYING LOVE

DEC 25 1935   Carl A Barn

A Town Called Claus

One of the most eccentric towns in the state and a place of weird and usually happy memories for legions of Hoosiers who grew up in the '60s and '70s is the town called Santa Claus. It's a strange place to be on a July afternoon when temperatures are in the nineties, but there doesn't seem to be any other state where such a surreal little village could exist!

Santa Claus, which sits in the southern part of the state, was founded in 1852 with the name of Santa Fe. Within a few days, however, the small town discovered that another town in Indiana had chosen that name first. According to reports, the first Santa Fe threatened legal action against the second, forcing a group of local business owners to come up with a new name. The story goes that their meeting was held on Christmas Eve at the local church (which also served as the town hall and school) and in the middle of it, the church doors inexplicably blew open and those assembled inside heard sleigh bells in the darkness.

A small girl who had been brought to the meeting by her father shouted, "It's Santa Claus!" The men burst into laughter but decided the Christmas symbol would make a wonderful name for their new town. There's another version of the story that claims the adults had been drinking during the long meeting, and by the time they heard the sleigh bells, they were ready for anything. Regardless of what really happened, Santa Claus it was.

The commercial potential of the name was not realized until 1935, when Santa Claus Town—believed to be the world's first theme park—opened its doors. Unfortunately, it's been replaced by the more politically correct Holiday World, where Santa shares time with the Easter Bunny, the Fourth of July, and the park's mascot, a longtime favorite in the lore of Christmas: Holidog! You remember him in the "Night Before Christmas" poem, right?

But this slightly tacky theme park is not really the small town's claim to fame. Every year, the post office here receives about 200,000 holiday cards to be postmarked from this famous town and a half million or more letters that are simply addressed to Santa Claus. Believe it or not, each Santa letter is answered personally by a contingent of "elves," local volunteers who want to maintain the spirit of the village.

And that's not the only strange thing about this town. Otherwise ordinary businesses and homes have been modified to look like castles, snow-covered lodges, and dwellings for elves. They rest along Noel Street, Candy Cane Lane, Prancer Drive, and other festively named streets. Even the town's fire department has gotten into the act. The fire truck is named Rudolph and has a red light for its "nose."

The Santa Claus War

It was not always ho-ho and holiday cheer in the town of Santa Claus, however. On the outskirts, you might come across a crumbling statue of Santa sitting atop a hill. Not so strange, considering the town's name. And yet there's something weird about the statue. In fact, it looks more than a little like a tombstone. So why is it there? Is it a town limits marker? A misplaced holiday decoration? Neither. The fact is that the decaying statue, as well as the abandoned ruins hidden in the woods behind it, are victims of the infamous Santa Claus War, one of the fiercest battles ever fought in Indiana.

It all began in the late 1920s, when the mountain of letters sent each year by hopeful children to the Santa Claus post office attracted the attention of businessman Milton Harris. Looking around the small town, Harris thought it odd that even though it bore the name Santa Claus, jolly old Saint Nick was nowhere to be found. He felt that needed to change, and, working with Postmaster James Martin, he came up with a unique idea. They would create a magical place called Santa Claus Town.

Nowadays theme parks are everywhere, but they didn't exist in those days. So it's safe to say that Harris and Martin were straying into uncharted ground. But that didn't stop them. Harris began by purchasing or leasing, it's not clear which, close to one thousand acres around the town. They then started to look for corporate sponsorship for the buildings they were planning on creating, including a candy castle, a toy village, and of course, Santa's workshop.

While all this was going on, another one of Santa's helpers rode into town, a man by the name of Carl

Barrett. Barrett claimed to be repulsed by what he felt was too much commercialism in the Harris and Martin project (although some say he was just jealous that they stood to make so much money). Whatever the reason, he grabbed a piece of land less than a half mile from Santa Claus Town and announced his plans to open his own Santa Claus Park. The war was on!

The two contenders spent the next few years filing lawsuits against each other, Harris and Martin alleging that they actually held a lease on the land Barrett had purchased, while Barrett denied their claims. As this was going on, Harris and Martin also announced they had reached an agreement with the Curtiss Candy Company, makers of Baby Ruth and Butterfinger, to help with their Santa's Candy Castle and that they would also be featuring products such as Lionel trains and Daisy air rifles in their Santa Claus Town.

Harris countered this corporate sponsorship by asking children, in the true spirit of Christmas, to send him their pennies so he could erect a solid granite statue of Santa Claus on the hill; the statue would also serve as the entrance to his Santa Claus Park. Incredibly, the pennies came pouring in, and Barrett eventually had enough money to begin building the statue of Santa.

Harris and Martin were the first to officially open a themed attraction in America when they dedicated the main building in their Santa Claus Town, Santa's Candy Castle, on December 22, 1935. Barrett meanwhile busied himself creating his Santa Claus statue along with

Santa's Candy Castle
Tour the 70 year old Castle &
Buy Discount Holiday World Tickets
Just 1 mile Past

building a log cabin, a wishing well, and other buildings for his park. Then came his crowning achievement, his answer to the crass commercialism of his rivals. Three days after the dedication of Santa's Candy Castle, on December 25, 1935, Barrett unveiled his solid granite statue, built with the kiddies' pennies. Everyone who saw it remarked that the children must have been very generous, for the statue stood over twenty feet tall and was estimated to weigh close to forty tons. It depicted Santa carrying a bulging sack full of toys and was mounted on a pedestal bearing the inscription DEDICATED TO THE CHILDREN OF THE WORLD IN MEMORY OF AN UNDYING LOVE. The pedestal also bore Barrett's signature, the date of the dedication, as well as other quotes, religious and otherwise, on the other sides. All of this was then mounted on a giant brass star of Bethlehem, which pointed toward the East.

Santa Claus Cracks

Over the next few years, Barrett continued to battle Harris and Martin in court for control of Santa Claus. Harris and Martin continued adding more buildings (and sponsors) to their Santa Claus Town, while Barrett relied on the power of his granite Santa Claus to bring people to his park. But then people started noticing something strange about the statue; it was cracking. As parts of the pedestal began to crumble, it became obvious that the statue was not made out of granite. Rather, it was simply concrete. Needless to say, this did not sit well with the people who had been led to believe it was solid granite, nor with all the children who had given their hard-earned pennies for the creation of the statue.

Then the Santa Claus War was put on hold when an even bigger war broke out: World War II.

There wasn't room for Santa Claus attractions during those tough days, and things were quiet in the town for a while. At the end of the war, Barrett and the Harris and Martin team attempted to resurrect their respective attractions, but now there was a new elf in town, Louis J. Koch. On August 3, 1946, Koch opened his own theme park, Santa Claus Land, which would eventually include such spectacular things as a roller coaster and even a water park. The attraction was later renamed Holiday World and featured areas revolving around Halloween, July 4, and even Thanksgiving.

Holiday World thrived, but the other two theme parks fell into ruin. Barrett's Santa Claus Park was abandoned first, while Santa Claus Town was eventually sold off and most of its buildings were either demolished or made into apartments.

Recently, Santa's Candy Castle was renovated and reopened as a stand-alone attraction. Santa Claus Park was not so lucky. Sure, the town of Santa Claus created a replica of Barrett's statue and proudly displays it in the center of town, but the original still sits atop a lonely hill, surrounded by a weed-choked metal fence and reindeer that have lost their antlers. And a short ways up the bumpy path behind the statue, the woods are slowly reclaiming Santa Claus Park, piece by holly-jolly piece.

Leavenworth, a Town That Wouldn't Give Up Its Seat

County seats have come and gone in Indiana. In the earlier days of the state, towns would spring up, seeming to have promise of a great future. But railroads would bypass communities, or once thriving roads would be diminished by other highways, and that promise would wither. In many counties, the seats of government changed to go along with the changing times. Residents of the "de-seated" towns were seldom happy about the changes, but little could be done—at least in most cases.

There was one town in Indiana history that refused to give up the fight. Its residents battled against losing their place as county seat for more than two years. Eventually, the new county government had to be set up at gunpoint!

By the early 1890s, the town of Leavenworth had been the county seat of Crawford County for more than fifty years. But traffic on the Ohio River had waned, and increased trade farther inland, in the town of English, brought a desire for a new courthouse there. A petition was created that called for the relocation of the county seat from Leavenworth to English, and it was circulated in a very unusual way: by a contingent of armed men! A skirmish line formed across the county in December 1893, and the men supporting the petition marched through the countryside to gather signatures.

There were many who said that the men, who armed themselves with rifles, pistols, knives, and hatchets, intimidated people into signing the petition. Others claimed the names were simply signed by the men from English and then attested to by other skirmishers. In spite of this, the commissioners at Leavenworth accepted the petition and English became the new county seat. But it was not to happen without a fight!

The people of Leavenworth organized against the move. They left their guns at home, however, and chose to fight their battles in court. The case moved through several courts, but finally the English petition was passed. English began construction of its courthouse, and by April 1895, it had everything that a county seat should have—except for the records and the county officials, which Leavenworth refused to surrender. Administrators in English berated Leavenworth and issued writs, letters, and complaints, but to no avail. Finally, the townsmen gave a man named Jack Goodman the authority to do whatever it took to make English the county seat, and on April 24, he acted.

In the darkest hours of the night, he gathered wagons, riders, guns, and men and they marched from English to Leavenworth. When the courthouse there opened the next morning at eight a.m., Goodman's "army" forced its way into the building at gunpoint and loaded all the county records into their wagons. County officials were dragged from the building and escorted into the wagons as well. Everything was hauled back to English, and within a few hours, the town had made its courthouse operational. It was now filled with records, filing cabinets, desks—and, of course, officials to fill the desks, issue the licenses, and carry out the day-to-day operations of the county seat.

Jack Goodman's army, believed to have numbered 478 men on foot, 82 cavalry riders, and 96 wagons, had managed to succeed where the law, documents, and harsh words had failed. They fought a battle to rescue their rightful place as the county seat—and they never had to fire a shot.

Even *if you have never been afraid* of walking alone in the moonlight, you might be by the time you finish this chapter. For legend has it that wild things lurk in the dark woods and remote regions of Indiana. These strange creatures can be found on land, in the water, or perhaps even in your own backyard.

Sightings and stories abound, yet proof that these legendary creatures have actually set foot in the state—or at least evidence that satisfies mainstream science—remains elusive. But cryptozoologists—researchers who study unknown creatures—know that there are more things in the world than science can account for. So before you laugh and dismiss out of hand Indiana's many tales of terrifying beasts, read on. And if you ever find yourself stranded in the forest or along a back road in Indiana, keep watching over your shoulder.

You never know what might be sneaking up on you!

Bizarre Beasts

Bigfoot Walks in Indiana

For more than a century, reports have filtered out of rural Indiana about strange, humanlike beasts that resemble a cross between a human being and an ape. Most witnesses tell of their odd appearance and the horrible odor that emanates from them. The stories of these creatures, which have come to be called Bigfoot, have been passed down through generations and have been chronicled by both professional and amateur researchers.

According to eyewitnesses, the creatures are usually seen wandering alone. They reportedly are omnivores, are largely nocturnal, and are less active during cold weather. They average around seven feet in height, with unusually powerful limbs that are described as being proportioned more like those of people than apes. However, their broad shoulders, short necks, flat faces and noses, sloped foreheads, ridged brows, and cone-shaped heads make them appear more animal-like. The creatures are most commonly reported as being covered in dark, auburn-colored hair, although reports of brown, black, and even white and silver hair occasionally crop up. Their footprints range in size from twelve to twenty-two inches long—most commonly eighteen inches—and are around seven inches wide.

Without a doubt, America's most famous Bigfoot sightings have taken place in the Pacific Northwest, but such creatures do turn up in Indiana as well.

Oldfoot

The first report of a mysterious apelike creature in Indiana dates back to December 1839, when settlers around Fish Lake in LaPorte County spotted a "wild child" in the woods. The creature was said to be about four feet tall and covered with light, chestnut-colored hair. It moved quickly and made frightening noises, like a combination of a bark and a scream. Witnesses also claimed to have seen

it swimming in the lake and foraging for food along the shoreline.

It would be four decades before another sighting was reported, this time near Lafayette in July 1883. Mrs. Frank Coffman, a local farmer's wife, was walking through the woods when she saw a strange creature eating bark from a tree. She said that it appeared to be female, with long black hair on her head and short gray hair covering her body. A hunting party of over a hundred men pursued the creature for more than half a mile, but she was too fast for them. Several of the men also noted that the creature used tree limbs and branches to travel above the ground with great speed. When the animal reached a nearby swamp, she vanished and was not seen again.

More than sixty years later another Hoosier Bigfoot encounter was reported. In July 1949, two dozen local residents saw a "big hairy beast" at Thorntown. They said it looked like a tall gorilla with protruding teeth. Two fishermen got close to the creature, but it became angry and chased them away. The sightings continued for several days, and then the monster disappeared.

Four years later, in the summer of 1953, a group of people had a close encounter with a creature near Winamac. They described it as being at least seven feet tall and covered with long, dark hair. It walked on two legs. Several children who saw it said the beast had only one eye. A witness later reported that he had grabbed his rifle and prepared to shoot the monster, but he'd been afraid to fire because it was like "shooting a man."

During the 1960s, Bigfoot appeared in at least ten locations throughout Indiana. Most of the encounters boasted multiple witnesses and huge tracks left behind at the scene. The monsters ranged from five to ten feet in height, and one of them, a creature seen near French Lick, earned the nickname Fluorescent Freddie because of his glowing red eyes.

Bigfoot and the UFOs

The weirdest Bigfoot encounter of the 1960s occurred near Rising Sun on May 19, 1969. The previous day, a farmer named Lester Keiser said that his power had gone out, while his neighbors reported seeing several UFOs in the sky overhead. Then, at seven thirty p.m. on May 19, Keiser's son, George, claimed he saw a shaggy, black creature standing in the barnyard. He described it as being a little under six feet tall and very apelike. As George approached it, the beast grunted at him, leaped over a ditch, and took off, running into the forest. The Keisers later made plaster casts of its footprints, which had four toes on them.

The 1970s were even stranger in Indiana—at least when it came to Bigfoot reports. There were at least thirty-five alleged encounters with hairy creatures of unknown origin during the decade. They included familiar descriptions: The beasts ranged from seven to twelve feet tall and were covered with hair. But now the creatures also smelled like sewage or dead fish. In two cases, witnesses reported seeing monsters in connection with UFO sightings, and one woman, Jackie Tharp, claimed that a hairy creature grabbed her by the arm in December 1977. It ran away when she screamed, leaving thirteen-inch-long tracks behind.

In early August 1972, Bigfoot reportedly laid siege to a farm owned by Randy and Lou Rogers outside Roachdale. Initially, the couple claimed to have heard sounds of growling coming from the woods, followed by neighbors' reports of seeing UFOs in the area. One night, a foul-smelling prowler began creeping around the Rogers farmhouse, pounding on the walls and knocking on the windows. Randy borrowed a gun from a friend and stood guard, reporting numerous sightings of a seven-foot-tall creature over the next three weeks. He said the monster walked upright but never left any footprints, even in fresh mud. Sometimes, it peered into the windows at Lou when she was cooking, and since it seemed harmless, she started putting plates of leftovers out on the porch for it at night. The plate was always licked clean the next morning.

The story of the creature went public on August 22. When a predator killed sixty chickens on Carter Burdine's nearby farm, he blamed the attack on the Rogers creature. Burdine said that he shot at the monster when it returned to kill more chickens, but it got away unharmed. Over the next two weeks, more than fifty local sightings were reported, but, eventually, the monster vanished.

Large, Hairy, and Screaming: Encounters Through the Millennium

Thirty-four Bigfoot encounters surfaced in Indiana in the 1980s. One of the most curious took place in southern Knox County in October 1981. After two sightings of a large, unfamiliar creature along the White River, Terry and Mary Harper reported that a prowler had attacked their home on South Fifteenth Street in Vincennes. According to the Harpers, the creature had ripped and gnawed at their aluminum siding and had torn off part of the back door's metal trim. Whatever it was, it left blood, scratch marks, teeth marks, and tufts of white hair behind at the scene. Sheriff's deputies informed the Harpers that the blood they found was "not human," but they made no further attempt to identify its source. And in the winter of 1988, witnesses in Vermillion County allegedly recovered "unusual hair" from the woods after they saw a monster that let out some "diabolical screams." No analysis was done to identify the origins of that hair, either.

The 1990s saw eighteen separate Bigfoot encounters. Most reports described the creatures as simply being "large," but occasionally more details were added. A Kosciusko witness saw Bigfoot in his own yard and said that its nose was "very wet." The creature approached him and touched his arm, leaving his sleeve damp, then ran away.

There have already been more than thirty-nine Indiana Bigfoot reports in the new millennium, including actual sightings, as well as instances of tracks, sounds, and odors. A remarkable similarity characterizes most of the descriptions, although a Vigo County fisherman reported seeing a Bigfoot "family" near Seeleyville in October 2001.

On January 30, 2002, Penny Howell and Dale Moore saw an apelike creature crouching alongside Chapel Hill Road, near the entrance to Monroe County's Hardin Ridge Recreation Area. They said that the monster was about five feet tall, but weighed at least two hundred pounds. It was covered with black hair, except for a patch of white on its face and neck. The creature left four-toed tracks behind in some wet clay, with claw marks that were more than an inch long. Controversy later erupted over this sighting: The tracks were dismissed as marks left by everything from a bear to a big cat to a dog, but in the end, no one came up with a definitive answer.

What are these strange creatures? Are they actually some sort of cross between a human being and an ape? Are they a new species altogether—or an old one that has managed to survive in secret, only rarely brushing elbows with humans? Whatever these Indiana mystery monsters are, they certainly have a devoted following. Those who pursue them often concentrate their searches in areas where Bigfoot creatures have reportedly left their footprints—Lawrence, Monroe, and Perry counties, which lie within or adjacent to the rugged Hoosier National Forest. This protected wilderness area covers some four hundred square miles in south-central Indiana, and sightings regularly occur in this region.

Phantom Panthers & Mysterious Cats

Officials still maintain that there are no big cats left in Indiana, that hunters reportedly killed the last one in 1851. So why do people still report seeing panthers and cougars roaming the state, and why do many of these sightings involve black panthers—a breed of big cat that has never been known to exist in Indiana, or even North America, at all?

The panthers have appeared at regular intervals (or "flaps") and then disappear without a trace. Legends and folklore have traced their appearance to wrecked circus trains and escapees from local zoos, and this may account for some of them. But is that the whole answer? Many people still wonder where these massive animals came from. And why they keep showing up in Indiana!

Early Panther Sightings

Phantom big cat reports in Indiana date back as far as 1877. In that year, a young woman named Mary Crane was viciously mauled by one of these creatures near Rising Sun. The predator escaped, but left six-inch pawprints at the scene.

Thirty years later, in 1908, residents of Gibson and Pike counties worried about a panther that was being spotted in the area. Hunters tried to track it through the swamps, but the only "creature" they managed to capture was a hobo who had been camping out in the woods.

Then in July 1947, residents of Fountain City began reporting wild, unearthly screaming that was frightening their cattle at night. A policeman named Louis Daniels saw a large cat while out with his family for a drive near Centerville. He described it as "the strangest, most vicious-looking thing . . . long front legs, a large head with small pointed ears, and small glittering eyes. We all remarked that it was the most ferocious, evil-looking

thing we had ever seen." This event would be the precursor of a major panther flap in 1948, which became known as the Year of the Varmint.

1948: Vintage Cat Flap

The big cat, or some other unseen predator, returned in July 1948. It killed seven hogs on the farm of Dorten Moore, who arranged a stakeout with three sheriff's deputies in case the thing returned. The panther did not come back to Moore's farm but struck at neighbor Harold Erskine's farm instead. That night, Erskine heard some strange screams and found another slaughtered pig. Another farmer caught a glimpse of the creature as it chased him from his own barn.

On August 1, 1948, conservation officer Charles Cornelius and game warden Clifford Fath spotted a large cat on a country road. Fath was driving when he saw the "varmint" sitting in the middle of the road, and he swerved to avoid it. The cat, which the men guessed weighed as much as three hundred pounds, charged Fath's car, slamming into the side of it and then escaping into the woods. The officers summoned assistance and tracked the animal with dogs. After a long chase, they managed to tree the cat and open fire on it through the canopy of leaves overhead. Somehow, the cat escaped.

On the evening of August 5, two married couples and their children were fishing in a pool below Elkhorn Falls, south of Richmond, when a huge cat emerged from the woods. One of the men ran to a nearby home and called the police. The cat was gone by the time Deputy Jack Witherby arrived, but he examined the tracks left behind. He said, with some assurance, "They are like nothing I have ever seen before."

It got even weirder two days later when brothers Arthur and Howard Turner saw two large cats on their farm near Richmond. The larger cat was brown, with a shaggy mane, and the smaller cat was black. Arthur Turner shot at them with his rifle, but the cats escaped without injury. The animals did leave tracks behind, but the Turners' hunting dogs refused to follow them.

On August 11, James Leo found a huge black cat sitting on the back porch of his home in Pennville, just west of Richmond. He ran into the house to get a knife with which to defend himself, but when he came back out, the panther was gone. He called the police to report the incident and, later that night, called them again to report that he had shot at a "varmint" from his bedroom window. He told the police dispatcher, "I know I hit him but I'm too scared to go out and see what I hit." Officers investigated but found no cat, tracks, or blood at the scene.

On August 22, more livestock was killed at the farm of Orris Tate near Sand Creek. He found a series of five-inch pawprints surrounding a fatally mauled pig. Six days later, "something" attacked Henry Foreman Jr. while he was cutting tobacco on his farm near Peppertown. The animal ripped Foreman's clothing and gashed one arm. It fled before the farmer could get a good look at it, but he noticed that it was dark yellow in color. This incident sparked more sightings in the immediate area, but search parties turned up no clues.

The last sighting in 1948 occurred on September 11. Two men repairing a barn roof saw an unknown animal "about the size of a wolf with yellow spots" wandering out in a field. It left without menacing the men or the nearby livestock.

More Recent Big Cat Sightings

A number of big cat sightings occurred toward the end of the twentieth century and have continued into recent times. In late September 2003, a black panther was reported near Albion. Those who spotted the creature—but failed to capture or photograph it—included several law-enforcement officers, a police dispatcher, and a number of townspeople.

In May 2005, during a phantom panther flap in Monroe County, Kristina Vosburgh saw a large black cat cross Tapp Road in front of her car. She said that it looked a lot like a cougar, except that it was black. She said, "I know that it's almost impossible for a cougar to be in Bloomington, but that's what it looked like."

In early July 2005, another woman spotted a sleek black cat in broad daylight. The creature was pacing along a rural roadway in Elkhart County. The witness reported: "It was completely black . . . and I watched it for a few minutes until it strolled out of sight toward the woods. I was glad it stayed in the road and didn't veer from its path to bother the horses."

Livestock belonging to Sherry Rohan of Whitehall were not so lucky. On January 31, 2006, a black cat that was larger than her German shepherd invaded her pigpen and killed seven hogs. More animals were mauled and threatened in Monroe County in March 2006. An unseen animal savaged three of Susan Pauly's dogs, killing an adult Labrador retriever. State Department

of Natural Resources officials blamed the incident on coyotes or wild dogs, but locals were already talking about a black panther. An employee of the Grandview Elementary School, located near the Morgan-Monroe State Forest, recently tried to videotape a large black panther as it crossed her backyard. Unfortunately, her batteries failed and she was unable to record any evidence of its presence.

We're Not Lion about This

Scores of residents accept the idea that black panthers often turn up within the state, but if these same people were asked to believe that an African lion once terrorized Indiana, would they be so open-minded? According to accounts from 1962, a lion did turn up here, and for a brief time, it was the terror of the region.

In June of that year, three years before Monument City was flooded to create the Salamonie Reservoir, a local farmer named Ed Moorman survived an attack by a cat that he and other witnesses claimed was an "African lioness." After two more sightings, Moorman summoned Sheriff Harry Walter, whose deputies discovered nothing.

On January 25, Moorman found ten of his pigs slaughtered and their hearts and livers devoured. Moorman called the sheriff again, but the search proved fruitless once more.

Other locals, who claimed to have heard "bloodcurdling howls" in the night, theorized that the lion was an escapee from some unnamed zoo or circus, but no big cats were reported missing anywhere in the Midwest.

Ed Moorman, along with other armed men, was present when the cat made its last appearance a short time later near Huntington. Unfortunately, two cameramen from an Indianapolis television station spooked the lion, and it disappeared once more.

Catlike Creature of Tippecanoe River

The monsters that lurked along the Tippecanoe River in the early 1870s were not aquatic beasts, but rather something strange and completely unfamiliar that terrorized the region from Atwood to Bloomingsburg. They wreaked havoc on local farms, slaughtering livestock and eluding the hunters who dared to chase them.

An account from 1872 stated, "For some months past this vicinity has been infested with two of the most uncouth looking animals that were ever seen, and so piercing were their hideous screams that it shook everybody with awe who heard them."

On December 12, 1871, two local men, J. H. DeBolt and Del Latham, set out with weapons and a half-dozen dogs to try to track down the creatures. After a two-mile pursuit, they met the beasts in a thicket, where a fight to the death took place. The hunters wounded both monsters with rifle shots and then attacked them with knives. Despite help from their dogs, both men were badly wounded in the skirmish. Latham suffered a fractured skull when his rifle misfired, and one of DeBolt's arms was nearly severed. Still, Latham managed to kill one of the creatures with a shot to the head, but the second one escaped. DeBolt lost his arm, but both men recovered from their injuries.

According to an account at the time, at the site of the melee, friends of the hunters "found the ground strewed with blood, bloody knives, broken firearms, pieces of wearing

apparel and dead dogs, all presenting scenes of a blood struggle. The animal killed was found to be six feet nine inches in height, and weighed 217 pounds. Its hide was taken and can be seen at the store in Bloomingsburg. The teeth and feet are on exhibition at the office of Dr. Hall, in Tipton."

Tragically, no evidence of this creature remains today. The beast's remains have long since vanished. But what were these creatures? The accounts never say whether they were humanlike or catlike, leaving an unsolved mystery in the wake of the story.

Around the world, more than eight hundred lakes and rivers have produced stories, legends, and reports of mysterious monsters. Scotland's Loch Ness, with its stories of Nessie, may be the most famous, but it's certainly not the only one. Dozens and dozens of North American lakes and rivers boast their own strange creatures, and, as it turns out, Indiana harbors more than her share!

Oscar—the Beast of Busco

Indiana's most famous bizarro may be a mysterious snapping turtle that makes its home near Churubusco. This titanic terrapin, which has been dubbed Oscar, has earned a place of honor in Indiana lore as the Beast of Busco.

Churubusco is a peaceful little town about fifteen miles north of Fort Wayne in Allen County. Its unusual name came from the town of Churubusco in Mexico, where America had won a battle during the Mexican War around the same time that the Indiana community was first settled, in 1847. As time passed, it was not the unusual name that attracted visitors. It was Churubusco's most famous resident, a turtle named Oscar.

According to local lore, a man named Oscar Fulk was the first to sight the Beast of Busco, in 1898. He was swimming in a lake on his farm (later named Fulk Lake in his honor) when he saw the immense turtle, swam up to it, and even carved his name on the creature's shell, thus branding him Oscar. The beast would not be seen again until 1914—sixteen years later—but everyone seemed to know he was out there. After that sighting, Oscar would not resurface again until the 1940s.

Fort Wayne resident Gale Harris purchased the Fulk farm from the old man's descendants in November 1947. Harris knew the story of the giant turtle but never gave it much thought until July 27, 1948, when his brother-in-law and a friend went fishing on the lake. The anglers returned with tales of seeing huge waves caused by something in the water and then seeing a huge turtle "going away like it was a submarine." The life span of snapping turtles in the wild is unknown, so it's possible that this was indeed the original Oscar.

A few months later, Harris saw Oscar for himself while he was patching the roof of his barn with the help of his pastor. He looked out toward Fulk Lake and saw something that looked like a big head moving through the water. Both men ignored it, but a second sighting the next morning persuaded them to investigate. They went down to the lake and saw a huge turtle, its shell approximately six feet long and four or five feet wide.

In the coming months, Harris saw the creature many times and once grabbed its tail while he was out on a boat with his son. Oscar did not take kindly to this. He capsized the boat, knocking Harris and his boy into the water, but he didn't bother them any more. He simply turned around and swam away.

In early March of 1949, a local newspaper, the *Columbia City Commercial Mail,* demanded a hunt for Oscar with headlines like FIVE HUNDRED POUND TURTLE WOULD MAKE LOTS OF GOOD TURTLE SOUP. A few days after this headline ran, the newspaper reported that a hunting party of about thirty men managed to lasso Oscar's hind leg with a chain, but the turtle escaped. The next day a neighbor blamed Oscar for snatching one of his cattle, but at that point, editors were bored with the story and declared that Oscar was "a dead issue as far as this paper is concerned."

Undeterred by the competition's lack of interest

in Oscar, the *Fort Wayne Journal Gazette* published its first story about the tremendous turtle that same day. In this story, a newsman for the paper, Cliff Milnor, coined the name Beast of Busco. This story inspired more efforts to capture, or protect, Oscar. On March 14, Churubusco's Community Club started a Turtle Committee to study the problem, while Indiana's Society for the Prevention of Cruelty to Animals protested plans to kill him. On March 18, Woodrow Rigsby, a diver from Fort Wayne arrived to search Fulk Lake, but he almost drowned in front of 750 people who turned out to watch.

The search continued with mostly comic results. Another diver, Walter Johnson, became trapped in the lake when he sank up to his chest in mud. Gale Harris allegedly netted Oscar on April 24, but the slippery creature managed to escape again. Hunters dredged the lake with nets and hooks, but found nothing. On May 9, after trying everything else, they brought a female turtle to the lake in hopes of seducing Oscar. She failed to get his attention.

Frustrated by a lack of results, Gale Harris began draining Fulk Lake in September 1949. The water was pumped into a ditch that fed nearby White Lake. After a week, most of the water was gone but there was still no sign of Oscar. Hunters managed to trap a fifty-two-pound snapping turtle, but they found nothing as large as the Beast of Busco—until October 9. That afternoon, with Fulk Lake now just five feet deep, Gale Harris claimed another successful harpooning

of the creature. And once again, Oscar managed to capsize his boat and escape.

The hunt was abandoned in January 1950, when a ruptured dam flooded the site with water that had been previously pumped out. Years later, Harris would voice his belief that Oscar had escaped from Fulk Lake using an underground channel that fed into another lake. Although far-fetched, this might explain another giant turtle sighting that occurred in Black Oak Swamp (south of Gary) in July 1950. Whether this was Oscar, or another giant creature, it was never seen again.

Oscar's story left a lasting impression on the town of Churubusco, and even today, the image of a smiling turtle graces official city letterhead. In April 1950, eighteen local civic groups organized Turtle Days, an annual event that includes turtle races, a parade, and even the election of a Turtle Queen. By 1971, Churubusco's summer festival was billed as "the world's greatest celebration for a turtle." Today, a sign outside of town declares Churubusco to be TURTLE TOWN USA.

In spite of all of this attention, the mystery of Oscar—just how he got there and where he went—remains unsolved. But he holds a special place in the hearts of animal fanciers as one of the most colorful, and beloved, of all of Indiana's bizarre beasts.

Churubusco—Loch Ness, U.S.A.!

The story I have is the story of my hometown. It is the story of Churubusco (Busco). We are the "Loch Ness of the U.S.A." Here is our story I hope you enjoy.

The Beast of Busco (Oscar) is a turtle so giant you could set a table for 6 on his back, with a mouth so large he could eat a soccer ball. You might think this was a story that interested a few yokels down at the local brew dispensary, but radio and newspapers across the nation fell in love with the story. Some European papers even picked it up. The story began in July 1948, when two men from Churubusco, Ora Blue and Charley Wilson, went fishing in Fulk Lake on Gale Harris' property. When they finished, they told Harris about a giant turtle they'd seen. According to Churubusco resident Rusty Reed, a turtle expert, the original report was a hoax. He based that on a conversation he had with Blue. "Charley Wilson was known to tell tall tales and Gale Harris was known to believe anything," Reed said. So when the newspapers reported the sighting of a large Turtle on Harris' farm, the two fishermen enjoyed a laugh. Except that Harris now claimed to have seen the turtle himself, and it was every bit as big, if not bigger, than Wilson and Blue had reported.

This wasn't the first time a large turtle had been sighted in Fulk Lake. The original owner of the property, Oscar Fulk, claimed to have spotted a giant turtle in 1898. Another sighting came in 1914, and I have heard the Indians knew of the turtle long before us. During the first days of March in 1949, Harris saw the turtle again. A group of townspeople suggested capturing it, and according to newspaper reports they just about caught Oscar on the first day. A trap of stakes and chicken wire penned the beast in about ten feet of water. A movie (now apparently vanished) showed the turtle swimming just below the surface.

But you don't catch a legend that easily. Oscar flexed some muscle and waltzed out of the trap. On March 7th, the Columbia City newspaper reported the search. The next day, reporters from Fort Wayne showed up. One was a young reporter from United Press International, who sent the story across the wires. Timing is everything, and the timing was perfect for such a story. Americans were ready for a happy story. On March 9th, newspapers across the nation ran the story of the giant turtle. For more on this story, you may just have to visit our two stoplight little town of Churubusco. We celebrate our town every June, and remember Oscar in doing this. We would love to have you visit our small town that at one time had the world watching us. In my opinion Oscar still lives, but under the protection of the town. We will never tell, for his safety.—*Robert Green*

Lake Manitou Monster

Lake Manitou, near Rochester in Fulton County, had an evil reputation with the Native American population long before the first white settlers arrived. The name, which means "Devil's Lake" in Pottawatomi, referred to an Indian legend of a devil-snake that inhabited the lake.

Fulton County's early settlers heard the legends when they first came here, but dismissed them until July 1838, when four local fishermen reported seeing a creature in the water that was at least sixty feet long. Soon after, a blacksmith named John Lindsey was riding along the lakefront and saw an animal raise its head three or four feet above the water. A local newspaper, the *Logansport Telegraph*, reported: "The head he described as being about three feet across the frontal bone, and having something of the contour of a beef's head, but the neck tapering, and having the character of the serpent; color dingy, and with bright yellow spots. It turned its head from side to side with an easy motion, in apparent survey of the surrounding objects."

Lake Manitou's monster was not seen again for eleven years. In May 1849, a fisherman reported that he had harpooned "a very remarkably long fish." It measured about seven feet long, which was far shorter than the monster that had been reported earlier, but still much longer than the small, inland lake should have contained. Could this have been the monster known to the Indians?

Most people thought so until 1969, when a woman named Carole Utter and her teenage son saw a "huge fish" surface near their boat. She stated that the creature was longer than her fourteen-foot fishing boat and that she did not see all of it in the water. Utter's uncle later told her a number of people he knew, including several veteran fishermen, had also seen the creature—and that most had vowed never to fish in Lake Manitou again.

The creature continued to be sighted throughout the 1970s and into the 1980s, but recently the waters here have been strangely quiet. Is the creature still lurking out there beneath the surface, waiting to put in another chilling appearance?

Dogtown Lizard Man

This strange creature, felt but never seen, brings eerie images of the famed Creature from the Black Lagoon of horror movie fame. On August 21, 1955, Mrs. Darwin Johnson and her friend, Mrs. Chris Lamble, went swimming in the Ohio River near Dogtown, which is a few miles upriver from Evansville. While hanging onto an inner tube about fifteen feet from the shore, Mrs. Johnson felt the distinct pressure of a hand grab her left leg and pull her underwater. She kicked free, but the unseen assailant grabbed her and yanked her down beneath the surface once more. Again, she fought her way free, but the attacker—whoever or whatever it was—kept a firm grip on her leg. It was only when Mrs. Lamble swam over to try to help her friend that the hand released its hold.

Mrs. Johnson said that the hand that grabbed her had clawed fingers and what felt like a "furry" palm. Investigator Terry Colvin confirmed that Johnson's leg bore a green stain, shaped like a palm print, which could not be removed for several days.

When the Evansville newspaper ran a short article on the incident, several locals claimed that they had recently seen a "shiny oval" hovering above the river where the attack had occurred. The UFO sightings brought a U.S. Air Force officer to the Johnson house. He grilled Mrs. Johnson for several hours and reportedly took copious notes.

Over the years, it has been suggested that what Mrs. Johnson felt on the mysterious hand could have been scales rather than fur, and the idea of the "lizard man" was born.

Mud Mermaids

In October 1894, another weird story filtered out of Vevay, located on the Ohio River in Switzerland County. According to the story, "two nondescript creatures horrible in appearance and habit" had been discovered on the river's bank. Locals dubbed them the "mud mermaids" and claimed they were amphibious in nature, like huge lizards with human features. They allegedly subsisted on a diet of fish, mussels, and other aquatic prey. The mermaids—or the mermaid and merman; they seemed to be a mated pair—were first seen in 1891. Witnesses said that their faces were "strikingly human" but they had doglike ears and "bore no signs of intelligence."

Weird Menagerie of Water Monsters

On April 22, 1892, the *Vincennes Commercial Weekly* reported that a local resident named Isaac Daines had spotted a sixty-foot, serpentlike creature in Horseshoe Pond, which was located about six miles south of Vincennes. Other witnesses included Daines's wife, his hired hands, and several neighbors.

Daines described the creature as being black on its back and sides, inhabiting the water but staying close to shore, and gliding through the pond like a snake swimming. Whenever he tried to approach the creature, it became alarmed and quickly swam away. He had tried to kill it several times but had failed on every occasion.

Daines told the newspaper that his next plan was to recruit a "firing squad" of locals, all armed with Winchester rifles, to attack the creature all at once. Unfortunately (or fortunately for the monster), the plan never came to fruition. Soon after, the beast vanished and was never spotted again.

In June 1892, another "serpent" was seen in Big Swan Pond, also close to Vincennes. This beast was smaller—only about twenty-five feet in length—and had a white head, which it carried above the water as it swam. It was reported to be "spotted red and yellow, like the side of a large water snake." The witnesses who saw this monster were said to be men of "good repute and veracity." By the time a hunt was organized, this creature had also disappeared.

In August 1904, newspapers reported that a strange beast was dwelling in a local swamp near Converse in Miami County. The swamp was located at the back of Frem Pence's farm and was first reported by a neighbor and her daughters, who were picking wild raspberries nearby. They were frightened by the sound of loud screams and then saw their dogs running away as quickly as they could. The woman and her girls followed suit and went to fetch her husband. He returned to the area, shotgun in hand, and found the bodies of two dead hogs, presumably the victims of some sort of attack. Whatever had killed them seemed to have come out of the water.

Two weeks later, another berry-picking party returned from the swamp with more tales of strange noises. One of the women in the group claimed that she had seen something black coming out of the water near some bushes. It made the same bloodcurdling noise the other women had heard. This time, a group of hunters scoured the area but found nothing out of the ordinary. Whatever it was—if it was anything at all—was lost in the swamp.

The out-of-place and unusual animals of Indiana could create an entire menagerie for one of the weirdest sideshows that ever played a county fair in the state. We have seen everything here — mysterious panthers, lions, alligators, human-like beasts, and more. But no chronicle of Indiana's weird animal reports would be complete without one last look at some of the really, really strange creatures encountered in the state!

Hoosier Werewolves

Surprisingly, werewolves hold a time-honored spot in *Weird Indiana* history.

The mythological belief in werewolves has been with us for centuries. Many historians and folklorists have pondered the origins of the belief in lycanthropy, or the human ability to change into animals, such as wolves, bears, big cats, and other dangerous creatures. The transformation of human into wolf is the best known, largely due to Old World traditions of wolves being feared as predators. There are many historical accounts of wolves preying on human beings during wars and hard winters in Europe, although not all accounts can be taken as fact. However, true accounts were prevalent enough that the French had a word for the wolf that has acquired a taste for human flesh — the werewolf or the *loup-garou*.

Indiana's werewolf stories date back to the first French trappers who wandered the land. Wherever French explorers traveled in the early days of the region, their *loup-garou* followed and, if their stories are to be believed, it was a hungry monster made of flesh and blood.

But not all these creatures were deadly. For instance, the White Eagle werewolf was actually said to befriend a hunter named Soudenière and nurse him through a terrible illness. At Vincennes, a werewolf rescued a farmer named Jacques Cabassier after his horse plunged into an icy river. Another intervened to help American forces defeat British soldiers during the Revolutionary War.

It's easy to chalk up these tales to someone's overactive imagination, but werewolf sightings continue to this day in Illinois and Wisconsin. In light of these stories, we may not want to be too quick to dismiss them. There are certainly stranger things lurking out there in the woods and fields of Indiana.

Red-Eyed Headless Monster

Renowned weird researcher Charles Fort uncovered a report of one strange Indiana sighting that allegedly occurred in September of 1891. According to the story, two ice deliverymen in Crawfordsville saw a "seemingly headless monster" soaring overhead in the early morning hours. It was about twenty feet long and eight feet wide, they said. Its noisy flight awakened a Methodist minister, the Reverend G. W. Switzer, who lived nearby. He also observed the creature from his bedroom window.

According to a story reported in the *Indianapolis Journal* on September 5, 1891, hundreds of residents of Crawfordsville got the scare of their lives when they saw the massive headless flying monster circle their town. The next evening the creature appeared again before hundreds of residents. They spoke of its single red eye and the screams it let out.

The Jackson Dragon

According to a newspaper report from 1879, a farmer named Jacob Rishel was passing through a field in Jackson Township on August 16 and noticed something very peculiar. He saw tall grass waving about in an erratic manner, like a small whirlwind, and turned to get away from the disturbance. He became very frightened when the grass began moving in his direction, and his fright turned to absolute terror when the grass parted to reveal a "huge reptile or monster the like of which he had never seen before."

Rishel ran for his life but the monster kept pace with him, coming so close that the farmer could feel its breath. It seemed to be a huge snake, and yet it had horns protruding from its head above each eye. After a breathless chase, Rishel managed to make it to his barn, grab a scythe off the wall, and then turn to confront the beast. His first blow severed one of its horns. He was able to kill the monster by cutting off its head after it became snagged in the prongs of a reaping machine.

Rishel then contacted several of his friends and they examined the beast. Describing it as a snake, they measured it: It was about thirty-four feet in length and about "as thick as a barrel." The head was remarkably small and flat, and the color was akin to that of a garter snake, with a dark green stripe running down its back. A newspaper account stated, "The snake was skinned and the skin sent to Chicago, where it will be stuffed and placed on exhibition."

Needless to say, the trophy never reached Chicago, and no record of it remains today.

Local Heroes and Villains

A *surprising number* of odd people, strange characters, and, yes, all-around weird folks seem to make their home right here in Indiana. Every small town, big city, and village at the edge of the cornfield seems to have its own "characters": eccentric, one-of-a-kind residents who make their mark on Indiana history in ways both big and small.

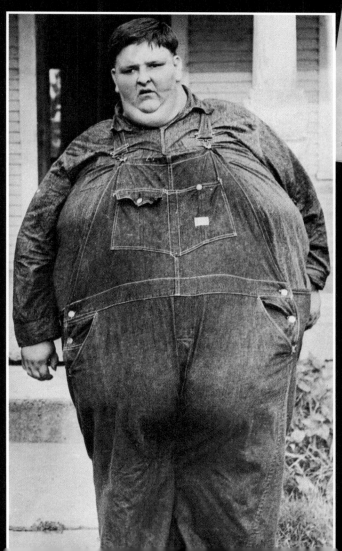

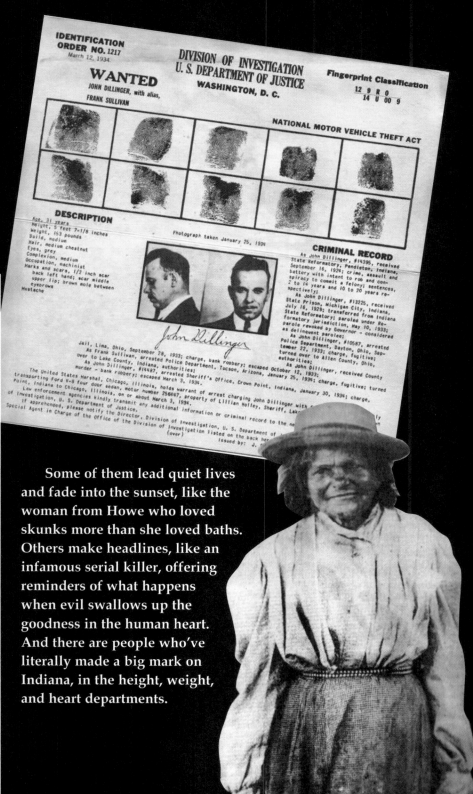

Some of them lead quiet lives and fade into the sunset, like the woman from Howe who loved skunks more than she loved baths. Others make headlines, like an infamous serial killer, offering reminders of what happens when evil swallows up the goodness in the human heart. And there are people who've literally made a big mark on Indiana, in the height, weight, and heart departments.

LaPorte's Black Widow

One of the most macabre chapters in Indiana history started with a fire. On April 28, 1908, a blaze broke out on a forty-eight-acre farm just outside LaPorte. The flames quickly engulfed the farmhouse, and nothing could be done to save the building or its residents: owner Belle Gunness and her three children. When the heat had subsided enough for rescuers to go in, firefighters found the charred remains of four corpses lying on a mattress in the basement. Three of the bodies were those of children, the smallest of which, a boy, was laying across the arm of a headless, adult female body.

The location of the corpses and the apparent decapitation of the adult female immediately gave rise to the suspicion of murder. It did not take long for police to name a suspect: a former hired hand at the farm named Ray Lamphere. He had worked for Belle for more than a year, but the two had a falling out, and in the months before the fire Belle had told the police several times that Lamphere was stalking her and making threats against her and her family. He had been charged with trespassing twice (and convicted once).

Lamphere was found a few hours later at a nearby farm and arrested. He admitted traveling near Belle's farm that morning—even to seeing the fire from a distance—but he steadfastly maintained that he had nothing to do with starting it. The story might have ended with the trial and possible execution of a disgruntled hired hand, but it was about to take a horrific turn.

On May 1, 1908, a Norwegian farmer named Asle Helgelein arrived in LaPorte in search of news about his brother, Andrew, a farmer from Aberdeen, South Dakota. He had left his home on January 2, telling his family that he would be gone for about a week. When he did not return, Asle searched through his brother's belongings in

Belle Gunness and Ray Lamphere

Aberdeen and found several letters from Belle Gunness. One letter urged Andrew to sell his farm and move to LaPorte, where the two would share the "finest home in Northern Indiana." In another letter, she insisted that they keep their communications a secret from his family, and asked him to "sell all that you can get cash for, and if you have much left you can easily bring it with you whereas we will soon sell it here and get a good price for everything."

His suspicions aroused, Asle Helgelein wrote to the LaPorte police, who replied that a man fitting his brother's description had been seen in LaPorte in the company of Mrs. Gunness. Communications with Andrew's bank in Aberdeen also revealed that he had sent money to be collected at the First National Bank of LaPorte.

Asle Helgelein also wrote to Mrs. Gunness, who replied that Andrew had been her guest in January, but had left to go to Chicago, and then perhaps to Norway. In a subsequent reply, she reiterated her story, said she was also concerned about Andrew's whereabouts, and invited Asle to visit her farm in May.

Next, Asle received a letter from the First National Bank of LaPorte that included a newspaper article concerning the fire and subsequent discovery of four bodies. Alarmed, he immediately boarded a train to LaPorte. The following day, Asle searched through the burnt debris of the farmhouse, with the help of the local sheriff, for signs of his brother, but they found nothing. The next day, however, the men discovered something that would change the course of the investigation—and LaPorte history—forever.

A Hole in the Story

Asle Helgelein asked one of the farmhands if he knew about any holes that had been dug on the property in the early spring. The man remembered one in the garden, which he had filled in that March, after Mrs. Gunness had dumped rubbish into it. He showed them where the hole was, and the men started to dig.

After only a few feet, they became aware of a foul odor. Digging a few more feet, they uncovered a gunnysack, in which they were shocked to discover the neck and arm of Andrew Helgelein. Digging in another soft spot of earth a few feet away revealed the skeleton of what appeared to be a young woman. Beneath the skeleton was a rotted mattress, and when this was removed, the searchers found the remains of three other people: a large man and two children about twelve years old. The bodies were moved into an outbuilding for safekeeping.

The LaPorte farmhouse ablaze on April 28, 1908

Word spread about what was developing in LaPorte, and by May 10 an estimated fifteen thousand people from across the Midwest converged on the site to witness what had become one of the largest murder investigations in Indiana history. More bodies were discovered—most in a severe state of decay—all removed from holes and soft spots in the ground. A carnival-like atmosphere pervaded the area, with vendors hawking ice cream and lemonade to picnicking spectators. At least one vendor was sold out of postcards bearing a picture of the gruesome remains of Andrew Helgelein.

It was immediately clear that many of the murders could not have been the work of Ray Lamphere. Instead, the crimes appeared to have been carried out by Belle Gunness. There was evidence that she had not died in the fire; rather, according to this scenario, she had murdered her children and an unknown woman to take her place, set the fire, and then fled the scene. Giving rise to these suspicions were the missing head on the adult female body and the fact that the burned woman's remains showed that she was of a slighter build than hefty Belle. Some thought the skull might have been charred to ashes by the intense heat, but others noted that the children's bodies, though badly burned, had remained intact.

Also suspect were Belle's actions before the fire. Several days earlier a neighbor saw Belle drive past her farm with an unknown woman in her carriage, a woman whose stature was smaller than Belle's. The woman was dressed in traveling attire and was never seen again. And the day before the fire, Belle Gunness went into town, withdrew part of her savings from a local bank, and purchased five gallons of kerosene oil. Innocent-seeming actions at the time, which, in retrospect, took on sinister implications.

How could Belle have committed such crimes with apparent impunity, and how long had she been at it? Investigating her life provides some tantalizing details. She was born Brynhild Paulsdatter Storset in 1858, in Norway. She arrived in New York in September 1881, made her way to Chicago, and moved into her sister's home. While there, perhaps in an effort to become more "American," she became known to friends and neighbors as Belle.

Belle married Mads Sorenson

Searching the remains of the Gunness farmhouse

The remains of one of Gunness's victims

sometime between 1883 and 1889. A confectionery store they operated burned down in 1898, the first of a series of mysterious fires that seemed to follow Belle throughout her life. They took the insurance money and moved to the Chicago neighborhood of Austin, where they boarded foster children and possibly had several children of their own. At least two of these children died mysteriously of "acute colitis," but the symptoms were consistent with poisoning. Child mortality in those days was high, and no concrete evidence exists today to indicate that the deaths were murders. But future events make their deaths a possible precursor of things to come.

In 1900, Mads Sorenson died suddenly of what his death certificate listed as a "cerebral hemorrhage." But his symptoms indicated the possibility of strychnine poisoning. More suspicious, he died on the one day that two of his life insurance policies overlapped. This meant that only in the event of his death on that day would Belle be able to collect on both policies, which she promptly did. Mads's brother demanded that his body be exhumed for an autopsy, and the authorities complied, based on the "coincidental" timing of his death. Official results were inconclusive, but the autopsy did not include an

examination of the brain or the stomach—key to proving a case of poisoning.

However inconclusive the official results might have been, Gunness became an outcast in Chicago's close-knit Norwegian community. Perhaps to escape this stigma, she left the Windy City to visit a cousin in Minnesota. While there, she worked out a land trade between her property in Chicago and the LaPorte farm, which she moved into in November 1901 with her three children.

The oldest child was a beautiful young girl named Jenny Oleson, who had lived with Gunness for some years after her mother died. The younger girls, Lucy and Myrtle, shared Gunness's last name, and she referred to them as "her own," but their birth certificates list only a father's name and none for the mother. After her death, it was rumored that over the years Gunness had agreed to "adopt" a number of children and raise them to adulthood (for a fee). But no records exist of such informal agreements, and the whereabouts and fate of these children are unknown.

The following April, Belle married Peter Gunness. They seemed happy, but only eight months after their marriage, he died in a manner so bizarre that it resulted in an inquest. Belle testified that late one night Peter had gone to the kitchen to get a pair of shoes he had left behind the stove to warm. While bending over to pick up the shoes, he knocked a pot of scalding hot water from the stove, spilling it over his head and face. This made him stand up abruptly, knocking a sausage grinder off a high shelf and onto the back of his head, partially crushing his skull.

Peter's autopsy showed wounds that fit Belle's

description of events, but many suspected foul play. There wasn't enough evidence to bring a murder charge against her, however, and the inquest ended with an open verdict. Once again Belle, financially bolstered by her latest late husband's life insurance money, resumed the life of a widow. In 1903, she would give birth to Peter's son, Philip.

Fishing for a Victim?

Two years after Peter's death, Belle placed the first of what would be many matrimonial advertisements in a national Norwegian newspaper. One ad, which can be found in the LaPorte Historical Museum, reads:

> Wanted—A woman who owns a beautifully located and valuable farm in first class condition wants a good and reliable man as partner in the same. Some little cash is required for which will be furnished first class security.

With many single or widowed Scandinavian men in America at the time, the advertisement must have been enticing. It will never be known how many men responded or actually made the journey to LaPorte in search of the "first class security" Belle promised, but it is known that at least four men were murdered and buried on the premises.

It was not simply gentleman suitors who met their end at the Gunness farm. Sadly, the body of the young woman that had been uncovered during the initial excavation was positively identified as that of Jenny Oleson. Neighbors recalled that she had disappeared from the farm shortly after she and a local boy seemed to develop a romantic relationship. At that time, Belle claimed that Jenny had gone east to college. However, a coroner confirmed that Jenny Oleson had never left town.

In the end, the bodies of twelve men, women, and children were uncovered at the farm, but the number buried there could actually be higher. Many other bodies may lie beneath the soil around the farm or at the bottom of an adjacent pond where Gunness had been seen dumping sacks. She may have also fed the dismembered remains of her victims to her hogs. Whatever the case, it will never be truly known exactly how many lives ended at the hand of Belle Gunness.

"I Know Things About That Woman"

Despite his pleas of innocence, to many people only Ray Lamphere had the motive and opportunity to set the fire that killed the family. In addition to Belle's accusations of stalking, only days before the fire Lamphere reportedly told another local that "I know things about that woman, and she will pay me for it or suffer."

He refused, however, to officially reveal anything he knew about her whereabouts. His trial occurred in November 1908, with the prosecution intending to prove that Gunness died in a fire Ray Lamphere had set out of revenge, and the defense promising to remove all doubt that Belle Gunness was not dead at all. The prosecution brought in witnesses claiming to have seen Belle Gunness alive—after the fire—including a neighboring family who testified that they had seen Belle on her property several times in early July 1908.

On November 27, the jury convicted Lamphere of arson but acquitted him of murder. The jury foreman followed the verdict with a statement from the jury. They believed the woman found dead in the basement was Belle Gunness and had decided the case on "an entirely different proposition."

Whatever their motivation, the jury had spared Ray Lamphere's life. He was sentenced to "between two and twenty years" in the state prison at Michigan City, where upon arrival he is said to have quipped to a guard, "I am better off here than I would be if I were with her." And he'd often tell his cellmate, Harry Myers, "She's out there, Harry," as he'd stare idly out their window.

The truth of Lamphere's statement will never be known. A little more than a year into his sentence, he died of liver failure. With him died the last hope the world had of definitely discovering the fate of Belle Gunness.

Seeing Belles

Within weeks of the fire at the Gunness home, the tale of Belle Gunness appeared in newspapers around the world, with one English paper referring to her as the "American Lady Blue Beard." When the press reported that she might have escaped the fire, Belle Gunness sightings proliferated. One matronly lady, bound for New York to visit family, was removed from her railcar and questioned by local authorities for several hours because a fellow passenger

thought she resembled Belle. Other reports came from California, Florida—even Norway and Paris. Reports of sightings continued for many years afterward, but none ever proved to be the infamous Black Widow.

One particularly intriguing possibility came in 1931, when a seventy-one-year-old woman going by the name of Esther Carlson was arrested in Los Angeles for the poisoning murder of a man for whom she was caring. She was under investigation for the deaths of several other men by similar means. According to one press report, investigators examining a trunk in her room found, lying at the bottom, a picture of Belle Gunness with three of her children.

Ms. Carlson died in jail before she could stand trial, and before any connection between her and Belle Gunness could be confirmed. However, two former LaPorte residents, then living in Los Angeles, were allowed to view her body at the morgue and are said to have come away convinced that the body they saw there was that of Belle Gunness.

Belle's life, crimes, and eventual fate are as much open to speculation as they were that dark morning when flames engulfed the farmhouse on the outskirts of LaPorte. Her legend lives on in museum displays, in books and articles, and most of all in tales that will continue to be told about the most prolific female serial killer in American history—Indiana's own Belle Gunness, the Black Widow of LaPorte.

Indiana's Favorite Bank Robber

One of the most famous bank robbers in American history was a native son of Indiana. In 1934, he was front-page news across the country for his daring robberies throughout the Hoosier State and the Midwest. Despite his chosen career path, the "Gentleman Bandit" is surprisingly beloved, and the number of post-death sightings of him are probably second only to Elvis's.

John Herbert Dillinger was born in Indianapolis in 1903 and was, by all accounts, a quiet child with good grades who was well liked by his friends and teachers. He was an excellent athlete, especially when it came to baseball. He did, however, have a minor brush with the authorities in the sixth grade, when he stole coal from the Pennsylvania Railroad yards and sold it to his neighbors.

After an abbreviated stint in the navy (he deserted), Dillinger made his way back to his home state. Seems the good boy had turned bad by then, because in September 1924 he and a friend botched a robbery in Mooresville. Dillinger was caught and received concurrent sentences of up to ten to twenty years in prison, to be served at the Indiana State Reformatory.

In the reformatory, Dillinger befriended some bank robbers, refined his trade with them, and when he was freed in May 1933 began robbing small banks in Indiana towns like New Carlisle,

Daleville, Montpelier, and Bluffton. Then he tackled a larger bank in downtown Indianapolis. With the resulting take, he arranged a prison break for his friends, still behind bars.

Dillinger did have a strange sense of fair play. Five months later the gang robbed the Central National Bank in Greencastle. As the robbers left the bank, Dillinger saw an old farmer standing at one of the tellers' windows. In front of him on the counter was a small stack of bills. Dillinger asked the farmer if the money belonged to him or to the bank.

"It's mine," the farmer replied nervously.

"Keep it," Dillinger said. "We only want the bank's."

After a robbery in Milwaukee, Wisconsin, the gang decided to winter in Daytona Beach, Florida, and then moved on to Tucson, Arizona. During this time, two unknown men robbed the First National Bank of East Chicago, Indiana. Dillinger and gang member John Hamilton were accused of the crime: Dillinger was said to have killed a policeman during the attempt, something he always denied.

It was in Tucson that the gang was identified and arrested. Dillinger was extradited to Indiana to stand trial for the East Chicago robbery—the one robbery that he probably didn't commit. He was sent to the "escapeproof" Lake County Jail in Crown Point, but proved his

It's Dillinger-proof

John Dillinger's gang was known to ride along the Lincoln Highway, one of the few paved highways in the state at the time. The highway went right through the heart of Goshen, and residents there soon realized that the main intersection in the center of town was a bank-robber's dream—a four-way intersection with banks on three sides. The town knew they had to do something other than wait for the worst, so they constructed what they called a "bulletproof police booth."

The booth was made of limestone and came complete with a watchtower, bulletproof glass, and holes through which guns could be poked to fire away at passing renegade gangsters. It even had a sink and running water. It was built at the fourth corner of the intersection, in front of the courthouse, facing the banks.

It's still there today, should Dillinger's ghost decide to make an appearance.

prowess once again. He broke out in March 1934 and put together a new gang, including former Capone gunman Lester Gillis—a.k.a. Baby Face Nelson.

After a series of robberies, the gang decided to lay low in the quiet Wisconsin resort of Little Bohemia. But someone tipped off the FBI, whose agents raided a lodge there on April 22. It wasn't the right lodge, however, and the federal agents killed one man and wounded two others—nobody connected to Dillinger. The gang escaped into the woods along the lake.

Now under the harsh glare of public criticism for their screwup, the FBI placed a shoot-to-kill order on Dillinger's head, along with a $10,000 reward. Five states in which Dillinger had committed bank robberies also ponied up rewards. Newspapers covered Dillinger every day, and in the following months, six men who resembled him were arrested or almost shot. Everyone was looking for Dillinger, but he was nowhere to be found.

In May, he appeared at his parents' home for Sunday chicken dinner and reportedly told his father that he was leaving on a long trip, and the family wouldn't have to worry about him any more. He also gave his father a large sum of money to cover his own funeral expenses. Then he disappeared.

He may or may not have had plastic surgery during this time to alter the contours of his face. He was rumored to have robbed a bank in South Bend in June, but this may be another case of Dillinger's getting credit

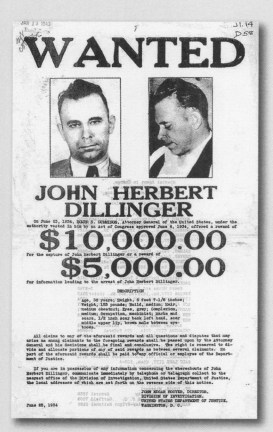

for someone else's work.

In early July, a detective with the notoriously corrupt East Chicago, Indiana, Police Department made a deal with the FBI: to get Dillinger, dead—not alive. The plan went down on July 22, 1934, after Dillinger left the Biograph Theater in Chicago, apparently on a movie date with a woman and a friend. When he realized that many law-enforcement officials were waiting for him, he took off down an alley, but it was too late. He was fatally wounded by two bullets, courtesy of the FBI. Or was he?

There's much debate as to whether the FBI shot Dillinger or if another man was set up to take

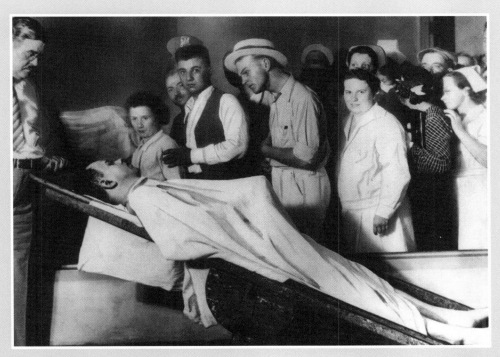

the hit. The conspiracy theories surrounding Dillinger's death still fly like the bullets said to have stopped him dead in his tracks.

Those who doubt that the dead man was actually Dillinger question the motives behind the hit, citing Dillinger's lack of awareness that he was being targeted that night, for certainly he was so well-connected someone would have tipped him off, and the many inconsistencies in the autopsy report: The corpse didn't have the same eye color, height, weight, scars, or general health as Dillinger.

The man who many feel was actually killed that night was named Jimmy Lawrence: a small-time criminal who disappeared the night of the shooting. Lawrence lived near the Biograph Theater and often went there. He also bore an uncanny resemblance to John Dillinger. Could Lawrence have gone on a movie date, not knowing that the FBI was lying in wait for Dillinger there?

Some writers, including respected crime writer Jay Robert Nash, have suggested that this is exactly what happened. Nash reported in his book *Dillinger: Dead or Alive?* that Dillinger's attorney, along with other parties, rigged the whole affair. Nash believes the FBI agents shot Lawrence instead of Dillinger, and when they realized their mistake, covered it up.

So what happened to the real John Dillinger? According to testimony from a Dillinger friend and fellow bank robber named James "Blackie" Audett, Dillinger was hiding in nearby Illinois at the time of the shooting. He and Audett escaped a few hours after the shooting, taking the northern route, through Wisconsin and Minnesota. Audett claimed that he left Dillinger at an Indian reservation out west.

Audett told Nash that he saw Dillinger on the West Coast several times prior to 1974, and claimed Dillinger was still alive right up until Audett's own death in 1979. But Nash could never persuade him to reveal where Dillinger was living. Nash also learned that the bank robber's family had received a letter from someone claiming to be Dillinger; the letter contained enough private information to convince them that it was genuine.

Regardless of who was really dead or alive, the man identified as John Dillinger was buried at the Crown Hill Cemetery in Indianapolis on July 25, 1934. John Dillinger Sr. declined an offer of $10,000 for the corpse, and to make sure his son would not fall victim to body snatchers, he filled the plot with concrete and scrap metal. The father didn't place a stone on the grave for two years. The stone that was eventually put into place was soon chipped away to nothing. The marker that rests on the grave today is the fourth replacement.

Diana of the Dunes

Around 1915, the area that is now Dunes State Park was mostly uninhabited wilderness along the shoreline of Lake Michigan. Fishermen and swimmers visited, but few dared to venture into the dense forest that hugged the shore for miles in every direction. It was the perfect place to hide if you wanted to escape from the bonds of society, and that's exactly what a young woman did in the early twentieth century.

Not long after the woman arrived in the Dunes, fishermen along the beach near Chesterton reported catching glimpses of a beautiful, naked woman swimming in the lake. The story spread that the woman was living like a hermit along the beach, and her notoriety grew. She was compared to the ancient Greek goddess Diana—hence the name.

All who encountered "Diana" described her the same way. She was small, slender, and lovely, with dark hair and skin that was tanned brown from the sun. She was also shy, elusive, and avoided all contact with the outside world. Those who got close enough to speak to her found her quite timid. She evaded their questions and offered no information about herself. The only thing she wanted, she said in a quiet, sweet voice, was to be by herself.

Regardless of Diana's desire to remain anonymous, word of her unusual lifestyle filtered beyond the surrounding communities. People shared stories about her origins, her true identity, her beauty, and her reclusive ways, making her into a larger-than-life figure. It was only a matter of time before Diana of the Dunes started attracting visitors.

Within a year of her arrival, the quiet of the Dunes was disrupted by scores of curiosity seekers, all hoping to catch a glimpse of the bronzed goddess. Diana was eventually tracked down to the abandoned fisherman's cottage she lived in and called Driftwood. A few visitors managed to evade the wild dog she had adopted and spoke to her,

All who encountered "Diana" described her the same way. She was small, slender, and lovely, with dark hair and skin that was tanned brown from the sun. She was also shy, elusive, and avoided all contact with the outside world.

including a newspaper reporter from Chicago.

Diana was actually Alice Marble Grey, the daughter of a prominent Chicago family. Alice was a cultured and educated woman who had traveled extensively. She had graduated with honors from the University of Chicago and had worked as an editorial secretary for a popular magazine.

Why did she abandon the comforts of society for the solitude of this lakeshore wilderness? The question can never be answered authoritatively. There's a claim that she came because of a broken love affair, but it's more likely that her deteriorating eyesight made work impossible. She sought refuge in the rough land she had enjoyed as a child on summer vacations, settling into a peaceful life. She borrowed books from the library, walked in the woods, and swam naked in the chilly waters of Lake Michigan. She was said to have kept extensive journals of her life in the Dunes.

In 1920, Alice met a drifter named Paul Wilson, and he moved into the cabin with her. He was an unemployed boat builder, and despite a checkered past, he seemed to make Alice happy. He repaired Alice's ramshackle home, fished, and did odd jobs to earn money for the two of them. His presence seemed to discourage sightseers.

Things started to fall apart in 1922, when the body of a man, who had been burned and beaten, was found on the beach by hikers, and an autopsy revealed that someone with great strength had strangled him. Police suspected that Wilson had a hand in the murder and questioned him. He said he was innocent, but deepened the mystery by claiming to have seen a "gun-toting hermit" on the beach. The "hermit" was never found, and Wilson was eventually let go because there was not enough evidence to hold him.

Then Wilson and Grey were evicted from their home to make way for a housing development that later became Ogden Dunes. They moved to Michigan City, where Wilson sold handmade furniture and she conducted nature tours.

Grey died in February 1925, shortly after the birth of her second daughter. The official cause of death was said to be uremic poisoning, a common complication of pregnancy in those days. Wilson was prevented from

burning her body on a funeral pyre in the Dunes, as he wished to do, and had to give her a more traditional funeral. He broke down beside her casket and then became angry with reporters swarming around and asking questions. He pulled out a gun and fired several shots into the air. No one was injured, but Wilson was jailed for a few days, missing Alice's burial in an unmarked grave at Gary's Oak Hill Cemetery. In death, she found the anonymity she had so desperately craved in life. The fate of her daughters is unknown, but some believe that her family took them in.

So ended Alice Grey's life, but the legend of Diana of the Dunes lives on. Hikers who venture into the woods beyond the lake tell stories of seeing a strange woman wandering through the trees in front of them, but she always disappears, leaving no sign that she was ever there. The truth of such tales is unknown. However, we would like to think that Grey returns to the place she loved so much, where the trials and pain of her lonely and sad life are forgotten, at least for a time, as she strolls along her beloved beach or disappears into the waters of the lake.

Smell of a Legend: The Skunk Lady of Howe

In 1925, the *LaGrange Standard* reported on the one time existence, somewhere in Elkhart, of a photo of a woman with the caption: "If you want to see the dirtiest woman in the world, go to Howe."

That's a pretty mean thing to say about anyone, but in this case it was true: In a filthy, unfurnished shack alongside a forgotten road in Howe, there once lived a woman well known for both her lack of cleanliness and her love of skunks and other animals. In the early part of the twentieth century, people would come from miles around to see (and smell) her.

Rather than turn her nose up at the attention, this woman would pretty her face up with some soot and greet her visitors with gusto, performing little dances and songs for spare change. She wore the same tattered old clothing every day, and tame skunks dangled from her shoulders like a living fur stole. If they sprayed a little, it wasn't a big deal: The scent was probably lost in the pervasive odor of the place.

The woman was Christina Hand D'Sullivan, but around northeastern Indiana they called her Chrissy (or Crissy) the Skunk Lady. She was born in the mid-1800s, and just around the time she hit her teens, the story goes that her father (or both her parents) drowned in a fishing/drinking accident in a local lake. But Chrissy was a tough little bit of Limburger who could take care of herself. She was described in a 1956 newspaper article as having "a man's coarse features and brawny shoulders,"

a "pudgy and powerful" frame, and a "bull-strong" voice with which she apparently showed off her mastery of off-color language. Accounts posted on the LaGrange County Historical Society's Web site say that she snagged a few sensory-deprived husbands. The most official-looking marriage was to a man named D'Sullivan, who apparently liked his drink so much that he passed out on the railroad tracks one night and was killed by an oncoming train.

But Chrissy did not lack for companionship: cats, dogs, chickens, guinea pigs, lizards, snakes, and skunks all shared her home and grounds. She raised baby skunks in boxes inside her shack. She especially loved a skunk named Old Rover and would carry him around in her arms.

The people of Howe weren't crazy about the stream of gawkers who came to visit Chrissy, but they recognized that she was simply an eccentric who didn't need to be institutionalized. They seem to have looked after her, especially later in her life, when they helped her clean up her act, moving her into a new place and giving her—gulp—a bath. Chrissy died only a month or so after that, in November 1925, and there are those who think it was the bath that did her in. She was buried at Riverside Cemetery, near where her shack once stood (it is no more). Sometime after she died, the town put up a monument to Chrissy in the cemetery. It marks the general place she was buried: The exact location was forgotten long before anyone could have sniffed it out.

Soldier Woman

Residents in and around Greensburg often came to the home of Civil War veteran John Finnern to listen to stories of battle—but it was not John they came to hear. The recollections and adventures so many wanted to relive were the war stories told by his wife, Elizabeth!

Elizabeth Cain Finnern could tell the most exciting stories because during the war she posed as a Union soldier and fought for more than six months before her masquerade was discovered. Even after it was learned that the gallant soldier was actually a woman, Elizabeth remained with the fighting unit, leaving only to nurse her wounded husband and other sick and injured men.

What led her to carry out this elaborate ruse and risk her life on the bloody battlefields of the Civil War?

John and Elizabeth Finnern came to America from Germany in the 1850s and not long after found their adopted country embroiled in a civil war. Anxious to protect the freedoms he had recently acquired, John enlisted in the Union Army in 1861. He planned to leave Elizabeth behind on their Ohio farm, but she refused to stay alone; instead, she volunteered as a nurse-laundress for the military.

There are different stories as to how Elizabeth ended up as a soldier on the field of battle. Some say that she simply donned a federal uniform she found in a storeroom and joined her husband on the battlefield.

She spent the next several months disguised as a man, never leaving John's side. She lived as a soldier, carrying a rifle, enduring long marches, going without food, and taking part in several battles. She also cared for the wounded and helped with amputations, leading many to believe that other soldiers may have been aware of her secret.

The Finnerns fought side by side at the battles of Corinth, Pocahontas, and Huntsville, Alabama; Harrison, Missouri; and Pulaski, Fort Donaldson, and Chattanooga, Tennessee, among others. When John was wounded at the battle of Arkansas Post, Elizabeth reportedly charged the Confederate lines and gunned down the man who had wounded him. Another Ohio soldier who had followed after her managed to save Elizabeth from death or capture.

It was at this point that her real identity was revealed, but she didn't let this stop her from caring for her husband—and saving hundreds of other lives. Following John to the hospital, Elizabeth was stunned to find that he was among more than seven hundred wounded men. The unit was disorganized and had no director, so she took over the supervision of the doctors, nurses, and scarce medical supplies. Not only was she credited with renovating the hospital, but she successfully battled an outbreak of scarlet fever as well.

When John was mustered out of the service in September 1864, the couple moved to Indiana. In the years that followed, they enjoyed great fame there as a result of their wartime exploits. After John's death in 1905, Elizabeth became a recluse. Few people visited her, and the town of Greensburg largely forgot about her. One winter she became desperately ill; luckily, one of her few remaining visitors was a female doctor whom she had inspired as a child years before. She nursed Elizabeth back to health and then helped her to apply to President Theodore Roosevelt for a pension as a soldier's widow.

Elizabeth died in July 1907, the pension funds largely unspent. Since Elizabeth had no family to pass the funds on to, her doctor friend put it to fitting use: a Bedford stone monument to mark the graves of two battlefield soldiers named John and Elizabeth Finnern.

The Other Kool-Aid Man

One of the most horrific stories of the 1970s was the mass suicide of the People's Temple cult in the jungles of Guyana, in South America. The name of the cult's leader, Jim Jones, became known all over the world and phrases like "drinking the Kool-Aid" became synonymous with brainwashing, suicide, and horror. You might be shocked (or maybe not!) to learn that the People's Temple—and Jim Jones—got their start in Indiana.

Jim Jones was born in May 1931 in the small town of Crete, near the Indiana–Ohio border. His mother believed she was the reincarnation of Mark Twain and told family and friends that her dead mother had come to her in a dream and proclaimed that she would give birth to the world's savior—a notion Jim must have filed away for future reference.

The family moved to the South Side of Lynn in 1934. Young Jim was always trailed by an assortment of stray dogs, cats, and other animals, and, at first, he was happy to let them run free. Soon, however, he built cages for them in his family's barn, and the captive animals slowly disappeared, one by one. Everyone pitied Jim's loss, but at the same time he was developing into a junior mad scientist, using the barn as a lab in which he experimented, for example, with grafting chicken legs to ducks. It is not comforting to imagine the likely fates of his animal friends.

Neighbors recalled that Jim could be talked into delivering profanity-filled diatribes for the price of a nickel, until a local minister capitalized on the boy's verbal talents to turn him into a child preacher. Jones brought this newfound talent home. He set up altars in the barn and preached to the other kids, attracting his "congregation" by offering lemonade and punch during the hot summer months. But once, the precocious preacher locked some of his friends in the hayloft when they threatened to leave his "church." He seemed never to outgrow this tendency toward entrapment.

Jones started off as a student pastor in Indianapolis in the summer of 1951, but soon began his own ministry. As a guest minister at a nearby church, he became known for miraculous healings that included yanking "cancerous blobs" from supposedly sick parishioners. A new, larger church Jones started in 1956 would eventually become the People's Temple. Early on, he did good things for the poor, actively recruited African American members, and helped integrate at least one Indianapolis hospital. In 1961, the governor appointed Jones director of the Indianapolis Human Rights Commission.

But Jim Jones hadn't outgrown his dark side. When he felt his congregation was being inattentive, he would throw his Bible on the ground and spit on it, raging that "too many people are looking at this and not at me!" He also devised an elaborate scheme whereby People's Temple members ran local businesses that channeled money back into the church; this piqued the interest of tax investigators and creditors.

In 1965, Jones and a hundred members of his congregation left Indiana for Ukiah, California, supposedly to avoid the upcoming nuclear holocaust. Jones gained

more followers in California, but eventually came under suspicion there for dubious fund-raising methods, brainwashing of congregants, and other tax and legal issues. Once again Jones devised a plan to stay ahead of the authorities. This time he moved the People's Temple out of California and into an agricultural commune he named Jonestown, in Guyana.

Conditions at Jonestown were miserable, but once there, cult members were not allowed to warn anyone back in the States not to come there. Word did filter back to California, however, and California Congressman Leo J. Ryan decided to personally visit Jonestown. He arrived with a group of reporters and was not happy with what he found there. Many People's Temple members wanted to defect, and when Ryan, his party, and some of the defectors left for a nearby airport, Jones sent a heavily armed hit squad to wipe them out. Ryan and three newsmen were among those killed.

Jones was sitting on his green throne when he got word that the hit squad had not killed everyone in Ryan's group. That's when he decided to proceed with a mass suicide—something the cult had rehearsed frequently since they'd arrived in Guyana. Jones ordered the preparation of the infamous large tub of strawberry-flavored Kool-Aid laced with cyanide, telling his followers that dying with dignity was better than being killed by the Guyana Defense Force.

Many followers realized that this was not a rehearsal

and, after seeing babies succumb to the poison, resisted. They were held down and forced to drink the deadly brew, or even injected with it. In the end, 912 people died at Jonestown. Authorities, alerted by the few survivors who managed to escape, found decaying bodies in piles reaching thirty feet high.

Cyanide poisoning is a horribly painful way to die, and Jones must have heard the agonized screams and tortured moans of his followers. At some point he decided that he would rather die faster and with less pain, and he was found dead on his throne with a bullet in his brain. Yet two mysteries still surround his death. The gun that killed him was found in another building some distance away from the throne. But, if he shot himself, as was the prevalent theory, how did the gun move? Or was it murder, and if so, who pulled the trigger? The other strange thing is that his bloodstains—around the throne and podium—could never be eradicated, no matter how much effort was expended to remove them.

Bigger Than Life Hoosiers

John Hanson Craig

Surely a man who weighed nearly half a ton knew more about eating than just about anyone else. With that in mind, John Hanson Craig, a Guilford Township native, opened a combination candy shop and lunch counter in Danville during the height of his popularity as one of the heaviest people ever to live in Indiana.

Craig was born in Iowa in 1847, weighing 11 pounds. By the time he was a year old, he was up to 77 pounds, and at two he tipped the scales at 206 pounds, enough to earn the weight title in Barnum's Baby Show in New York and win his parents $1,000. He'd eventually stand six feet five inches tall and reach 907 pounds.

Craig traveled with circuses and sideshows for many years, using Danville as his headquarters. While touring with P. T. Barnum's company, he met "Fat Lady" Mary Jan Kesler of Hendricks County, who weighed more than 700 pounds. They married in 1869 and also toured at times with their own company, always returning to Danville to check in on the restaurant and a small zoo Craig operated out of their home.

Kesler died as a result of poor health and fatigue in October 1881, leaving Craig free to meet his second wife, a petite woman named Jennie Ryan. They had a daughter, whom they named Helen, but the marriage was rocky. The couple divorced in 1893, remarried three months later, then separated for good in the spring of 1894.

Ryan left Helen behind with Craig, but he died that summer. Craig's manager, William Roddy, took care of Helen until her mother returned to Danville. Shortly thereafter, Roddy and Jennie were married and left the area. Whatever became of them is unknown.

A Danville tailor once displayed one of Craig's enormous suits in his store window, causing a sensation when three young men borrowed the suit and walked around the town square wearing it—all at the same time.

Baby Ruth

Indiana native

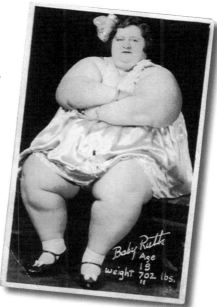

Baby Ruth, whose weight peaked at 815 pounds, was a major attraction for the Royal American Shows and the Ringling Brothers Circus. Born Ruth Smith in Kempton in 1904, she didn't want to follow in the footsteps of her mother, a well-known circus fat lady in her day. Ruth attended secretarial school and tried to work for a telegraph company, but then weighed 400 pounds and was too large for the equipment. She also tried a job as a stenographer in a lawyer's office, but people kept barging into the office to look at her. With a sigh, Smith took up where her mother had left off—with the Ringling Brothers Circus.

While working in the sideshow, she met a balloon salesman at Madison Square Garden. He took one look at the 697-pound Baby Ruth and dubbed her "my woman." They married, and Ruth was happy—but not completely. Though she reportedly earned nearly $300 a day, she yearned to lead a normal life. Unfortunately, she continued to grow at a rate of more than 40 pounds a year.

In 1942, she checked into a hospital in Tampa, Florida, to have tumors removed from the insides of her knees. The surgery had to be postponed when the hospital bed she was lying on collapsed. Ruth returned to the hospital with her own specially made bed and successfully underwent the operation. Then, as she was recovering from the anesthesia, she started to vomit. Nurses tried but could not turn over Ruth's eight-hundred-pound body, and she choked to death.

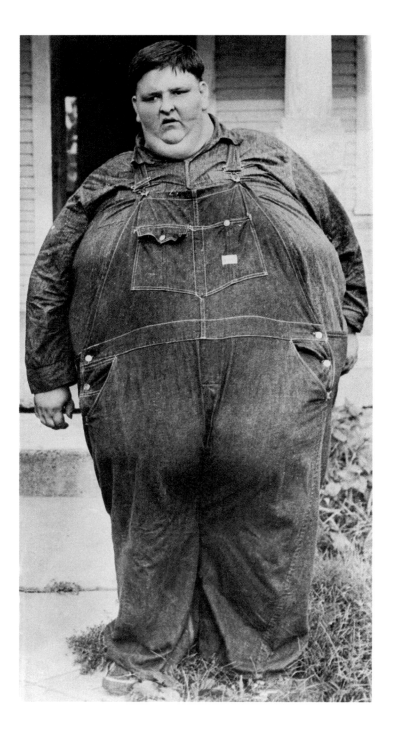

Robert Earl Hughes

Indiana was the location of the bizarre early death of another larger-than-life performer, Robert Earl Hughes. He was born in 1926 in Illinois and developed normally until the age of three, when a bout with whooping cough may have upset his endocrine balance. He began to gain weight much faster than normal: He was 203 pounds by the age of six, 378 pounds at ten, 693 pounds at eighteen, 896 pounds at twenty-five—and he kept putting on the pounds. In February 1958, Hughes weighed an incredible 1,069 pounds—the record to this day as the heaviest man who ever lived.

Hughes's quest to find work eventually led to the sideshow circuit, where he spent the rest of his life. He had an easygoing manner and was popular with the other performers and the public.

In July 1958, Hughes was in Indiana with the Gooding Brothers Amusement Company when he contracted a case of three-day measles. Even simple ailments can be serious for a person of his size, and he was rushed to the nearby Bremen Community Hospital in a carnival truck. At the hospital, they found that no doorways or corridors were large enough to allow him to pass and no bed could support his weight. Carnival workers retrieved Hughes's custom-made trailer, where he stayed during treatment.

Within a few days, the measles began to clear up, but then Hughes developed uremia. His kidneys stopped functioning normally, allowing poisons to accumulate in his blood. Hughes died on July 10, weighing 1,041 pounds, a number that was etched on his tombstone for eternity.

Sandy Allen

Shelby County native Sandy Allen stands just a hair above seven feet seven inches tall and holds the record as the tallest woman who has ever lived. She's been described as having a sense of humor even bigger than she is: If you ask her what she had for breakfast, she'll often tell you that she ate "short people."

Born in 1955, Allen was a normal-sized infant but says that by the time she was eleven, she was taller than Michael Jordan. In fact, if she hadn't had an operation on her malfunctioning pituitary gland when she was nineteen (and seven feet tall at the time), she might have rivaled the height of Robert Wadlow, an Illinois native who holds the record as the world's tallest person at eight feet eleven and a half inches.

Allen's mother essentially abandoned her when she was six, and she was raised by her grandmother. Despite years of teasing and ridicule about her height, she grew into a warm, caring woman with great compassion for others.

She wears a size 22 shoe, which necessitates specially made footwear (as does most of her wardrobe), but her favorite is a pair of sneakers she received as a gift from the Indiana Pacers basketball team. During her lifetime, Allen has traveled the world, been on dozens of talk shows, made two movies, and written a book called *Cast a Giant Shadow*.

These days, Allen is mostly confined to a wheelchair and resides at a convalescent home in Shelbyville. Her height and weight (450 pounds) make walking difficult, but a custom-made van helps her remain on the lecture circuit. She may not get around as much as she used to, but she feels that every trip or appearance, no matter how tough, is worth it. Each one of them gives her one more chance to say, "It's okay to be different."

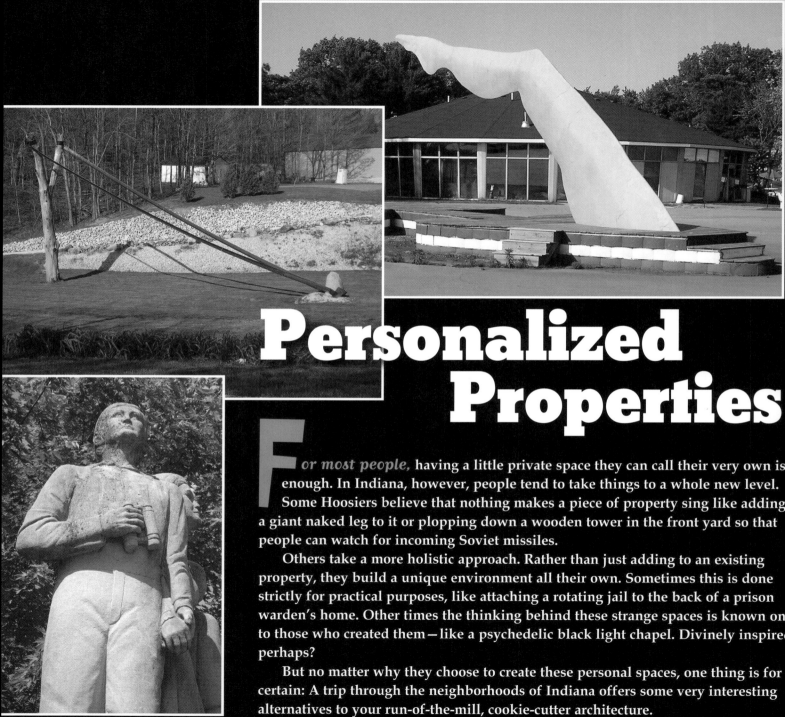

Personalized Properties

For most people, having a little private space they can call their very own is enough. In Indiana, however, people tend to take things to a whole new level.

Some Hoosiers believe that nothing makes a piece of property sing like adding a giant naked leg to it or plopping down a wooden tower in the front yard so that people can watch for incoming Soviet missiles.

Others take a more holistic approach. Rather than just adding to an existing property, they build a unique environment all their own. Sometimes this is done strictly for practical purposes, like attaching a rotating jail to the back of a prison warden's home. Other times the thinking behind these strange spaces is known on to those who created them—like a psychedelic black light chapel. Divinely inspire perhaps?

But no matter why they choose to create these personal spaces, one thing is for certain: A trip through the neighborhoods of Indiana offers some very interesting alternatives to your run-of-the-mill, cookie-cutter architecture.

Chain Saw Garden

While passing through Milltown, home of the infamous Shoe Tree (see "Roadside Oddities"), we ran into a young couple, Travis and Angela, who put us on to one of the town's lesser known attractions, the Chain Saw Garden. Before you knew it, we were following them down the road in search of the site. And sure enough, we found it. Sitting alongside the road on a very sharp turn was the 66 Chain Saw Garden—row after row of chain saws planted in the ground. Yup, actual chain saws. So for the sake of the locals, let's all hope that Leatherface doesn't ever travel Indiana's Route 66.

Collection of Outhouses

Most people think that if you've seen one outhouse, you've seen them all. In fact, most people don't really have a desire to see more than one outhouse, let alone own one. But then again, most people aren't like Hy Goldenberg from Huntington Township.

According to legend, Goldenberg once ordered a single outhouse, but was shipped two by mistake. Apparently, he believed that two of anything was a collection, and thus started searching far and wide for unique outhouses. Little by little, the long driveway up to his house started to be lined with these structures. Not just ordinary outhouses, though. Rather, the ones in Goldenberg's collection all had something unusual about them, from weathervanes on top to multiple windows, entrances, and in some cases, seats. There was even a concrete outhouse.

In 1995, Goldenberg donated forty-one acres of his property to the state to use as a nature preserve. Dubbed the Tel-Hy Nature Preserve, the area allowed lots of people to view some of the gems of the collection. Of the dozens of outhouses that once adorned the Goldenberg property, today only about twelve still make their homes there; the remaining outhouses have been moved to the historical society in downtown Huntington. Our personal favorite was the two-seater structure, which was apparently also a favorite of Santa Claus . . . or at least of his head. We're not sure how the rest of Santa's body felt about the whole thing.

Giant Slingshot

Out on the back roads of Barnard stands what might be the most unique home security system we've ever seen: a twenty-foot-high, thirty-foot-long slingshot sitting in the front yard. We're not sure how big a creature has to be to warrant bringing them down with a thirty-foot slingshot. But then again, we probably don't want to know.

Homemade Roller Coaster

What do you do when you love roller coasters but can't stand driving several hours to the nearest amusement park and then waiting in long lines to ride one? Well, if you're John Ivers from Bruceville, the answer is easy: Just build your own roller coaster in your backyard.

We can only imagine how the conversation went when John first told his wife, Sharon, of his plans. Obviously, she didn't kick up too much of a fuss, because after he spent a year working on it, the roller coaster known as the Blue Flash was completed in 2001.

The structure measures 180 feet in length and climbs to a height of 20 feet; a ride on the Blue Flash lasts a mere fifteen seconds with speeds that don't get above 25 mph. Not impressed? Then how about the fact that to ride the Blue Flash you have to sit in a late 1970s–model bucket seat and the only thing holding you in the seat is an old, frayed cloth lap belt? Oh yeah, and did we mention the Blue Flash comes complete with a 360-degree loop?

Incredibly, there were no blueprints or plans for the ride. Ivers didn't even try to model it after another roller coaster. He simply thought up an idea and ran with it, welding together bits and pieces of scrap metal in the very barn over which the Blue Flash now climbs.

So did I ride it? You bet! It was an experience I'll never forget! As Ivers fastened the belt, he warned "lean to the right" when the 360-degree loop approached. With that, he started

the motor up and pushed the chair off toward the lift. The chair linked up to a chain, and I was pulled up the twenty-odd feet, which meant up and over the barn, where gravity would kick in.

The initial climb seemed to take forever; sitting in a bucket seat on wheels and climbing up over a barn creates a very slow-moving, surreal atmosphere. Just as the chair crested the hill, a thought ran through my head, What am I doing? This thing is homemade! The question was never answered, because suddenly the seat banked to the left and immediately dropped down toward the loop. That went by so fast it's hard to remember it. There was only a split-second feeling of flipping through the air, and then it was over. Oh yeah, and I totally forgot to lean to the right.

Everyone who successfully survives a ride on the Blue Flash is given the opportunity to sign their name in Ivers's book alongside the names of all the other riders—literally hundreds of people from all over the world. As I walked away from the roller coaster and headed toward my car, I couldn't resist taking one last look. When I did, I recalled the words John Ivers uttered as he was unbuckling me from the bucket seat: "That's a lot of ride."

It was, indeed. But Ivers isn't done. He's currently nearing completion on another more "family friendly" roller coaster and even has plans to build a Ferris wheel. Wonder what all that's going to do to the resale value of his house? *—Jim Willis*

Naked Leg Sundial of Sun Aura Resort

So you say you were too young (or too shy) to hang out at a real-life '70s-style nudist camp? Well, you're in luck, because one still exists. So come along with us to the town of Roselawn. Don't bother to pack, because you won't need anything to wear!

The nudist camp Club Zoro opened in the early 1930s. It was the creation of Alois Knapp, a Chicago lawyer and editor of *Sunshine and Health* magazine, one of the first nudist magazines ever published. Over the years, Club Zoro had many different owners, until it came to be acquired by Dale and Mary Drost in 1968. But it wasn't Mr. or Mrs. Drost who had the biggest plans for the club. It was their son, Dick.

With big naked dreams in his head, Dick set about remodeling and revamping the club his parents had purchased. He began by renaming the place Naked City and then set his sights on creating all sorts of "theme nights" to attract more customers. His most famous was his annual Erin Go Bra-less Dance, which was held every St. Patrick's Day. It was also during this time that Dick began putting up, how shall we say, unique structures on the property, including a giant circular mirrored building that housed a restaurant, a sauna, and the main office (among other things, we're sure). Far and away the strangest structure that went up on the site was the giant woman's leg—all sixty-three feet of it—that functioned as a sundial.

The bottom fell out of Naked City in 1985 when Dick Drost was charged with molesting a thirteen-year-old girl and with showing obscene materials to minors. On March 24, 1986, Drost pleaded guilty to almost a dozen sex-related misdemeanors in exchange for being given a ten-year suspended sentence. However, part of the agreement was that Drost leave the state of Indiana and not return for ten years. Shortly after sentencing, Drost shut down Naked City and moved to California, leaving the leg sundial all alone . . . and naked.

After sitting abandoned for several years, Naked City was reopened as the Sun Aura Resort, which continues to operate to this day. Yes, the leg is still there keeping time, and she's even got a fresh coat of semi-neon-pink paint on her. As for the rest of the resort, it could use a bit of updating. In fact, when you walk around, you might think you had wandered onto the set of a 1970s TV show, if not for the naked people driving way too fast in their golf carts.

As we were leaving, we couldn't help but notice the small sign posted on the fence telling guests they needed to be dressed beyond that point. Proving that at the Sun Aura Resort, you can check out any time you like, but you can't leave until you put your pants back on.

Sanctuary of the Sea

If you're in the vicinity of Terre Haute and decide to tour the grounds of Saint Mary-of-the-Woods College, you will come across many memorials and shrines dedicated to saints. But as you are standing in front of the oldest shrine on campus, the St. Anne's Chapel, you just might find yourself asking, "So what's the deal with all the shells?"

It all started back in 1840, when the Sisters of Providence, headed up by the Blessed Mother Theodore Guerin, arrived in the area and began building the campus. Years earlier other settlers had arrived in the region and were attempting not only to survive but also to establish a congregation. So the Sisters of Providence were welcomed with open arms, and the campus slowly began to take shape.

In 1843, Mother Theodore was returning to the United States after a stay in France. Her mode of transportation home was the ship *Nashville*. Halfway through the journey, the *Nashville* ran into weather so severe that it seemed the ship would capsize at any moment. Full of fear, Mother Theodore began praying to Saint Anne, the patroness of sailors, and she promised Saint Anne that if she were to make it safely home, she would erect a chapel in the saint's honor.

Needless to say, the *Nashville* miraculously survived

the storm and made it into port safely. Upon arriving back at Saint Mary-of-the-Woods, Mother Theodore wasted no time holding up her end of the bargain. By the following year, in July 1844, a small log cabin building, the Saint Anne's Chapel, was erected. And every year, on the anniversary of the feast of St. Anne, Mother Theodore would lead a procession to the chapel for services.

But over the years, the logs of the chapel began to rot, and the decision was made to replace them with stone. It was also at this time that the sisters got another idea. They decided to decorate the interior of the chapel with shells they would gather from the nearby Wabash River. All the sisters joined in, and before long the interior of the chapel was covered in shells. Some were simply pressed into the plaster as it was drying, while others were meticulously arranged to create works of art depicting the state of Indiana and even scenes from Mother Theodore's stormy night aboard the *Nashville*.

The final touch was a statue of Saint Anne herself that Mother Theodore had brought back with her from France. The statue was added to the chapel altar, and the new chapel was blessed and reopened in 1876. Today it still stands and represents the oldest shrine on the grounds of Saint Mary-of-the-Woods.

Providence Home's Geode Grotto

Sitting on four city blocks in Jasper, The Providence Home Geode Grotto was the inspiration of Father Philip Ottavi, Director of the Providence Home for retarded men. When some handball courts were removed from the property, Ottavi decided to build something spiritual. His design was based on the Grotto of Lourdes, France. He chose geodes as his primary building material because these geological rock formations are plentiful in south-central Indiana. They've been used in landscaping and homes since the 19th century and they also have religious symbolism. It took Father Philip and a crew of men from the Home about ten years (from around 1960 to 1970) to build the Grotto.

In addition to the many shrines, there are fountains, flower planters, benches, lampposts, birdbaths, and walls—all encrusted with geodes. Other materials, such as marble, granite, seashells, rosaries and pictures were also embedded into the planters, posts and sidewalks. The cave-like Mother of God Shrine features a marble statue of Mary and a ceiling with faux stalactites.—*Debra Jane Seltzer*

Ultraviolet Apocalypse

Religion comes to different people in many different ways. Some are born into it, while others wake up one morning and just start to see things in a different way. In Indiana, some people say that the Our Lady of Mount Carmel Monastery in Munster is the place to go if you want to see things in a different light—a black light, to be precise.

On the grounds of the monastery is a collection of shrines erected by the Carmelites, specifically by the Discalced ("barefoot") Carmelites. These were a group of monks who served under Allied command in the Free Polish Army during World War II. After the war, many of the men emigrated to America to spread the word among the American people. After arriving, the monks began collecting unique rocks, stones, and gems from all over Indiana to create shrines that would show the God-created beauty in all things.

A visit to the monastery begins at the grotto of the Holy Mother. Completed in 1954, the grotto is a multistoried building constructed from over two hundred and fifty tons of sponge rock from a strip mine in the Ozark Mountains. The focal point of the grotto is a large altar inset on the front of the building. However, barely visible off to the side is a small opening that leads to a catacomblike structure nestled behind the altar. As you wander through its passageways, you will come across religious icons and statues built into the walls of the grotto. At one stop is the fluorescent altar, which offers a sign of bigger glowing things to come.

Front and center on the altar is an alabaster statue, the *Mother of our Savior*, surrounded by stones and rocks. It's a very well lit scene, but with the aid of a good old-fashioned light switch you can turn off the lights and activate a black light. This allows some words "hidden" in

the stones to pop out in all their neon glory: "hail" and "queen." Just be sure to read from the bottom left and work your way around, otherwise you'll see the secret message as "liah queen."

On Your Knees!

As you leave the grotto, you begin your walk along the stations of the cross. To reach a re-created Calvary, the place where Jesus was crucified, you are asked to climb the Holy Stairs. But since these stairs are holy, you are asked to climb them on your knees and be reverent about it too. Should you choose not to, there are a set of ordinary feet-climbing stairs to the left of the Holy Stairs.

Neon Second Coming

After coming down from viewing the crucifixion, you enter the Holy Sepulchre Chapel, which is made up to represent Jesus' tomb. It's quite a surreal feeling to walk down into the darkness and come upon a pair of angels guarding the pathway. Farther down, the hallway opens up into what is supposed to be the tomb, complete with a stone figure of Christ on his deathbed amid a lot of folding chairs. As you make your way to the back stairs and prepare to leave the chapel, make sure to turn to the right. Tucked away in a corner is the amazingly disturbing Memorial Chapel. The scene itself is a simple one: Jesus rising from the dead and the end of the world. An angel blows his trumpet while hands reach up from graves and yellow crosses fill the sky above your head. It's a strange enough scene until you take into account that all of this is the result of black lights, and then things really get trippy. As you stare at the neon stones and try to take everything

in, you half expect to hear "The Dark Side of the Moon" start coming from speakers hidden within the rocks. But it doesn't. So you take your leave and return to the outside world with the newfound realization that if and when it's time for the second coming of Christ, you better have a black light if you want to see it.

Rotating Jail

There are some people who claim that our current legal system is flawed and that our jails are nothing more than revolving doors for criminals to pass through. We're not sure about that, but we do know there's a jail in Crawfordsville where not only do the doors revolve, but the whole jail does too!

In the 1800s, jails were starting to become overcrowded. This posed the problem of not only where to put all the prisoners but also where to find the jailers who could keep the bad guys behind bars. Something had to be done that would allow fewer guards

to watch over more prisoners. Two men, Benjamin Haugh and William Brown, were put to the task of designing and building a jail that could be operated safely by one person. The result was the world's first rotating jail.

When it was completed in 1882, the Crawfordsville Jail was unlike anything that had been seen before. Four stories tall, the jail itself was attached to the warden's house and consisted of a two-story turntablelike structure as well as a basement to house the turning mechanism and an attic for sick prisoners. There were sixteen pie-shaped cells, each originally designed to hold two prisoners, making the total capacity a grand total of thirty-two. Each cell had a single door that, when opened, allowed prisoners access to the outside circle of the floor.

Here's how the rotating aspect of the jail came into play. Each time the jailer rotated the structure, a single cell door would line up with the door to the jailer's quarters. This allowed the jailer to interact (through the bars) with the inmates one or two at a time without fear of being overpowered by the other prisoners. Amazingly, even though the cell block weighed well over fifty-four-thousand pounds, the whole thing could be turned by applying a mere thirteen pounds of pressure to the crank mechanism.

Third Time's the Charm

Over the years, the jail started a collection of strange memorabilia from its time in operation. Most are nothing more than prisoners' drawings on the cell walls or, in one case, a scrawled profession of innocence. But the strangest piece of memorabilia is an iron ring from which the prisoner John W. C. Coffee was hanged in 1885. Officially, Coffee was the first man hanged from the scaffolding of the rotating jail. Although technically, Coffee's was the first, second, and third hanging at the jail.

Convicted of multiple counts of murder, Coffee was scheduled to be hanged on the afternoon of Friday, October 16, from scaffolding erected at the jail. After he was led to the scaffolding and fitted with the noose, the trapdoor opened at twelve twenty-six p.m., and Coffee fell through, prepared to meet his maker. But the rope broke, and Coffee fell to the ground. Sobbing uncontrollably, the prisoner was lifted up and again positioned over the trapdoor until a new rope could be located. At twelve forty, a second noose was placed around Coffee's neck, and the trapdoor was sprung again. This time, he hung suspended in the air, semiconscious, for approximately one minute before everyone concluded things weren't working. So they undid the noose and carried the man back up onto the scaffold. When doctors checked Coffee's pulse and found that he was still alive, officers simply stood him up, placed the noose back around his neck, and sprung the trapdoor a third and final time. As if this story wasn't bizarre enough, there's an odd footnote. As Coffee was hanging there, a mere seconds away from death, he uttered his final words: "Hold on, I have more to tell." What that "more" was, the world will never know.

After the Coffee debacle, the county carried out only one more hanging at the jail. In 1885, John C. Henning officially became the second, and last, man hanged at the jail, after being convicted of murder.

She Still Spins

By the time the 1960s rolled around, conditions at the jail had deteriorated, and in 1967 the Montgomery County Grand Jury shut it down for good. It seemed only a matter of time before the rotating jail would have a date with the wrecking ball. But fate stepped in, and in 1975 the building was officially listed on the National Register of Historic Places. It has since been taken over by a concerned group of people who have fixed it up and even offer tours, complete with giving the old jail a spin. All of which makes the Crawfordsville Jail the world's first rotating jail and the only one that is still operational.

Crawfordsville Star.

VOL. XIV—NO. 37.

CRAWFORDSVILLE, INDIANA, THURSDAY, OCT. 15, 1885.

$1.50 PER YEAR

JOHN W. C. COFFEE.

JAMES M. DENNIS.

JAMES McMULLEN.

THE AWFUL DROP!

HAS FALLEN WITH ITS HUMAN FREIGHT, AND THE HANGMAN'S TREE IS ACCURSED WITH ITS LAWFUL FRUIT.

Also John W. C. Coffee, Tortured by Evilling Hope and the Cruel Hangman's Rope; Lamenting the Deep Damnation of a

Black, Voidless Future, Throws Himself Upon the Mercy of His Creator and Takes the Awful Leap that Spans the Length Between Life and Eternity.

HIS CASE NOW BEFORE A HIGHER TRIBUNAL BEYOND ALL APPEAL WHERE GENTLE MERCY, SWEET CHARITY AND GODLIKE LOVE SHALL SOFTEN AND CHASTEN THE PUNISHMENT OF THE TORTURED SOUL.

THE EXECUTION OF JOHN W.

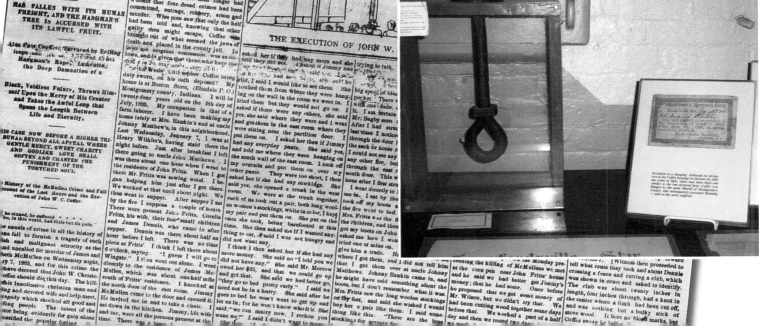

Backyard Watchtower—Cairo

By the beginning of the 1950s, all of America knew one thing: The Russians were coming. Worse, they were going to announce their arrival by launching missiles at us. Radar warning systems that could track incoming missiles (or even low-flying airplanes, for that matter) had not yet been invented. So how were we to defend ourselves?

In an attempt to counteract this impending doom, the United States Air Force created Operation Skywatch. But unlike most military operations, this one would rely on civilian participation. The idea was to rally people across the United States into forming volunteer groups of what would be known as Ground Observation Corps. These groups would be responsible for manning Ground Observation Defense Posts twenty-four hours a day and reporting any suspicious air activity directly to the air force. Sounds great, except for a couple of things. For starters, the Ground Observation Defense Posts were to be nothing more than giant wooden observation towers.

And the Hoosier State would be where it all started. On August 16, 1952, the first Ground Observation Defense Post was commissioned in the tiny town of Cairo, just outside LaFayette. The site chosen for the tower was the backyard of Larry O'Connor, who also ran the local grocery store.

Designated Delta-Lima-Three Green (or DL3-G), the tower ended up being thirty feet tall with a twelve-foot-square platform on top from which to scan the skies. On the platform was a seven-by-seven cabin that would shield people from the elements should the weather turn bad. Once the tower was completed, the people of Cairo banded together and started watching the skies. Over the course of the next year, between ninety and one hundred twenty volunteers took turns manning the Ground Observation Defense Post in two-hour shifts.

With the end of the Korean War in 1954, the Ground Observations Corps was scaled back and eventually ceased operation. Twenty years later the Operation Skywatch tower was used only by amateur severe weather spotters and the occasional teenage couple seeking some privacy.

In 1976, a statue was commissioned to be placed at the base of the tower and the tower itself was reconstructed and given a makeover, which cost a bit more than planned. As a result, it wasn't until four years later, in 1980, that the statue was paid for and installed near the tower. Bearing the title *They Also Serve Who Stand and Watch*, the statue depicts a father, mother, and child holding hands and looking skyward. The father has his binoculars at the ready, should any Russian planes or missiles come blazing across the sky.

Giant House

When Jerry Alan Hostetler first bought his house on Kessler Boulevard in Indianapolis, back in the 1960s, it was a modest place, similar to all the others in the neighborhood. Back then, Hostetler was just starting to enjoy success with his construction and design business. Perhaps that was what put the idea into his head. What better way to show potential clients his company's capabilities than to show his own house?

It started simply enough with a few renovations to interior rooms. Neighbors didn't blink twice when Hostetler put on an addition. But then the house started to take on a life of its own. It grew and grew and grew. Entire walls were knocked out, and whole new wings were added on. Hostetler preferred to construct his growing abode in Gothic style, completed oddly enough with a variety of shaped windows. Storage sheds became bedrooms, which then became cottages. Glass walkways were installed to connect outbuildings to the main house. With a crew working year-round, the house quickly stretched to the property boundaries. When Hostetler couldn't build out anymore, he built up, adding whole new floors. And when he couldn't build up anymore, he bought out his neighbors, took over their houses, and connected them to his mother ship of a home.

At the peak of construction, Hostetler's house was an amazing 55,000 square feet. Supposedly, there were over fifteen bathrooms and fifty rooms, although Hostetler himself often told people he wasn't really sure how many there were. This was because the builder was in the habit of completing construction on a room and then turning right around and ripping it all apart again.

But all this mad construction doesn't come without a price. Unfortunately for Hostetler, the bills started piling up higher than the roof on his gargantuan house. Falling ill, he was unable to keep up his business, and before long, foreclosures started. Of course, this presented a whole slew of problems for real estate agents and potential buyers alike. For example, when Hostetler's property started being broken apart and returned to its original plot sizes, often what was left behind was a two-story house that had been renovated to the point where it consisted of only two rooms, one bathroom, and no kitchen. Not exactly a hot commodity.

As for Hostetler himself, he passed away quietly on August 28, 2006, at the age of sixty-six, leaving behind one giant house and an even bigger pile of debt. When his death was announced in the local newspaper, it seemed only a fitting ironic twist that the obituary of the man who spent his whole life building giant things would consist of merely two sentences.

Living Underground in Pendleton

Sometime in the early 1980s, Vic Cook decided he'd had enough of corporate America. Giant buildings were being built without any regard to the environment or future generations, and it was all too much for Cook to take. So he decided to literally become one with nature. He walked into the woods of Pendleton and began to build his dream home—more than twenty feet underground.

Cook spent the next decade and over twenty-six thousand hours building his environmentally friendly house. It's named the Earthship and nicknamed the Giant after Neil Armstrong's famous line "one giant leap for mankind" when he took man's first step on the moon.

Cook's house is a testament to the fact that people can indeed live off the land without giving up the comforts we have come to know and love. Using the earth itself for insulation, the Giant stays a nice, comfortable sixty-eight degrees all summer long. Even during the cold winter months, the ground keeps the house so warm and comfortable that Cook needs to only occasionally run a kerosene heater during the coldest nights of the year. The Giant is powered almost entirely by the sun through the use of generators, although Cook does keep kerosene and gasoline on hand for the generators just in case the weather turns cloudy for long periods of time.

For most people a lot of monthly income goes to utility bills such as electricity, water, and telephone. Not for Vic Cook. All of his electricity comes from solar-powered batteries, so there is no electric bill. As far as water, Cook does indeed have what could qualify as running water, but it doesn't come from city water pipes or even from a well. Instead, Cook collects rainwater in tanks located in the ceiling of the house. Good old-fashioned gravity allows the water to flow to different parts of the house whenever it is needed. Cook even has telephone service, but opts for only the very basic service, which costs him less than $20 a month. Oh yeah, and there's no monthly sewage or trash charges because Cook composts everything (and we mean everything).

But even though Cook gets most of what he needs directly from nature, Uncle Sam still wants his cut. So Cook is responsible for paying property taxes—a whole whopping $10. The cost is so low because the property does not have any utilities.

Like any man, one of Cook's favorite parts of the house is the refrigerator. But nothing in Cook's house is what we would call "normal." He actually built the refrigerator himself out of a hollow log. During the course of its six-week construction, he lined the inside of the log with a special type of insulation called Reflectix and used a solar-powered battery to pull cool air out of the ground and recirculate it through the refrigerator log. After its completion, Cook added a freezer, which uses a simple microchip to keep everything frozen solid.

But no man's home is truly his castle without being filled with electronics. The Giant is no exception and is filled with a big-screen television, several computers, and even a recording studio, all of which are run by solar power. And for those of you who want to build your own Giant but don't think you could survive without the World Wide Web, take heart. All the home's computers have Internet access, which allows Cook to surf the Web to his heart's content and even run a Web site dedicated to the Giant (www.giantearthship.com).

Cook takes every opportunity to educate others about his Earthship, and he opens the Giant up for tours beginning May 1 and running through the middle of October. Checks to pay for tours of this eco-friendly house can be made out to the Earthship Corporation.

Dan Patch

When driving through Oxford, you can't help but see the barn emblazoned with the giant words "Home of Dan Patch 1:55." But before you go scrambling for your Bible to see what words of wisdom lie in Dan Patch chapter 1, verse 55, relax. We're just talking about a record-setting horse.

Dan Patch, the horse, was born April 29, 1896, in Oxford and was owned by Joe Patchen. It's interesting to note that when Dan Patch was born, he had a deformed left hind leg that was so bad, his mother had to help keep him propped up. His owners had their doubts as to whether or not Dan Patch would ever be able to stand on his own, let alone race. But the horse proved them wrong big-time. His leg was corrected, and he was soon recognized as a horse of great potential.

In 1900, Dan Patch was sold to M. E. Sturgis for the incredible sum of $20,000. Sturgis immediately started training Dan Patch to race. The very first time he raced, later in 1900, he won. He won his next race too and the one after that. All that winning caught the eye of Marion W. Savage from Minnesota. In 1902, Savage bought Dan Patch and brought him back with him to Minnesota. From that point on, the young horse's life was never to be the same again.

One of the main reasons for this was that Savage was not only a man of considerable wealth but he also loved horse racing. To that end, Savage had constructed a huge farm and racetrack that locals often referred to as the Taj Mahal. Sitting on almost seven hundred acres, the farm consisted of heated barns, electric lighting, and of course, a state-of-the-art racetrack. The area was such a

sight to see that the town officially changed its name from Hamilton to Savage.

As Savage started putting Dan Patch through his paces, he noticed something: The horse would almost literally fly by any other horse on the track. It was as if the other horses were standing still. It got to the point where friends and neighbors would come from all over just to catch a glimpse of Dan Patch racing around the track. That's when Savage knew he was onto something, and he started showing Dan Patch at local and then state fairs. Sometimes Dan Patch would race other horses, and sometimes he would just run around the track. It didn't matter. People just loved to see the horse run.

The biggest day came on September 8, 1906, at the Minneapolis State Fairgrounds. That was the day when Dan Patch, in front of an estimated 93,000 fans, set the world record for horse racing by completing a mile in a mere one minute and fifty-five seconds. It was a record that would be equaled but never surpassed.

Once he set the record, Dan Patch went from being a local celebrity to an international one; people came from all over the world to meet him. Savage helped by selling everything from Dan Patch horseshoes and photographs to pieces of hair from the horse's tail. Dan Patch became so popular that not one but two songs were written about him: "The Dan Patch Two Step" and "The Dan Patch March." Heck, Dan Patch even became the only nonhuman member of Wesley United Methodist Church of Minneapolis.

Then, on July 4, 1916, the fabulous horse fell ill. Savage, who himself was going into the hospital for minor surgery, left specific instructions as to how to care for the horse he

had come to love. Sadly, on July 11, Dan Patch passed away from what was thought to be an enlarged heart. While in the hospital recovering from his surgery, Savage was notified of his horse's passing. In a strange twist, less than thirty-six hours later, M. W. Savage passed away too.

Dan Patch was buried in Savage, Minnesota, in an unmarked grave on the property of M. W. Savage, near the racetrack where he loved to run. Back in Oxford, Indiana, the owners of the barn where Dan Patch was born painted the now famous "Home of Dan Patch 1:55" on the roof as an eternal memorial to the horse that won the hearts of a nation. Years later a gravestone bearing Dan Patch's name and dates of birth and death was added to the front of the barn property, leading some to believe they had found the final resting place of the beloved horse. But they haven't.

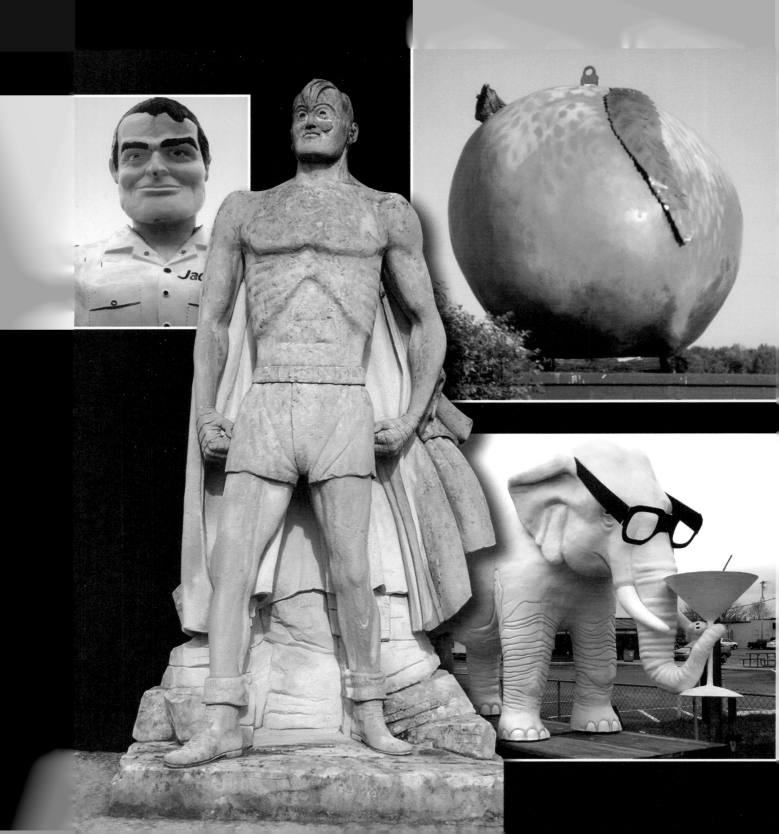

Roadside Oddities

indiana's state motto is The Crossroads of America, and with good reason. In Indianapolis alone, seven major interstate highways hit the city like a bull's-eye. That makes for a lot of asphalt, which could also make for a lot of tiresome driving. Good thing that the wonderful weird people of Indiana have made the decision to set out their personal bits of strangeness for us to marvel at, if only for a moment, from the seemingly endless pavement. Drive off the highways to some back roads, and things get even more peculiar—from giant statues to things that make you go, "What the . . . ?" Every odd object along the roadside has its own story to tell. And as diehard fans of the unusual, we are more than willing to listen.

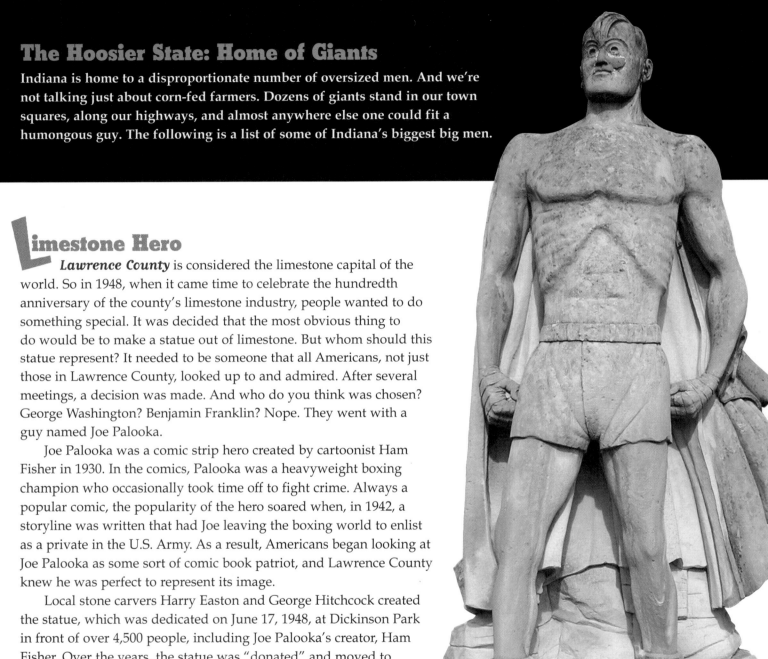

The Hoosier State: Home of Giants

Indiana is home to a disproportionate number of oversized men. And we're not talking just about corn-fed farmers. Dozens of giants stand in our town squares, along our highways, and almost anywhere else one could fit a humongous guy. The following is a list of some of Indiana's biggest big men.

Limestone Hero

Lawrence County is considered the limestone capital of the world. So in 1948, when it came time to celebrate the hundredth anniversary of the county's limestone industry, people wanted to do something special. It was decided that the most obvious thing to do would be to make a statue out of limestone. But whom should this statue represent? It needed to be someone that all Americans, not just those in Lawrence County, looked up to and admired. After several meetings, a decision was made. And who do you think was chosen? George Washington? Benjamin Franklin? Nope. They went with a guy named Joe Palooka.

Joe Palooka was a comic strip hero created by cartoonist Ham Fisher in 1930. In the comics, Palooka was a heavyweight boxing champion who occasionally took time off to fight crime. Always a popular comic, the popularity of the hero soared when, in 1942, a storyline was written that had Joe leaving the boxing world to enlist as a private in the U.S. Army. As a result, Americans began looking at Joe Palooka as some sort of comic book patriot, and Lawrence County knew he was perfect to represent its image.

Local stone carvers Harry Easton and George Hitchcock created the statue, which was dedicated on June 17, 1948, at Dickinson Park in front of over 4,500 people, including Joe Palooka's creator, Ham Fisher. Over the years, the statue was "donated" and moved to several different locations throughout Lawrence County until 1984, when it was moved to its current location on Main Street in Oolitic.

Big Jack, Yorktown's Muffler Man

Located right along exit ramp 41 of Interstate 69 in Yorktown is a classic thirty-foot-tall Muffler Man known as Jack RV. Jack's name is a bit odd, especially since he's standing in front of an equipment rental store with nary an RV in sight. Things start to make a bit more sense when you learn that years ago, the rental store was actually known as Jack Smith & Sons RV Sales. In fact, Jack the Giant Muffler Man once held an RV in his right hand and a BIG JACK sign dangled from his left. Alas, once the building was sold, Jack RV was stripped of his wares and left to stand alongside the highway empty-handed . . . for now. Of course, his loss raises the question, How big does something have to be to take something away from a thirty-foot-tall man?

Frankenstein's Muffler Man

For several decades now, Ralph's Muffler Shop in downtown Indianapolis has been home to Mr. Bendo, the area's favorite Muffler Man. Or perhaps a more fitting term for Mr. Bendo is Dr. Frankenstein's Muffler Man—because Mr. Bendo appears to have been cobbled together using parts of several different Muffler Man designs.

Look at Mr. Bendo's legs and lower body: clearly Muffler Man material. And yet his head is not the standard Muffler Man "issue" and is instead the noggin used for the lumberjack models. And check out Mr. Bendo's arms, especially the way the hands are positioned. There's no way they could hold a muffler. But Muffler Man conspiracy lovers claim that this guy's arms are actually a variation of International Fiberglass's Indian model, despite the fact that the right hand on the Indian versions is open and extended while Mr. Bendo's right hand is closed. The mystery deepens even more if you talk to old-timers in the neighborhood, who swear that at one time Mr. Bendo did indeed hold a muffler in his hands.

Uncle Sam Wants You (to Buy a Chrysler)

Standing outside the parking lot of Eastgate Chrysler (okay, actually he's chained to a lamppost), is an oversized Uncle Sam. In the grand scheme of giant roadside oddities, this guy's sort of at the low end of the scale. Still, he does have a crazy look in his eyes, which is probably why he's chained up. There's no telling what sort of damage this guy could do if he ever got loose.

There were rumors of a second, even bigger Uncle Sam at the car lot; however, he was not to be found when we visited. Of course, we did visit in November, so perhaps Big Sam was out encouraging people to vote in the upcoming election.

Propane Piggy

As we crested a hill on U.S. 31 in Kokomo, we were struck by a site that made us wonder why we hadn't heard the news that Pink Floyd was in town. Peering out at us from around the Mittler Supply building was a giant pink pig. It wasn't until we got closer that we realized the enormous pig was actually a painted propane tank.

So what's the connection between pigs and propane? Not sure. But we didn't stick around to ask. We've found that whenever we come across giant things that are gassy, it's best to just hold your nose, take a picture, and move on as quickly as possible.

Big Ol' Ben—Kokomo

When he came into the world in January 1902, Old Ben (probably known as Young Ben at the time) tipped the scales at a whopping 135 pounds. For obvious reasons, he became known as the world's largest calf.

But Ben didn't stop there. By most accounts, Ben ate no more than all his barnyard buddies on the Murphy farm, halfway between Bunker Hill and Miami. Nevertheless, he kept on growing at an alarming rate. By the time he was a mere eighteen months old, he had already swelled to almost 1,800 pounds. When his third birthday rolled around, Ben was pushing a massive 4,000 pounds. It's no wonder that Mike and John Murphy, Ben's "parents," began showing him at county and state fairs.

In 1910, Ben slipped and fell on a patch of ice, suffering an injury so severe that the poor animal had to be put down. At the time of his death, Old Ben was six feet four inches tall, weighed a little over 4,700 pounds, and from tip of his nose to tip of his tail he measured sixteen feet two inches.

After his death, the Murphy family decided they wanted to keep Ben around and made arrangements to save the hide so that a taxidermist could stuff and preserve it. The rest of Ben was shipped off to a hot dog manufacturer in Indianapolis.

The Murphys kept Old Ben on display in their barn until 1919, when they sold their farm and moved. Before leaving, they made the decision to part ways with Ben, and the city of Kokomo became his new owner. The city

moved Ben out to Highland Park and gave him a home right next to the world's largest sycamore stump. He's pretty easy to find, since he's located off Old Ben Drive, which might make Ben the world's only giant stuffed steer to have a street named after him.

Giant Pink-Eyed Elephant

If you pull into the Wagon Wheel Liquor Store in Fortville for a "fill up," what you see in the parking lot might be enough to make you swear off the sauce for a while. Sitting just to the right of the store's front entrance is a giant pink elephant holding a martini glass, complete with olive, in his trunk. He's also got bloodshot eyes, a clear sign that he's had one too many elephant-size martinis. And if that's not enough, for no apparent reason this elephant appears to be sporting Drew Carey's eyeglasses. The giant pink pachyderm has been sitting outside the store and sending people to AA for several decades. As an added bonus, the elephant is on a trailer and can be rented out. For what, we're not sure.

Big Peach

At the entrance to a produce stand in Bruceville stands this enormous peach. Those with hearty appetites might be a bit disappointed, as all the produce for sale at the stand is of normal size.

World's Largest Egg . . . or Is It?

Mentone is one of the world's top egg producers. And by the looks of what's sitting on Main Street, Mentone produces some pretty darn big eggs.

This giant egg was built by Hugh Rickel in 1946 to coincide with the local egg festival. Pouring concrete over a steel frame, Rickel created an egg-squisite piece of artwork, weighing in at three thousand pounds and standing over ten feet in height. Lest anyone forget the enormity of the situation (and the egg), Rickel proudly emblazoned the phrase, MENTONE INDIANA: THE EGG BASKET OF THE MIDWEST across the front of the egg. Soon people began flocking to the tiny town of Mentone to marvel at this giant egg. Some even declared it to be the largest egg in the world. That's when the controversy began. Seems that the town of Winlock, Washington, has a giant egg of its own that it is pretty darn proud of too. The town even paints it from time to time (which technically might make it an Easter egg). Sometimes it even decorates the egg with stars and stripes à la the American flag. Of course, the egg sits on a pedestal proudly proclaiming that it is the WORLD'S LARGEST EGG.

So how do these eggs stack up? Well, the Winlock egg is almost two feet higher than the one in Mentone. But what the Mentone egg lacks in height it makes up for in volume, as it's a good eighteen hundred pounds heavier than the one in Winlock. This is due mainly to the fact that the Winlock egg is made of fiberglass, while the Mentone one is comprised mainly of concrete. That's also the reason the townspeople of Winlock think the Mentone egg is bogus. They claim that the egg in Mentone doesn't classify as an egg, since it is made out of concrete. Although, with all due respect to the people of Winlock, we don't remember real eggs being made of fiberglass either. But then again, we've led a somewhat sheltered life.

So which town is home to the world's largest egg? The debate continues. As for us, we think both towns are a little cracked.

Giant Candle

Next time the lights in Centerville go out, people won't need to go fumbling around looking for a flashlight. They have a giant candle to light the way for them.

Created in the fall of 2006 outside the Warm Glow Candle Company, it dwarfs even the store itself. What's more, at night the wick lights up and flickers, illuminating cars as they travel along I-70 and serving as a beacon for all those in search of the perfect apple-butter–scented candle.

Long's Big Stuff

Standing near Long's Furniture World in Franklin is a rocking chair that's so large it's been given a name: Big John.

But this is no ordinary giant chair. Apparently, it's been acknowledged by *Guinness World Records* as being the largest in the world. As for the odd name of the chair, it's sort of the namesake of store owner, John D. Long, who had the chair built. However, there may be some rocking-chair–loving giant roaming around Amity. As evidence, we point to the fact that there's a giant-size dresser standing outside the store entrance. By the looks of the tie hanging out of it, whoever used it last left in a hurry.

Sneakering Around New Carlisle

Bigfoot is apparently running rampant in New Carlisle. And he's lost his sneakers in the process—two giant sneakers, each capable of squashing a bug . . . a Volkswagen Bug.

Originally the sneakers were part of a pair constructed in 1991 by artists Todd Anders and Gary Abner as elements of an outdoor advertising campaign for Reebok. As a tie-in with the NCAA Championships, the sneakers were placed inside a giant shoebox and then mounted onto a billboard under the tagline NBA STARTER KIT.

After the billboard had run its course, the sneakers made their way over to the Basketball Hall of Fame in New Castle. One of the sneakers (top right) was then donated to the Steve Alford Inn, owned by none other than, you guessed it, Steve Alford—the former Indiana Hoosier basketball star.

Over the years, both sneakers have received paint jobs in order to remove or replace the Reebok logo. The Hall of Fame sneaker now sports a Hall of Fame logo, while the sneaker outside Steve Alford's now has an Iowa Hawkeyes logo to reflect Alford's current position as head coach of the Iowa Hawkeyes basketball team.

Dig This!

We're not sure what sort of plants Habig Gardening Centers have been digging up recently. But based on the size of their trowels, we think it's safe to say they're pretty big.

There are two Habig Gardening Centers in Indianapolis, each with its very own giant trowel. This one's sitting near the corner of College and Fifty-second.

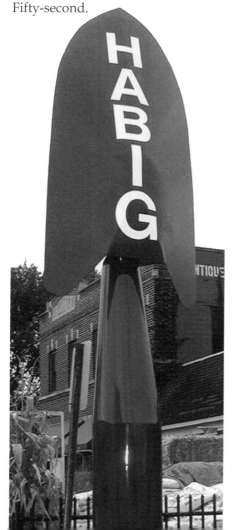

Biggest Ball of Paint

Flip through any *Guinness World Records* and you'll come across some pretty weird achievements: most goldfish swallowed, world's largest pancake, world's largest ball of paint. Ball of paint? Yup, and believe it or not, it's hidden away in Alexandria and has to be one of the coolest world's records ever. That's because this award winner is interactive and visitors have the unique opportunity to roll up their sleeves, roll on some paint, and become part of this world's record. So how did it come to be?

Back in the 1960s, Mike Carmichael was spending his summer vacation working in a paint store. One day, while he was playing catch in the store with a friend, the baseball knocked over a can of paint. Mike thought it would be cool to paint the ball with one thousand coats, record the colors, and then see what the end results looked like. So he spent his remaining years of high school painting that baseball every chance he had. He even wrapped the ball with a wire to make it easier to handle.

After he reached one thousand coats, Carmichael gave the ball to one of his teachers, who kept it a while and then donated it to the Alumni Museum of the Knightstown Children's Home. He eventually decided he wanted the ball back, but when he contacted the museum, they wouldn't return it. So since he couldn't have his ball of paint back, Carmichael decided to do the next best thing: make an even bigger ball of paint!

On New Year's Day, January 1, 1977, Mike and his son, three-year-old Mike junior, applied the first coat. He even made sure someone was there to take a picture and capture what he was sure would be a historic moment. He had learned a lesson from his first ball-painting experience, and this time he stuck a metal plug into the ball to make it easier to handle and paint. After the first coat, Carmichael would paint the ball in the evenings and on weekends. And his wife, Glenda, would add a coat whenever she had some free time. Before long, he was showing his newly painted ball to family and friends, all of whom wanted to take their turns applying a coat. Pretty soon, coat number one thousand was only a memory, and the ball kept growing and growing as more and more people showed up to gaze in wonderment at it . . . and paint it, of course.

When it reached 17,994 coats, Guinness came calling and officially awarded Carmichael the record for the world's largest ball of paint. But at that point, Carmichael saw no reason to stop and just kept right on painting.

Seems the ball had gotten so big, it had taken on a life of its own; it was now something of a national celebrity and was visited by other celebrities such as Tom Greene and members of the Indianapolis Colts.

Carmichael weighs the ball roughly once a year, so it's hard to get an exact weight, but currently it is hovering somewhere in the 2,300-pound range. Recently, the ball got so big it had to be moved into its own quarters; it took up residence in a barnlike structure, where it was suspended from the ceiling. Carmichael put on a wall a running tally of how many coats of each color are on the ball so visitors can track which colors are the favorites. Recently he even got Sherwin-Williams to endorse the ball and supply him with all the paint he needs, so the possibilities are endless.

Enter *Weird Indiana*.

When we arrived at the Carmichael's place in the spring of 2007, we were honored to have the chance to put our own personalized coat on the world's largest ball of paint. For the record, we were coat number 20,216, and we have a certificate to prove it! Of course, we couldn't pass up the opportunity to give the world's largest ball of paint its very own coat of weirdness—the *Weird Indiana* logo! And so it shall remain, at least until someone else comes along to paint coat number 20,217. If you're planning on being in the Alexandria area, give the Carmichaels a call beforehand. We hear Mike just might have a paint roller with your name on it.

These Bib Overalls were owned and worn by Robert Wadlow "The Gentle Giant". They were an exact fit.

Miami County Museum

Located along North Broadway in Peru, the Miami County Museum currently houses over seventy thousand items related to the history of Miami County, including more than a few weird and wonderful relics!

The Gentle Giant

The man who would become known as the Gentle Giant, Robert Pershing Wadlow, was born in Alton in 1918. At the time of his birth, Wadlow was a normal eight pounds eight ounces. His height was not recorded at the time. It wasn't long before Wadlow's growth spurts made people realize he was turning into something big. The first time his height was recorded was when he turned five. At that time, he was five feet four and weighed in at a little over one hundred pounds.

By the time his thirteenth birthday rolled around, Wadlow had grown to an incredible seven four and was pushing three hundred pounds. At the time of his death on July 15, 1940, at the young age of twenty-two, Wadlow had topped out at 8 feet, 11.1 inches tall, making him the tallest person in history according to *Guinness World Records*.

The overalls on display at the museum are a pair worn by Wadlow. They were an exact fit.

Big Charley

There was a time, beginning in the 1870s and continuing into the 1940s, that Peru, Indiana, was considered the circus capital

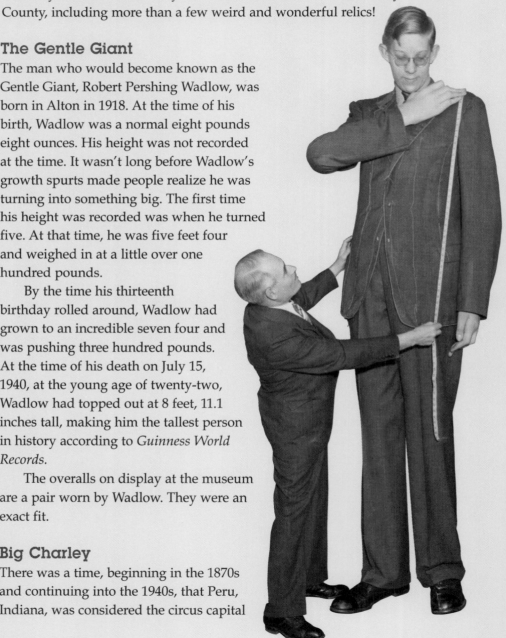

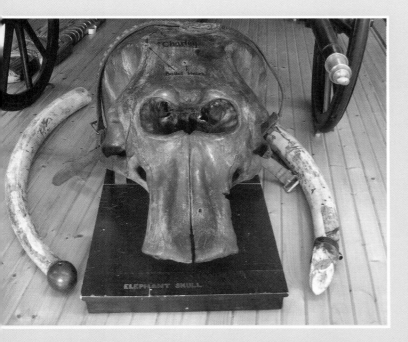

of the world. This was because Peru was a railroad hub, which made the shuttling of circus supplies, including livestock, easier. Many of the world's most famous circuses, Ringling Bros. included, made Peru and the area surrounding the town their winter headquarters. Because so many circuses were camped together, it wasn't uncommon for workers, and even whole acts, to move from circus to circus if the money was right. So when the J. H. LaPearl Circus went bankrupt, Benjamin Wallace took the opportunity to purchase most of their equipment and animals, including an elephant named Big Charley, and incorporate them into his shows.

On the morning of April 25, 1901, trainer Henry Hoffman took Charley down to the banks of the Mississinewa River. But on this day, Charley wasn't in the mood for a bath or even a drink, so he just stood there. Hoffman then did what most trainers would do and started prodding Charley with a metal hook. This didn't set well with Charley either, and he responded by smacking Hoffman with his trunk, sending the man flying into the river. Afterward Charley calmly walked over to the entrance gate and waited to be let back into the camp.

Now most people would agree that when an elephant uses his trunk to launch you into a river, it's probably a good idea to leave that elephant alone for a while. Unfortunately for Henry Hoffman, he was not like most people. So after pulling himself out of the river and onto a nearby wooden raft, he began yelling at Charley and ordering him to return to the water. For Charley, that was the last straw. The enormous elephant suddenly charged Hoffman, who barely had time to throw up his arms in defense before he was scooped up in Charley's trunk. The crowd gathering along the water's edge could only look on in horror as Charley repeatedly slammed Hoffman against the wooden raft. When Hoffman's muffled cries finally ceased, Charley tossed the man's body into the river and slowly made his way back to the camp.

As can be imagined, panic swept through the camp. Someone managed to reach Benjamin Wallace by phone. He immediately gave the word to have Charley killed before he could harm anyone else. Believe it or not, there was actually a procedure set in place for times when animals got out of control and had to be put down. First, two enormous pills containing the poison strychnine were tossed near Charley, who ate one of them but ignored the second. The crowd waited a few minutes for the poison to take effect and then quickly decided to go to Plan B—gather up all the firearms in the camp and unload them on Charley. Incredibly, the elephant was hit by over two dozen bullets before two well-placed shots to the skull finally brought the giant beast down.

Today visitors to the Miami County Museum can see all that remains of Big Charley: his tusks and skull, on which someone has written "Bullet Holes," with arrows directing you to the holes.

Cole Porter Museum

Born in Peru on December 18, 1919, Cole Porter was destined to stand out among the crowd. He was a musical genius who wrote a slew of successful shows such as *Anything Goes* and *Kiss Me Kate* and gave the world such memorable songs as "Begin the Beguine," "I Get a Kick Out of You," and "I've Got You Under My Skin." But while the Cole Porter Museum contains many objects related to Porter's musical career, two of the most interesting items on display have nothing to do with music.

In 1937, a horse fell on Porter, severely fracturing both his legs. As a result, he was practically crippled and spent the remaining years of his life in excruciating pain. One of the museum's displays features a custom-built sofa Porter had made extra deep to accommodate his legs.

Another item of interest is Cole's customized 1955 Cadillac Fleetwood. The car was featured in the book *Travels with Cole* and has appeared in TV shows and movies, most notably *The Godfather.* Some of the custom work done on the vehicle includes the Cole Porter logo on the side doors and red leather interior upholstery. Porter chose the color because he believed that in the event his dog, Hildegarde, had an "accident" in the car, it would not be as noticeable on the dark leather.

Bloody Dresses and Weird Animals

On the top floor of the Miami County Museum are displays designed to look like storefronts from days gone by: a music store, a photo shop, a dentist's office, even a combination furniture–coffin maker's place of business. Far and away, though, the weirdest items are found in the display made to look like the old Miami County Museum. Seems like everywhere you look in this exhibit, you're met with the sight of something you feel guilty about looking at . . . and yet you can't seem to stop staring at it.

The first bit of morbid curiosity in the display is a small pink calico dress stained with blood. Seems that back in 1853, Samuel Burns and his family were making their way from South Carolina to California. Somewhere in the Arizona desert, Burns's young daughter, Margaret, fell from a wagon and was crushed to death. She was buried the next day, but her family decided to keep the bloodstained dress she was wearing when she was killed. The dress was handed down from generation to generation before finding a home here at the museum.

On the opposite side of the display is a bizarre collection of stuffed animals, including a two-headed calf and a Siamese pig.

Rockin' Tree

Yellowwood State Forest in Brown County is literally teeming with wildlife. Hunters and hikers alike have ventured into the woods in search of all sorts of unique birds and animals that have come to call the area home. But far and away the weirdest inhabitant of the state forest is a four-hundred-pound rock that somehow managed to come to rest almost forty feet off the ground.

Nicknamed Gobbler's Rock after it was first spotted by a turkey hunter around 1999, the giant hunk of sandstone was estimated to be about four feet wide and roughly one foot thick. Somehow this stone behemoth became embedded in the branches roughly halfway up an eighty-foot-tall chestnut tree.

As to how this rock found its way into the tree, theories vary widely from pranksters and tornados to otherworldly explanations such as UFOs. Those who point to humans as responsible seem to leave out the fact that Gobbler's Rock is roughly a mile from any main road and that hoisting a rock to that height would certainly require a crane of some sort.

Sadly, in June 2006 a terrible storm ripped through the area, resulting in the rock and the tree crashing to earth as the tree was uprooted. Amazingly, the rock still remained embedded in the tree.

But the legend doesn't end there. There are reports of other trees hidden away in the over 23,000-acre state forest that boast rocks of their own. Known among locals as URBs—unexplained resting boulders—some of these rocks are rumored to be even higher off the ground than was Gobbler's Rock. All this leads many to wonder what's up inside Yellowwood State Forest.

Shoe Tree

Most people, when they find that they have too many shoes lying about, tidy up by hanging them on a shoe tree in their closet. The people of Milltown are no different. Except in their case, the shoe tree they use is an actual tree in the middle of the woods, from which literally hundreds of pairs of shoes are hanging.

Stop and ask anyone in Milltown where you can find a good shoe tree, and they'll send you to a little four-way intersection off in the woods. Not all the roads back there are paved, so it might get a little tricky. But you can always follow the directions to the tree, which are spray-painted on the road. If all else fails, just keep looking up, and you can't miss it. In fact, it's pretty hard to see the bark of the tree through all the leather and soles. There are some people who claim that there's a pair of NBA star Larry Bird's sneakers somewhere up there.

So why do so many people chuck their shoes into this tree? It's hard to say. For while there are several shoe trees scattered throughout the States, each with its own legends, there's no concrete story surrounding the Milltown Shoe Tree. The only one we could find was that some people believe that if you throw a pair of shoes into the tree, you'll have good luck, but only for a year. Perhaps that's why so many people tend to come back to the tree year after year clutching their worn-out shoes.

That luck, however, didn't spread to the tree itself, which was struck by lightning several years ago. The tree still stands, although it looks charred and pretty much dead. That hasn't stopped people from filling the dead branches with shoes, though. In fact, so many people have brought their footwear to the tree that they have started throwing them into the surrounding trees,

creating shoe trees at all four corners of the intersection. It's truly a surreal sight.

Naturally, we couldn't visit the famous Shoe Tree without leaving a pair of *Weird Indiana* shoes behind in tribute. Next time you're out there, see if you can spot them—third branch on the right.

Shoe Corner

There is a corner in Saint John where 109th Street meets Calumet Avenue. It's known as the Shoe Corner. People throw all kinds of shoes there, from baby shoes to boots to athletic shoes to sandals to dress shoes—you name it, it's there. Periodically, someone clears the shoes from the corner, but new shoes keep appearing. I don't know how long this tradition has been going on, at least five years that I know of.

When I first mentioned the shoes in the road to one of my friends who lives on Calumet Ave., he said "Oh yeah, that's the shoe corner," so it's very well known by locals. He's lived on the road all his life so it's possible the tradition is long-standing. He didn't know how it started or why it continues. The best time to visit the shoe corner is in the summer. It seems to collect more shoes in warm weather. If you visit, don't forget to take some shoes to contribute.—*Anonymous*

Roof Trees

Indiana has long been home to many a giant tree. But there's a tree in Greenville that towers over all the others. That's because the top of this tree is over 110 feet off the ground. Oh, yeah, and did we happen to mention the tree is growing on the roof of the courthouse?

It all started back in 1874, when construction began on the current courthouse. Shortly after it was completed, people started noticing a strange, branchlike object on top of it in the northeast corner. They originally thought a tree branch had simply blown up there. The problem was that over time, this branch grew. Soon it became clear that the branch was actually a sapling that somehow managed to take root on the courthouse roof. Stranger still was that one day people from the town saw another sapling pop up. And then another. And another. In the end, a total of five trees sprouted, and pretty soon everyone was proudly telling their friends about the grove of trees growing on the roof.

But as time went on and the trees continued to grow, people started getting nervous. After all, with five trees growing up there, wasn't it just a matter of time before they came crashing through the roof? So in the 1880s, workers were hired to scale the courthouse in order to cut back the trees and make them more "shrublike." When they were done, they had removed three of the five trees and cut back the other two considerably. The trees would have the last laugh, though. Because shortly after the workers descended, a new tree appeared, this time in the southwest corner of the roof. As it grew, another tree sprang up right alongside it. Of all the trees to grace the courthouse roof, these are the two that have remained to this day.

Most, sadly, eventually succumb to the elements (or the elevation) and die. But not without first growing to impressive heights. The largest tree was said to have been almost fifteen

feet high with a five-inch diameter. Granted, that's not too impressive for most trees, but then again, most trees don't take up residence on the roof, do they?

So how do these trees get up on the courthouse roof? No one is really sure. Theories have included everything from birds and strong winds carrying seeds up there to hints at courthouse employees themselves planting seedlings. As to what type of trees they are, it had long been assumed that they were large-tooth aspens. Recently, a sample from the trees was examined by foresters from Purdue University, who determined they were actually mulberry trees. Locals don't really seem to care what kind of trees they are, though. Most simply claim that they are a unique species known as Courthouse Roof Tree and leave it at that.

Studebaker Trees

Founded in the 1850s in South Bend, the Studebaker Company began by manufacturing industrial mining wagons. Beginning in 1902, Studebaker started partnering with other manufacturers to build gasoline-powered vehicles. By the time 1913 rolled around, Studebaker was ready to release the very first gasoline-powered cars under the now famous Studebaker name.

In 1926, Studebaker took roughly 840 acres in South Bend and turned it into the world's first-ever controlled automobile testing grounds. Dubbed the Million Dollar Outdoor Testing Laboratory, the area was used to test all aspects of Studebaker's cars, including crashes and how the vehicles operated in different weather conditions.

In order to make the testing grounds reflect natural driving conditions, Studebaker spent a lot of time developing different styles of terrains. In 1937, after watching some of the landscaping taking place, two Studebaker engineers, Michael de Blumenthal and Mel Niemier, got an idea. Since the aviation industry was growing in South Bend, what better way to advertise Studebaker than to create a sign that could be viewed from the air? With that in mind, the Civilian Conservation Corps, a Depression-era federal workforce, was called in. Over the course of the next month and a half they planted over eight thousand six-inch seedlings on the Studebaker property. But the seedlings were not placed haphazardly. Instead, they were placed in specific locations so that when they grew, the trees would form the word Studebaker when viewed from above by an airplane. Each of the letters was created using five rows of trees; three inner rows of red pine trees and two border rows of white pine trees. When completed, the entire sign was over a half mile long.

After Studebaker's manufacturing plant closed in 1963, the property, including the tree-sign, was purchased by the Bendix Corporation, which used the area for corporate events until they donated it to the St. Joseph County Parks and Recreation Department, which currently maintains the site. By the late 1980s, the tiny saplings had grown so much that each of the letters was now close to two hundred feet wide and two hundred and fifty feet in length. The trees have survived weather damage over the years, and now, thanks to programs such as Google Earth, all of us earthbound mortals can view the Studebaker sign in all its leafy glory.

The Head That Gave Birth to a Town

Brown County is home to a lot of small towns with weird names: Gnaw Bone, Bean Blossom, Dead Fall. Most of these make you wonder where the names originated. But there's one you don't have to worry about: Stone Head. And how will you know when you're in the town of Stone Head? Easy, just look for the stone head.

Seems that back in the 1800s there was a law on the books in Brown County that required all male residents to work at least six days a year on public works projects. In 1851, a gentleman by the name of Henry Cross came up with a unique idea in an attempt to get out of his six days' worth of hard labor. Cross proposed that he would carve three busts that could be placed as mile markers along the desolate road known as New Bellsville Pike so that travelers would know just how far they were from the nearest town. Area officials agreed, and Cross set to work carving the mile markers. Before long, they were placed alongside the road.

Legend has it that almost as soon as they made it to their new roadside homes, two of the three markers were destroyed or lost, leaving only the one that stood in front of Thomas A. Hendricks's house.

But this surviving bust did not fade into obscurity. As the years went by, people starting using it as a mile marker when giving directions ("turn left at the stone head"). Over time, not only the bust but also the area itself was being referred to as Stone Head. And the name, as they say, was set in stone.

Today, the somber bust still sits staring out at cars as they pass in front of Thomas Hendricks's house, which is now known as the House at Stone Head.

Roads Less Traveled

Have you ever come across a road that just seems a little off? It might be some place you've never seen before and know nothing about, yet you have no urge to linger there. We've all been intrigued by those odd stretches of roadway that give travelers a creeping sensation at the back of the neck.

But creepy sensations are just what *Weird Indiana* looks for. So we packed up the car for a journey into the dark side and tracked down some of the eeriest or most cursed places in the state. Read about them here, but if you go in search of these spots, be sure not to trespass on private property or get yourself into a situation that's dangerous. There's a reason why these are Indiana's roads less traveled. They can be hazardous to both your physical and mental health!

Reeder Road's Vanishing Girl

A *desolate* and gloomy stretch of highway in the northwestern part of the state, between Merrillville and Griffith, Reeder Road is surrounded on all sides by dark woods, swamps, occasional junkyards, and miles of barely inhabited land. It is a place that is, by night, largely avoided by the local populace. This road has a really grim reputation. In the 1980s, the headless body of a man was found dumped in the woods alongside Reeder Road, and it has been the scene of other, albeit less bloody, horrors since then.

Murders and headless corpses aside, the resident haunt of Reeder Road is the ghost of a mysterious young woman who hitches rides with unsuspecting male motorists. The most famous encounter occurred in the early 1970s when a young man, a senior at Griffith High School, picked up the girl as he was returning home from a date. It was a rainy night, and he was running late, trying to get home before his curfew, when he saw a young woman standing on the side of the road. She was waving her arms for help, and he pulled to a stop on the shoulder of the road.

The girl quickly got into the passenger seat and explained that her car had gone off the side of the road and she had been waiting a long time for a ride. Naturally, the guy offered to take her home. He couldn't help but notice that she looked miserable in her wet white dress and that she was very pretty. The girl gave him directions, and they started off toward her house. He wouldn't be able to miss it, she told him. It was a white clapboard house with a porch on the front. She knew the light would be on outside because her parents had to be worried sick.

As they drove along in the darkness, the young man tried to make conversation with the girl, but she didn't seem up to talking. He did see how cold she was, so he offered her his high school letterman's jacket, which was lying next to him on the seat. She gratefully accepted it, wearily wrapping it around her shoulders as she tried to stay warm.

The young man continued to drive, and then, ahead in the mist, he could make out the iron fence that surrounded Ross Cemetery. He could see some of the old tombstones reflecting in his headlights, and he slowed down, knowing that he needed to turn to make it to his passenger's house. Unsure of which way to go, he turned to the girl to ask her where to turn, but she was gone!

Without thinking, he slammed the brakes hard and swerved the car over to the side of the road. He sat there for a moment, breathing hard, then jumped out. In the dim glow of the car's dome light, he searched the front and back seats and even looked back down the road to see if he could see where she had jumped out. He found it hard to believe that she could have climbed out of the moving car without his seeing her, but the fact was, she was gone. The girl had simply vanished!

He slowly got back into the car, still not believing what had occurred. Had he imagined the whole thing? If so, then where had his letterman's jacket disappeared to? The last time he had seen it, it had been wrapped around the girl's shoulders. But when she vanished, she took the jacket with her.

The young man went home and spent a restless night, unable to shake the eerie feeling that the incident had given him. The following morning he decided to return to Reeder Road and retrace his route from the night before, hoping that it might make sense in the light of day. He drove the same roads that he had taken in the darkness, passing Ross Cemetery where the girl had disappeared, and eased up the road to the turn the girl had described to him. He went looking for the house she

has lived here in a long time."

He went on to recall that the family who had lived in the house had moved away about fifteen years earlier, when their daughter had been killed in an auto accident on Reeder Road. The car had run off the road into a ditch; the young girl was thrown through the windshield and killed. He told the young man, "I went to the funeral. She's buried at Ross Cemetery, not two miles from here. Sure a tragedy. Killed by a hot-rodding boyfriend on one of those back roads."

A few minutes later, still shaking from the story told to him by the old man, the boy slowly drove back to Reeder

said she lived in and found it, just around a bend in the road.

The old, ramshackle house was covered with peeling white shingles, and the poorly maintained porch leaned at a haphazard angle. The house looked abandoned, but the boy decided to knock on the door and see if anyone was home. Just as he was starting to walk across the yard to the porch, an old red pickup truck stopped on the road behind him and an elderly man asked the boy if he needed help. The young man explained to him that he had met someone who told him that she lived in the house, and he wanted to check on her.

The old man shook his head. He explained, "If someone said she lived here, then she was lying. Nobody

Road. He had no idea what made him do it, but when he reached the gates of Ross Cemetery, he stopped and got out. He walked among the graves for a few minutes, not really sure what he was looking for. Then a flash of color caught his eye.

He saw a headstone at the edge of the woods, and he walked toward it. Carved on the stone was the name of the girl the old man had told him about—the one who had been killed in the car wreck on Reeder Road.

But it was not the tombstone that the young man was looking at. He stared at what lay in front of it—an object that would haunt his dreams for many years to come.

It was a letterman's jacket, folded neatly on the ground atop the young girl's grave.

Terror in the Trestle at White Lick Creek

A *railroad trestle* near Avon has gained such notoriety that the road leading to it has been renamed Haunted Bridge Road. There are many tales about the identity of its resident specter, but perhaps the oldest story attached to the bridge originates in its construction. It is a tragic story of a man known as Dad Jones.

In the early twentieth century, new roadways and railroad lines were being built throughout Indiana to carry commerce, particularly between Indianapolis and Terre Haute. In 1907, the Inter-Urban Railroad was building a new railway line that would require the construction of a bridge over White Lick Creek. Building trestles and laying track was backbreaking and dangerous work, often done by temporary workers. These men were hungry to earn money, and because they weren't permanent railroad employees, their job safety was at best a secondary consideration for railroad officials. It was only a matter of time before a tragedy occurred.

On one hot August morning, workers were laboring to build the bridge. Wooden forms had been built to pour cement for the supporting pylons of the bridge, and the cement had been brought in by special railroad car.

Standing on the platform above the forms was an African American man known to his co-workers as Dad Jones. He was six feet five, and it was said that he was the strongest man on the crew. Because of this, or possibly because he was one of the few black workers, he was often given the most grueling and dangerous work.

At midmorning, Dad Jones waited impatiently for the second load of concrete to be lifted to him and his crew. When it arrived, he and a fellow worker grappled the heavy bucket to maneuver it over the form. Once it was in place, they tipped the bucket, and the cement began to flow into the form below. As it did, however, the wooden platform on which the workers were standing gave way. The other worker was thrown clear, but Dad Jones pitched forward, let out a hoarse yell, and fell headlong into the wet cement. He struggled for a moment, his giant fists beating a crescendo against the wooden form until the remainder of the cement in the bucket cascaded down onto him, sealing him forever in its embrace.

The entire incident happened too quickly to stop it, and according to the railroad foreman, not much could have been done anyway. The railroad was unwilling to stop construction and tear apart the cement pylon to find the body of a temporary laborer. Some workers objected, saying the spirit of the man would not rest unless given a proper burial, but the officials in charge scoffed at the idea and the work continued. The finished railway was gauged a complete success. The memory of Dad Jones's tragic end receded from the memory of all concerned.

Until the screaming began.

A local farmer was the first report it. On his way home from raccoon hunting one moonlit night, he found himself beneath the shadow of the White Lick Creek Bridge just as a train thundered over it. As the train crossed the first trestle, the man swore he heard, over the sound of the locomotive, a man's scream piercing the night. It came, he claimed, not from the train tracks, but from within the bridge itself.

Naturally, this report was met with some skepticism, but within a month, local teenagers corroborated it. They claimed to have been walking the rails one night when, approaching the bridge, they saw a train coming from the opposite direction. Jumping off the tracks, they stood by the bank of the creek and were unnerved to hear the sound of a man's hoarse scream over the sound of the locomotive. Further, they claimed the scream was accompanied by the noise of something pounding within the bridge.

The teenagers were so unnerved by what they'd heard

White Lick Creek Bridge. It seemed the track over the first pylon was gone. There was only a gaping hole where the track should have been. The supporting column had just disappeared.

Halting his train, the engineer grabbed a lantern and dismounted from his engine to investigate. But by the time he reached the bridge, the track was in its place, and no evidence of damage to the pylon could be found.

And then he heard the sounds . . . a dull thumping sound emanating from inside the bridge. He leaned down and peered under the bridge with his light, but he could see nothing. Then he heard a low moan echo in the darkness—a sound that a man might make in his dying moments.

The engineer jumped back onto the train and slowly inched the engine across the bridge. When he reached the other side, he pushed the throttle forward and steamed off at high speed. Soon other reports began to filter in from other railroad engineers—of low moans and a vaporous form suddenly appearing in the middle of the tracks. These reports became so routine that a new rule was instituted instructing engineers to slow their engines when approaching White Lick Creek Bridge. And again the matter was dismissed.

The spirit of Dad Jones cannot be so easily dismissed. As the decades passed, the spot became a common destination for teenagers out on a late-night lark. More than a few came away with a chilled spirit, claiming they had heard the screams and sometimes a hammering sound, as if someone within the bridge were seeking release. Even today, at odd moments, the moisture running off the concrete forms is said to take on the color of blood.

Suburbia encroaches upon the area today, yet the story lives on. And who knows—when the moon shines its cold light on a lonely railroad bridge near Avon, an unquiet spirit may live on too. A spirit that rages against its cruel fate and seeks an audience for its plaintive cries.

that they ran to town to awaken the local sheriff. He loaded the boys into his car and returned to the bridge. As the sheriff expected, all was quiet. He was sure the boys' story was fueled by imagination and perhaps some "liquid courage" they had imbibed. He was about to take them home when he noticed something. The moisture in the early morning air was condensing on the cool cement of the pylons and running down their sides in thin rivulets, a normal occurrence. But something appeared odd. He walked over and placed his hand in the moisture, and what he saw chilled his heart. The moisture running down the pylon was the color of blood!

Without telling the young men what he had seen, the sheriff drove them home. Then he returned to bed, determined to forget the event. However, the boys' story was not so easy to ignore, as more strange events occurred.

In one incident a railroad engineer who was pulling a single flatcar from Indianapolis saw something that caused his heart to skip a beat as he approached the

Do You Hear Him?

I grew up in the area of the haunted bridge and everyone knew the story. As a kid I used to play beneath the trestles on long summer afternoons, and we all saw the red color of the water as it ran down the side of the bridge. My older brother used to tell me the bridge was bleeding. When I was about 13, I snuck out of the house with my older brothers late one night and we went out to the bridge. We sat by the banks of the creek for a long time waiting for a train—I was not sure what we were waiting for because my brothers had not told me the story yet. Finally, at about 1:00 a.m., we heard a train approaching and we all got up and stood by the bottom of the bridge. Just as the train reached the near side of the bridge opposite us, my brother Pat put his hand on my shoulder and said, "Do you hear him?"

"Who?" I asked, suddenly uneasy, but no sooner had I said it than I heard the sound. At first I thought it was the sound of the engine putting on its brakes—kind of a high pitched sound, but then I realized it was human. Someone was screaming. It was a man's scream, and then it went low and turned into kind of a groan. I had no idea where it was coming from, but I knew I wanted out of there right then.

We all took off and ran. We didn't stop for probably half a mile. By then I had decided that my brothers had played a trick on me, and was about to accuse them. But when we stopped I looked at my brother Matt, and saw that he was white as a sheet.

Before I could say anything he turned to my other brother and said, "It really happened! I heard him! I never thought the story was real but I really did hear him!"

It took us ten minutes to calm down, but then as we walked home my brothers told me the story of the workman trapped in cement. Matt and I shared a room and I can tell you for a fact neither one of us slept that night. I am still not sure just what we heard, but I do know that it sounded like a man, and I know how it affected my brothers and me. Someone or something else was out there at night.—*Robert G.*

Ghostly Women of Cline Avenue

The far northwest corner of Indiana, known as the Calumet region, is an odd fit with the rest of the state. The cornfields and wild forested regions to the south yield to smokestacks and mammoth factories here. While many of the factories and refineries are now abandoned and silent, some do continue to operate. And as the area's fortunes come and go, so do the tales of otherworldly spirits roaming the region, possibly looking for the glories of yesteryear.

Two of the most famous resident ghosts are female specters that, according to legend, haunt the same stretch of Cline Avenue between Gary and Whiting. Cline is a roadway that travels from Gary almost to the Illinois border. A drive along it today provides a look at urban decay that seems to stretch forever from both sides. But if the stories are true, there is much more to this highway than first meets the eye.

A Weeping Mother

As Cline Avenue winds its way through the old Cudahee neighborhood of Gary, a dark and forbidding apparition is said to drift along the deserted street. Most of Cudahee has long since vanished, but in the 1940s it was a thriving community of mostly Mexican immigrants who had come north to work in the steel mills. Some believe they brought the spirit known as La Llorona along with them.

The tale of La Llorona involves a young widow who lived with her sons in a small town near Mexico City. She fell in love with a young nobleman, but he refused to marry her because of her children. The woman went mad and one night savagely murdered the children. She ran to her lover to tell him what she had done for his sake, but he was repulsed and frightened by her and threw her out of his house. Now completely insane, she roamed the streets with her children's blood on her hands and white dress, weeping and screaming. Before the authorities could apprehend her, her body was discovered facedown in a pool of muddy water.

For hundreds of years, the story of the bloody woman in white was told in Mexico City. Some believe this spirit came north to Indiana with the immigrants, but others believe the Mexican population simply gave the name of their legend to a ghost that already existed in Cudahee, the ghost of a woman whose children were killed in an auto accident in the early 1930s. After their funeral, she returned again and again to the spot where they had died and wandered the area, crying for them. She died, completely insane, many years ago, but her spirit continues to wander.

Whoever the Cline Avenue spirit may be, nearly all reports agree that she manifests at night. Motorists have frequently seen her there, standing by the side of the road. She seems to be weeping but always vanishes into the darkness when approached. Some say that she is short and thin with a dark complexion. Others maintain that she has what seems to be blood on her hands and dress. Still others claim she makes wild motions with her hands and screams something about

her children before she fades away into the night.

Despite the frequent sightings, the ghost remains elusive, always seeming to stay a step ahead of researchers and investigators who try to track her down. She still roams in the night, crying over the loss of her children.

Spirit of a Jilted Bride

La Llorona, or whoever she is, is not alone on Cline Avenue. Farther west, as the roadway nears Hammond, another spectral woman makes her presence known. According to legend, she is a young Polish woman whose story is one of ill-fated romance that has extended from this world to the next.

Motorists claim to have seen a beautiful blond girl wearing a wedding gown standing at the side of the road. She stares pitifully at the cars as they pass by her, then runs down the embankment toward the river.

This woman made the mistake of falling in love with a man of whom her parents did not approve. Instead of finding a suitor among the Polish men in her neighborhood, she fell for someone from neighboring Whiting, a man from one of the many Puerto Rican families who had recently moved into the area. Cross-cultural relationships like this were virtually unknown at the time, and the marriage would have been regarded as scandalous for all concerned.

The two were forced to meet in secret, hidden away from their families and friends. They often met on the banks of the Calumet River, just south of Cline Avenue as it approached the outskirts of Hammond. Today that area is an industrial wasteland, but back then the river still retained its natural beauty. The young lovers met here, walking hand in hand and dreaming about their future together.

Eventually, the two decided to marry. They found a priest in Griffith who was willing to go along with their plan, and in late September their long-awaited wedding day arrived.

The young woman told her parents that she would be working late that day, but instead she hurried to the dressmaker's for her wedding gown. Wearing it, she took a cab to the church and waited for the groom to appear.

But he never came.

No one knows what happened to the young man. Some say that he was killed in an accident as he rushed to the church, and others claim that he simply got cold feet and left the area, never to return. Whatever the case, the bride waited for more than two hours before she fled from the church, heartbroken and shattered, and hailed a taxi to take her back to Hammond.

But as she traveled along, she realized that she could not go home. If word of what had happened leaked out, she would be the subject of both scorn and ridicule in her community. Finally she told the driver to let her out along Cline Avenue, close to the Calumet River, where she and her lover used to meet. She jumped out of the cab and ran toward the water. The driver tried to stop her, but she plunged into the dark river and vanished from sight.

Two days later fishermen found her body in the river. Her grieving parents buried her in Hammond, but the legend states that her spirit can be seen on Cline Avenue as it passes close to the Calumet. Motorists claim to have seen a beautiful blond girl wearing a wedding gown standing at the side of the road. She stares pitifully at the cars as they pass by her, then runs down the embankment toward the river.

The stories of this forlorn young woman began in the 1950s and continue today. The poor Polish bride has become a fixture in local folklore and an integral part of the weird roads of Indiana.

Séance at Murder Tract

An area of land that follows the path of a treaty with the American Indians has become known as The Murder Tract because of the unusual number of disappearances and deaths that have occurred here through the years.

At the turn of the century, the local newspaper printed a story about a man who was returning home one evening along Treaty Line Road (the name has since been changed). Passing a house, he was startled to hear screams and a loud commotion coming from within, immediately followed by the occupants running in terror from it.

Entering the house, the man found the area in disarray with smashed furniture and even a large, oak table broken down the middle. The occupants, all showing signs of being beaten severely, claimed that they had been holding a séance that evening, when the spirit of a local man who had committed suicide a few weeks previously appeared to them. One of the participants was a local cobbler who recognized the shoes he had made for the man just days before his death. They said that a great howling arose within the room, and unseen spirits attacked them and tossed furniture and dishes about the room. –*Martin Stigleman*

Mooresville's Gravity Hill

Weird travelers know that "mystery spots" and "gravity hills" exist all over the country, but few of them draw the sort of attention that Kellar's Hill near Mooresville has managed to do over the years. Hoosiers have been perplexed by this anomaly ever since the road that crosses it was just a gravel lane and automobiles were a newfangled invention.

Gravity Hill (or Magnetic Hill, as some people call it) can be found just southwest of Mooresville, right off State Road 42. It has become a long-standing tradition for visitors to park their cars at the bottom of the hill, put them in neutral, and then coast backward (up the hill!) fifty to one hundred feet. At the top of the hill, they get out and try to push the cars back to the bottom. To their amazement, the automobiles refuse to budge.

Curiosity seekers also make the journey with buckets of water, which they pour onto the road and then sit back and watch as the water runs uphill.

Local folklore claims these weird happenings are caused by the spirit of a Native American whose bones are buried at the bottom of the hill, but debunkers say otherwise. A surveyor who investigated the hill claimed that its "crest" was actually eighteen inches lower than its apparent "bottom." An Indiana University professor also helped to spoil the fun by noting that the land contours, rock formations, and the angle of fences and utility poles create an optical illusion.

But that hasn't prevented people from coming to experience the hill for themselves. In fact, the steady

parade of traffic-stopping, bucket-carrying tourists prompted local law-enforcement officials to ask people not to stop in the middle of this busy roadway. As one article about the phenomenon said, "Heavy traffic coming at you may result in a different sort of gravity."

World's First Ferris Wheel

If you find yourself walking across Dunn's Bridge in the tiny town of Tefft, don't be surprised if you catch yourself marveling at the giant metal half-moon arches that make up the bridge. They seem strangely out of place, almost as if they were part of something bigger before they ended up stretching across the Kankakee River. And if the legend is true, they WERE part of something bigger. Much bigger. Would you believe a Ferris wheel? And would you believe it was the world's very first Ferris wheel?

The year was 1889, and Paris had just astonished the world when it unveiled the Eiffel Tower at the Exposition Universelle. Since the next World's Fair was to be held in Chicago in 1893 to celebrate the four hundredth anniversary of Christopher Columbus's discovery of America, planners knew they needed something that would top the Eiffel Tower. So they turned to George Washington Gale Ferris (yes, that's all one name), who designed and constructed the world's first Ferris wheel, and oh, what a wheel it was!

It stood an amazing 266 feet tall, weighed in at well over 70 tons, and was able to accommodate over 2,000 riders at one time. To do this, the wheel had 36 cars—each roughly the size of a Greyhound bus—capable of holding 60 people, 40 of whom had to stand. To turn the wheel required two 1,000-horsepower steam engines.

A ticket to ride the Ferris wheel cost fifty cents. For that price, a person could enjoy two full revolutions.

The Ferris wheel was such a huge success that it was moved to St. Louis and exhibited at the 1904 Louisiana Exposition. However, the cost of operating the wheel far outweighed the money made in ticket sales, so it was decided to demolish it. Tons of dynamite were strapped to the Ferris wheel on May 11, 1906, and by all accounts it blew up real good. The remains were then sold off as scrap. That's when things really started to get interesting.

According to legend, a farmer by the name of J. D. Dunn traveled to Chicago, bought parts of the scrapped wheel, and had them shipped back to his hometown of Tefft. Dunn, with the help of a carpenter and a blacksmith, fashioned the parts into a bridge across the portion of the Kankakee River that ran through his property. It's an interesting story, but there's a problem with the math. The legend says that Dunn went to Chicago "in 1894 after the Fair closed." The problem here is that the Ferris wheel was still in operation in 1894 and would be for another decade. But legends don't die easily. So some people still believe that Dunn purchased parts of the old Ferris wheel, but that they were original parts that had been replaced on the wheel after they wore out.

Further confusing things is the fact that the Eli Bridge Company, today considered one of the leaders in Ferris wheel construction, created a smaller version of the original wheel and toured it around the country. Some say that it's actually parts from this wheel, not the original,

that Dunn used to make his bridge.

So what do we think? Is this bridge really made from the world's first Ferris wheel? Hard to say. When you stand on the bridge, you notice all sorts of rivet holes that are there for no apparent reason. It's as if they were used at one point, but don't really serve a purpose on the present structure. The bridge certainly looks like it came from a Ferris wheel, but the size doesn't seem right. The first Ferris wheel was enormous, and these trusses just don't look big enough. It's a really cool story, though, and a weird-looking bridge to boot. For *Weird Indiana,* that's all that matters.

Ghost Rider of River Road

One of the oldest legends of Perry County, in the southern part of the state, tells of the ghost rider who once haunted River Road: a seldom-used thoroughfare today, but once a three-mile highway that was the only route between Cannelton and Tell City.

The first sighting of the ghost rider occurred on September 8, 1858, at the wedding of Amanda Brazee and Paul Schuster. Friends and family gathered at Mulberry Park, the Brazee's estate on River Road, for the happy event. But the festivities were interrupted by the appearance of a rider astride a fiery black horse. The rider wore a dark cloak, and he brandished a riding crop as his horse pounded down River Road, its hoofs flashing. The horseman stopped when he reached the wedding party, then reared his horse back and galloped off down the road. As the rider and his mount reached the edge of the property, they disappeared.

The strange story circulated in the area, and many laughed, saying the partygoers had far too much to drink during the celebration. But for years after it happened, many travelers reported their own encounters on the road with this menacing phantom, and it seems the rider may not have been simply the product of a whiskey bottle after all.

One night as a young man drove his buggy to Cannelton, the rider suddenly appeared on the road ahead of him. The young man reined in his team, pulled out his revolver, and opened fire, but found his bullets had no effect on the vision before him. He whipped his team and ran his buggy full speed all the way to Cannelton. When the man arrived home, he told his parents what had happened, and they later recalled that his face was as white as a sheet.

Around 1890, a young boy hurried along River Road from Tell City so that he could reach Cannelton before an approaching thunderstorm arrived. As he neared Mulberry Park, thunder rumbled loudly from above and a bolt of lightning flashed, brightly illuminating the road in front of him. He could see that just ahead, at the side of the road near the trees, was the dark figure of a horse and rider. The rider made no move toward the boy, but his presence was so frightening that the boy refused to go any closer to him. He turned and ran back in the direction that he came, waiting to go to Cannelton until long after sunrise.

Stories of the ghost rider continued for the next decade, fading away around 1900. Today River Road exists only as an overgrown passage hidden behind a flood wall that was erected in 1940. The stories may have stopped, but memories of the phantom rider still linger. No one knows who the ghostly figure was or why he terrorized River Road for almost fifty years. His appearances may have ceased, but those who encountered the horseman were never in doubt that he existed.

One night as a young man drove his buggy to Cannelton, the rider suddenly appeared on the road ahead of him. The young man reined in his team, pulled out his revolver, and opened fire, but found his bullets had no effect on the vision before him.

Even more impressive than Indiana's collection of haunted roads may be its plethora of haunted bridges. These spans dot the landscape, offering both passage to travelers and a collection of impressive legends.

What follows is a rundown of some of the Hoosier State's most talked-about bridges. The stories attached to them are some of the most chilling and macabre we've encountered over the whole state. What is it about these bridges that attracts such forces? Perhaps their height increases the level of fear they produce in folklore. Perhaps their status as structures that allow man to overcome nature intensifies the idea of supernatural forces around them. Perhaps they're just scary dark locales that are perfect breeding grounds for twisted tales.

Whatever the reasoning, Indiana has some of the most frightening bridges in the nation. Stop and take a little pride in that the next time you cross one of these spans — if you're not too scared.

Legend of Purple Head Bridge

Over the years, the Stangle's Bridge near Vincennes has earned the colorful nickname of the Purple Head Bridge. According to local legend, this strange designation began many years ago and involves the disembodied head of an American Indian.

The early days of the nineteenth century were bloody times on the American frontier. The territory that would someday be Indiana was about as far west as most dared travel if they valued their lives. Ongoing conflicts between the arriving white settlers and the American Indian tribes who occupied the region often led to bloodshed and death.

Many of these battles and massacres occurred along the Wabash River, including one that took place near Vincennes. In the midst of the fighting, one story goes, an Indian shaman was killed, and his body fell from the riverbank into the swiftly moving floodwaters of the Wabash. His tribesmen tried to retrieve his body, but it was swept away downstream and lost.

According to Native American tradition, a soul is unable to pass on to the next world without a proper burial. The Indians believed the shaman's spirit would be bound to the river for all time, unable to rest, forever haunting the place where his life came to an end.

Today, the narrow Stangle's Bridge, once used by the railroad, spans the Wabash River between Vincennes and St. Francisville. It's located, according to local lore, where the Indian shaman was killed centuries before and where his specter still haunts. Curiosity seekers often go to the center of the bridge and look down into the waters below, hoping to see a hand rise from the depths, reaching up to them as if from a drowning man looking for their help.

It is said that those who stay a little longer will then see the dead shaman's bloated and purple head as it comes up out of the water. The head is said to give off a luminous glow from the sockets where its eyes once were. At this point, even the most hardened ghost enthusiasts usually flee the bridge in terror!

The legend maintains that the purple head will continue to appear below the bridge until the shaman's body is found and he can be buried with the rest of his people, thus releasing his spirit from the river's dark depths.

Dog Face Bridge

There are many haunted bridges throughout the United States. There are also many ghost stories involving women and an equal number involving demonic dogs. Indiana may be home to the only site in the country that combines all of these into one of the strangest, darkest tales of haunting we have ever heard.

In San Pierre, at the end of Route 1100W, is a dead end and a dilapidated bridge. Beyond this is a dirt path that leads to a blocked-off second bridge. The reason these bridges are sealed off is tied in to the grisly events that purportedly happened here many years ago—and the strange creature that still looms in these woods as a result.

In the 1950s, the story goes, a young couple were driving over the first bridge. They were talking and therefore distracted, and didn't notice when a dog ran out of the woods and onto the bridge. By the time the man driving saw it, it was too late. He swerved in an effort to get out of the way and save the dog, but his effort merely spelled doom for all three. The car struck the dog, sending it flying off the bridge. The car itself followed, and both passengers died along with the dog.

The true gruesome nature of this tale doesn't reveal itself fully until you realize the condition of the deceased. While the man's remains were intact, the woman had been decapitated in the crash. Her head was located near the car, but her body was flung from the scene, never to be found. Conversely, the dog's body was found, but its head could not be located.

The bridges were sealed off, and the surrounding community did its best to move on from the terrible tragedy that took place here. This became harder when those visiting the bridges began reporting being terrorized by a twisted, evil monster—a creature that had the body of a woman and the head of a dog.

To this day, adventure seekers report being attacked by this evil amalgamation of two innocent souls whose mortal lives ended violently and prematurely. Many say that after they walk over the first bridge, but before they get to the second bridge, the monster reveals itself. If the visitor does not sprint back to his car fast enough to stay ahead of the beast, he may be attacked and killed.

Tunnelton Tunnel

For railroad companies, tunnels mean obstacles bypassed and time and money saved. But for others, tunnels mean adventure, mystery, and rites of passage. Such is the case in (ironically enough) Tunnelton, the home of a nearly two-thousand-foot-long train tunnel that burrows directly through a hill three miles outside town.

Known as the Big Tunnel, Tunnelton's tube was first used in 1856. Curious spectators would flock from miles to watch trains emerge from the hill. At first, part of the curiosity was in the various problems the tunnel experienced. Slow-moving trains meant that passengers, often dressed in their finest Sunday whites, would emerge blackened, having been covered in soot and smoke. The vibrations of the trains themselves often led to huge hunks of rock falling from the hillside, much to the delight of onlookers. Eventually, the tunnel walls were lined with brick to stop this problem.

Soon, the novelty of the tunnel wore off and its visitors were of a much less upright mentality. Local legend has long held that at least one murder victim's body was disposed of in the tunnel. Stories say that a man named Henry Dixon was murdered and placed in the darkest portion of the tunnel, right on the tracks. When the next train came through, the engineer didn't see the corpse, never slowed down, and completely destroyed his body. Because of the lack of a corpse, local officials were never able to convict his murderer, even though the identity of the guilty party was well known in the area.

These days, the tunnel is still in use, although far less frequently than it was in its glory days. It's mainly the stomping ground of fascinated teens who visit the place as a rite of passage. Graffiti covers the entrances and walls, and litter is scattered about. Teens often test one legend of the tunnel. It's said that Henry Dixon's spirit still haunts the darkest point of the tunnel. A person who makes it all the way to this middle point of darkness will experience one of two things—either Dixon will brush past and move on or he will mistake the visitor for his killer. If the latter occurs, Dixon will chase the person all the way out the other side.

If you do decide to visit the infamous Tunnelton Tunnel, be careful. Not only are there restless spirits to deal with, but the occasional train still rumbles through, making it very dangerous.

Crybaby Bridge

Pendleton, in Hancock County, is the home of a mysterious and macabre haunted bridge, just up the road from the Main Street Cemetery. It is haunted not by specters or visions, but by sounds—specifically, the sounds of crying babies said to have died on the spot.

Locals claim that if you park your car on the small bridge at night, the faint sounds of crying babies can be heard. Supposedly, these are the cries of children who were drowned in the river beneath the bridge.

The nearby cemetery is home to its own legend of a cursed child: A girl who was possessed by the devil in life is said to be buried there. A plant in the shape of a pitchfork grows above her grave.

Mystery Woman of the Embarrass River

The CSX Railroad crosses over the Embarrass River just west of Vincennes. On some occasions, the misty form of a woman appears near the middle of the bridge, only to disappear just as mysteriously. Some say she is the spirit of a young woman who learned that her fiancé died in combat during World War I. Rather than face life without her love, she ran into the path of a locomotive on the bridge. Today, her spirit returns to reenact her sad demise.

Hell's Gate

In the tiny town of Diamond is a tunnel that many say is the first in a series of seven gates that lead directly to hell itself. The stories of Hell's Gate are numerous and in many ways have no connection to each other. This makes anyone researching the place wonder, why are there so many dark, evil legends here? What about this unassuming town and unassuming tunnel has led to so many stories saying it is a central gathering point of mystical, dark forces? And ultimately, what is the truth about what happened here to cause the stories to spring up in the first place?

Many stories of Hell's Gate relate to a train crash that supposedly occurred at the site years ago. Some people say that if you sit in the tunnel of Hell's Gate and listen, you will eventually hear light music, laughter, and conversation—all followed by the unmistakable sound of twisting steel, screaming, and horror. People swear that this ever-repeating ethereal audio is the sound of a train accident happening over and over again in the netherworld, as it once did in reality at this site.

Another legend of Hell's Gate challenges the visitor to tempt the dark forces contained within. Supposedly, if someone flashes his car's lights three times, drives the length of the tunnel, then turns around and parks halfway through the tunnel, a strange and terrifying series of events commences. After a few minutes, the graffiti that lines the tunnel walls glows and re-forms itself. If in the process of this re-formation any of the graffiti happens to spell out the names of those in the visiting car, those people will die. Some report seeing pools of blood form on the walls and road while trying this. Still others have seen the ghosts of people hanging in the trees around the site.

Best of all, rumors abound that the tunnel in question, which many have visited, is the first in a series of seven similar haunted spots nearby. While we can find no definitive proof of these subsequent gates to hell, we can only imagine how terrifying they must be if the first such place has so many stories attached to it.

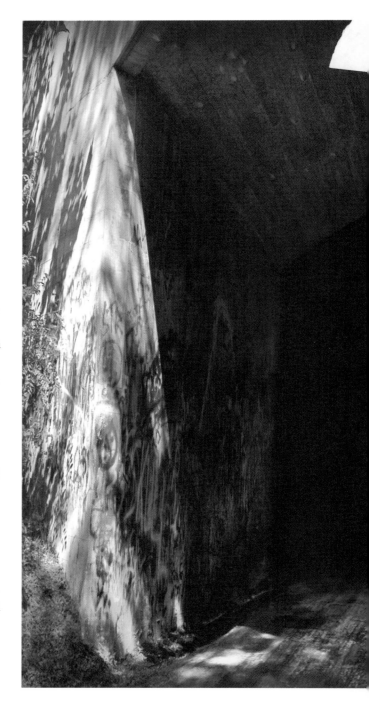

Hoosier Haunts

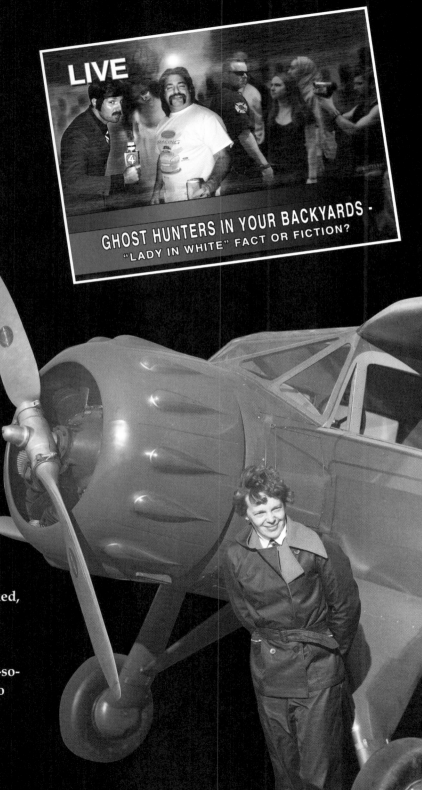

GHOST HUNTERS IN YOUR BACKYARDS -
"LADY IN WHITE" FACT OR FICTION?

LIVE

Indiana has long had a reputation as an utterly conventional, "white bread" midwestern state. From the industrial region of the northwest to the seemingly endless panorama of cornfields in its center to the rolling hills in the south, there is little in our state's geography to suggest the exotic or remarkable. Perhaps this accounts for the pragmatic nature of its residents. These descendants of practical farming settlers and immigrants were instilled with a matter-of-fact nature that leaves little room for whimsy or mystery. Yet scratch this thin veneer of rationality and you will find a darker, more mysterious realm. For beneath the no-nonsense façade of farm fields, small towns, and urban blight Indiana is replete with ghostly tales.

Some ghosts linger over old tragedies, unable to rest or forgive. Others seem to watch over places in which they were happy. Their stories are often overlooked, but they are as much a part of Indiana as is the smoke from steel mills or the harvest moon setting over a cornfield. Whether they are older than the state itself or are whispered tales of strange occurrences from our not-so-distant past, these stories hint that there is much more to Indiana than meets the eye.

The Gray Lady of Willard Library

Not every ghost can boast of a formal dance held in its honor, let alone a gala hosted by the governor of Indiana. Yet such is the renown of the Gray Lady of Willard Library in Evansville.

Opened in 1885, the Willard Library was the brainchild of local philanthropist Willard Carpenter. A successful businessman in Evansville, Carpenter built a strikingly ornate structure at the corner of First Avenue and Division and endowed it as a library "for the use of people of all classes and sexes, free of charge, forever." Almost 125 years later, the Willard Library continues to fulfill this noble purpose, serving as the only privately owned library in the state. In addition to its impressive earthly collections, the Willard Library seems to have collected an artifact from another time—the shadowy spirit of an unknown woman known as the Lady in Gray.

The first report of her presence came from a custodian in the 1930s. It was his custom to work until ten p.m., then leave, only to return at three a.m. to fire the basement furnace in preparation for the next day. One cold winter morning the man, armed with a flashlight, unlocked the door to the basement furnace area, entered, and found himself staring at a dark figure. Thinking it was a transient, the man shone his flashlight upward and was astonished to see that the figure was a woman in a long dress with a gray shawl draped over her shoulders, a costume reminiscent of the fashion of the late nineteenth century. The custodian's bewilderment turned to abject terror as the woman seemed to melt away before his eyes. In a moment, she was gone, and he stood alone and frightened. He had just encountered the Gray Lady. He would see her a few more times, but never got used to her and is said to have quit his job rather than endure further encounters.

Since his experience, many others claim to have caught a glimpse of the Gray Lady within the library. She has been seen crossing the main staircase to the second floor, in the employees' lounge, and in the tower attached to the corner of the building. It was her appearance in the tower that would cause considerable consternation with local police.

Twenty years ago the library installed motion detectors that would set off an alarm system if disturbed. The alarm company would then call the police and the library's director to alert them of a possible break-in. In the months after the system was installed, the detectors were frequently set off in the middle of the night, and apparently without cause, as subsequent searches of the premises by the police showed that no one was in the building.

Late one night Mr. Baker, the library director, was awakened by a call from the alarm company. He went to the building to open it up for police investigation and arrived to find a patrol car already waiting. He unlocked the front door and entered the library with one officer while another officer waited outside to catch any intruder trying to make a hasty exit.

As on previous occasions, the search of the building

Governor and Mrs. Robert D. Orr
on behalf of
The Trustees and Friends of Willard Library
request the pleasure of your company at a
high-spirit dinner dance to celebrate the
Library's 100th year
and in honor of its resident spirit,
the Lady in Gray.
Friday, the 18th of October, 1985,
7:00 PM at Willard Library.
Black tie. (Long gray veil optional.)
Spirits available at cash bar.
Reservations limited to 250.
Valet parking. Music by the Temple Airs.

was in vain. But when the two men left the library, they found the officer who had been standing outside impatiently waiting for them. "Did you catch her?" he asked excitedly, shining his flashlight toward the building.

"Who?" asked Mr. Baker, adding, "There is no one in the building."

"Of course there is!" exclaimed the policeman. "There was a woman in a long dress in the tower. I saw her clearly in the window!"

"Maybe you saw the Gray Lady," remarked Mr. Baker, somewhat sarcastically. He was thinking that perhaps the policeman's imagination had been affected by the local legends.

"Who is that?" asked the officer. He had never heard of the legend of which he had now become a part.

Though the Gray Lady has been seen and heard throughout the library, her favorite "haunt" is the basement children's section. The children's librarian, Margaret Maier, who worked there for over fifty years until her death in 1989, had the most frequent contact with the Gray Lady. In an interview just prior to her death, Ms. Maier reported first glimpsing the ghost in the early 1950s while working in the children's section. Her description of the ghost was similar to that of the night custodian's from years earlier—a woman dressed in a long skirt and blouse with a gray shawl wrapped around her shoulders. She often spotted the

ghost standing among the bookshelves or in the adjacent staff area; it would disappear into thin air moments after being observed. She also heard footsteps between the bookshelves and experienced objects disappearing from her desk when no one was in the area, only to have them reappear later in an unlikely spot.

It is fascinating to note that Ms. Maier seemed to form a kind of attachment to the gentle, elusive spirit, and perhaps this affection was returned. For when the children's section was closed temporarily for renovation, Ms. Maier and her sister were shocked to see the Gray Lady silently drift through their living room one evening. Another time, a visiting nephew saw a woman in Victorian dress ascending the staircase to the second floor of the house. When renovations were complete and the children's

abashed, the assistant librarian stared at the book at her feet and then stammered to the patron, "Well, perhaps I'm mistaken!"

The Gray Lady's identity is still a mystery. Some have suggested she might be the spirit of the daughter of library founder Willard Carpenter. Those who work in the library discount this, however, because it is known that the daughter was unhappy about her father's leaving a significant amount of his estate to the library. They say the spirit is possibly that of a former children's librarian who devoted her life to the library in its early days.

In recent years, the library has been investigated by paranormal research groups and has appeared on television shows that cater to the paranormal. Ghost hunters can try to spot the Gray Lady online by watching the "ghost cams" that have been set up in sighting hot spots such as the children's section and reference room (though the cameras aren't always functioning). She even has her own MySpace page.

Despite all the attention, the Gray Lady remains shy and obscure. Perhaps she disdains publicity and simply seeks the quiet and solitude afforded her by the library after hours. In any case, she still makes her presence known in the building at odd moments and in subtle ways. Far from the shrieking specters so often portrayed in the popular media, she is truly a lady—the now famous Gray Lady of the Willard Library.

section was reopened, the migratory spirit resumed her haunts at her former location.

Through the years, many who worked in and around the building have encountered this genteel, feminine ghost. Perhaps one of the more evocative incidents occurred to a children's librarian some years ago. A local kindergarten class visited, and instead of a story hour, they wanted to hear about the ghost. The librarian complied, but the next day a parent called and complained that the story scared her child into a sleepless night. The librarian decided to stop talking about the ghost and asked her staff to do likewise.

The next day an assistant librarian was working in the children's section when a woman from the community asked her if there had been any recent sightings of the Gray Lady. Remembering her supervisor's request, the assistant replied, "Oh no. We don't think she is here anymore." At that moment, a book from the top shelf seemed to jump off the bookcase, fly through the air, and land between the two women. Shocked and somewhat

Broadripple's Amicable Apparitions

In *the '90s* my wife and I rented an early 1900s farmhouse at the northeastern edge of Logansport. Little did we realize that the house and the surrounding 10 acres of property were already inhabited. It had three very active and mostly friendly spirits: an older woman, an elderly man and a five to eight-year-old child.

One morning, we rushed out to make an appointment in Kokomo. In our haste, we left some plates and silverware out to dry on the kitchen counter. We also left the bread undone, but folded the end under the package. When we returned that evening, we found the bread wrapped, tied and put away. The dishes were also put away. Like I said, a friendly ghost.

The basement was home to the child. This spirit stayed close to the stairs and particularly enjoyed hiding tools and then making them reappear, stacked neatly at the entry to a small pump room at the foot of the stairs. Sometimes, old tools that had never been in my kit appeared, many dating from the '30s. I could never shake the feeling that someone was always there watching what I was doing any time I ventured downstairs. It was more a sense of curiosity and intense interest than anything else.

The property also included a large barn, which I had hoped to use as a place to work out and

store things. Its residents included one gigantic groundhog and the ghost of an elderly man. While cleaning out the barn of many years of accumulated debris, I could hear muttering and occasionally comment or compliment. Unless the groundhog learned to speak, I think I was receiving encouragement in my endeavors from a previous owner.

Sadly, we moved out of the house when housing became available on the base I was stationed at. My wife was expecting, and the one and a half bedroom farmhouse was going to be too small for our needs. But I recently checked out a USGS aerial map of the area, and the house and property near the Broadripple Bridge is still there.—*JB Smith*

Mother of a Ghost Story: Stepp Cemetery

A secluded corner of Morgan Monroe State Forest near Bloomington is home to a small cemetery, its few tombstones weatherworn and illegible. Surrounded by the shadows and deep silence of the woods, Stepp Cemetery is as peaceful and beautiful a spot as one could wish to while away an eternity.

In one corner, next to a small grave, there was for many years a strange object that was the subject of speculation and tales. It was the stump of a fallen tree that had been carefully crafted into a sort of chair. It was known to generations of local teenagers as the Witch's Throne, but if legend is to be believed, it is not the seat of a witch but of a woman whose grief took her beyond the bounds of sanity and into the realm of Hoosier folklore.

The woman's real name has been forgotten over the years, but she is most often called Anna. Stories vary as to her origin, but most agree that she and Jacob, her husband, settled into a homestead not far from Stepp Cemetery in the early 1900s, in search of land and a new life. Life was not easy, but they managed to get along. And when Anna gave birth to a daughter named Emily, the family's happiness was complete.

But then Jacob died in an accident at the quarry and was buried in Stepp Cemetery. Circumstances did not allow Anna to become immobilized by grief, and she

threw herself into providing for herself and her growing daughter. She also became obsessed with protecting her. She walked her to school each day and kept a careful eye on her when the girl was home. Even when Emily turned sixteen, her mother maintained watch and control over her.

Emily was an obedient child, but it was only a matter of time before she would want to venture into the world. One day a young man who attended high school with her appeared at the cabin to ask Anna for permission to take Emily to a dance the following Saturday night. Anna's immediate instinct was to refuse, but the boy seemed nice and respectful. Reluctantly, Anna agreed, provided they return home by ten p.m.

The following Saturday evening was lovely, but the

air had a softness that foretold the possibility of rain. The young man led Emily to his car, and with a renewed promise to be home early, they drove down the road and into the gathering dusk. Anna felt a knot of anxiety tighten in her stomach, and as events turned out, this feeling might well have been prophetic.

True to indications, the clear spring evening gave way to rain by mid-evening, and the roads became slick. The couple stayed at the dance longer than they intended and were speeding home to comply with Emily's curfew when the car slid off the road and collided headlong with a tree. Emily was killed. She was buried at Stepp Cemetery, just a few steps from her father's grave.

Rumors have persisted of the sighting of a strange dark figure in the cemetery, seated at the Witch's Throne. Local teenagers believed that if you touched the throne beneath the light of a full moon, you would die an unnatural death within a year.

Emily's death was the final blow for Anna. She had lost her last shred of happiness in life, ironically due in part to the rigid curfew she herself had set. She became a recluse, subsisting on vegetables from her garden and no longer venturing into town or church. The few who saw her said she always wore mourning clothes—a long black dress and shawl—even in the summer. The only place she was ever seen outside her farm was Stepp Cemetery. She visited daily, sitting by Emily's grave for hours and talking to her daughter as though she were still alive.

Happenstance would soon provide Anna with a more comfortable setting for her visits. One spring, lightning struck a tree not far from Emily's grave. The blackened stump that remained had the vague form of a chair. Taking a sharp knife and hatchet with her to the cemetery, Anna carefully reshaped this stump to provide a natural chair on which to sit during her long visits there. Those passing by the cemetery began to report seeing a figure in black seated on her "throne" at one end of the graveyard. If approached, Anna would quickly walk away to a nearby grove of trees, where she would stare ominously at the intruders until their departure. Locals began to avoid the cemetery, saying the old lady who frequented it was crazy. It was best, all agreed, to leave the woman in black alone.

Eventually, Anna died. It is supposed she was buried near her husband and daughter, yet no headstone can be found there. However, if the stories that have sprung up after her death are to be believed, she left behind a memorial more macabre than any tombstone.

Since the early 1950s, rumors have persisted of the sighting of a strange dark figure in the cemetery, seated at the Witch's Throne. Local teenagers believed that if you touched the throne beneath the light of a full moon, you would die an unnatural death within a year. Many made nocturnal visits to the cemetery, most coming back disappointed. A few, however, returned shaken, swearing they witnessed a dark shape rise from the seat and advance toward them out of the gloom. Others have reported a curious phenomenon associated with the mound of earth next to the chair, which is reputed to be Emily's grave. It is said that an object placed here at nightfall will be moved to another spot by the next morning, even if watch is kept to prevent human intervention. Perhaps Anna still guards the grave of her beloved Emily.

The cemetery grounds were eventually incorporated into the Morgan Monroe State Forest and are under the guardianship of the Indiana Department of Natural Resources. It is said the chair has been vandalized and partially destroyed, but if the stories are true, no one will ever be able to remove the sad figure that occupies it.

Wistful Spirits of Tuckaway

Serene and secluded amid the busy thrum of city life, the quaint bungalow called Tuckaway sits in a picturesque neighborhood in northern Indianapolis. One would never guess the home hosted some of the most famous and historic figures of the twentieth century . . . or that its deceased former owners may still call it home.

The cottage, built in 1906 on what is rumored to be the site of an Indian burial ground, was purchased in 1910 by George Phillip Meier and his wife, Nellie Simmons Meier. The couple was already well known by the time they acquired their new home: he as a fashion designer, and she for her palmistry skills. In the ensuing decades, their home became renowned as a social gathering place, hosting some of the most famous figures of the first half of the twentieth century, including Eleanor Roosevelt, Walt Disney, Albert Einstein, George Washington Carver, and Isadora Duncan.

The Meiers lived happily at Tuckaway, and with their eventual passing the house came into the possession of their niece, Ruth Cannon. She made every attempt to maintain the home she loved, but the years and declining fortunes of its Meridian Park neighborhood seemed to doom the place. By the early 1970s, it sat empty and forlorn. It was then that the current owner, Ken Keene, purchased the house and its contents for just $12,500.

Mr. Keene knew Tuckaway's history, and he

was determined to restore it to its former glory. Every detail of the house's refurbishment—from the vintage furniture to the flooring and draperies—was carefully chosen to sweep the visitor back to a more refined era. It's of little surprise that such a loving restoration might encourage the appearance of a spirit or two.

Mr. Keene said that he was unaware of any ghostly presence at first, but soon heard reports that caught his attention. At one time, he rented rooms to nearby university students, and they began to share stories with him. The most striking thing, he says, is that many of these guests told the same stories over a thirty-year period.

According to Mr. Keene, guests reported waking from their sleep to see spectral faces suspended over their bed, peering down at them genially. The face of a woman is said to have smiled, winked, and then vanished. The faces, he says, are a good description of George and Nellie Meier. "Maybe they were just checking in on who was staying in their home," he added.

The Meiers have appeared at a few of the many costume parties Mr. Keene has hosted in the last thirty years, including a summer costume party with a 1920s theme. At that event, a young female guest asked Mr. Keene if she could look around upstairs. He said yes, and added that she should check out the upstairs sleeping porch. The woman headed upstairs while the other guests gathered around a piano, singing.

Their singing was soon interrupted by a bloodcurdling scream from upstairs. It was followed by the sound of the young woman's feet thumping down the stairs, after which she flew out the door and to her car. A friend of the terrified woman went outside to see what had happened. When she returned, she told Mr. Keene the strange story.

As her friend stood on the sleeping porch, she saw an older couple at the far end. They seemed to be dressed for the party, as they wore clothing dating from the 1920s. The man was in a white woolen suit with a white straw hat and had a well-groomed mustache. His companion was a plump woman nearly a foot shorter than he, with a pleasant round face.

The young woman assumed the pair were her host's parents, and so she approached the couple, extending her hand in greeting. They turned toward her, smiled warmly, and then disappeared before her eyes. It was this unorthodox departure that precipitated her hasty exit.

As Ken Keene heard the story, he realized that, once again, the description of the elderly couple fit well with that of the Meiers.

While most ghostly encounters at Tuckaway are of a pleasant nature, one time the phenomenon took a more frightening tone. It was January 1978, and two young men arrived at his door during one of the worst blizzards Indianapolis had seen. One of them was an acquaintance of Mr. Keene's and knew that he occasionally let out his extra bedrooms. They begged for lodgings for the night, and since Mr. Keene knew one of the young men, he welcomed them in.

Things began to get strange very quickly. While Mr. Keene and the young man he knew were out getting emergency groceries, and the other young man was alone in the house, pictures that were securely fastened to a wall began to swing wildly in unison. He was frightened enough to want to leave the house, but Mr. Keene and the man's friend calmed him down when they returned and convinced him not to run out into the snowy night.

The next morning, however, Mr. Keene woke up to find that the young man who'd witnessed the swinging pictures was gone. His friend frantically called around and found him at another home about ten miles away, to which he had trudged on foot in the blizzard. He took such extreme measures because he had awakened early that morning to an odd feeling. Sitting up abruptly, he knocked his head on the ceiling before looking down to find the bed floating several feet from the floor. Horrified, he rolled off the bed onto the floor below and then ran from the home.

Ken Keene later discovered that the young man in question had a criminal record, including charges of theft. He surmises the Meiers did not approve of his presence. If so, they must be credited with a novel way of getting rid of an unwanted houseguest!

Amelia Earhart Fades into Thin Air at Purdue

She was young and fearless, and her daring escapades caught the attention of a nation. She became a symbol of American spirit and helped redefine where women stood in society. And if the strange tales told about an airplane hangar at Purdue University Airport in West Lafayette are to be believed, her spirit still lingers where she lived some of her last and happiest days.

Most people are familiar with the story of Amelia Earhart, who in 1932 became the first woman and only the second person to pilot a solo plane across the Atlantic Ocean. She set a number of other aviation records until she disappeared in 1937 while trying to complete a flight around the world. What many in Indiana are unaware of, however, is their state's role in her life and death.

In the fall of 1935, Earhart spoke to a rapt audience at Purdue University. Among those who heard her was university president Dr. Edward C. Elliott, a visionary leader who long held a special interest in aviation, as well as a strong commitment to higher education for women. In Earhart, he saw a way to advance both interests, and at dinner after her talk he offered her a position at the school, which she accepted.

In November 1935, she assumed the role of visiting faculty member in the women's careers department, as well as adviser to the aeronautics department. She was to spend several weeks each semester on campus, giving lectures and interacting with the students, particularly the young women. This, it seems, Earhart did with some relish, as her husband, George Putnam, would later write, "[I think] she found her time at Purdue as one of the most satisfying adventures of her life."

Purdue's support went even further. When Earhart was planning her historic flight, Elliot volunteered to have the university supply her with a "flying laboratory." With his backing, other donations poured in, and by July 1936, the plane—a Lockheed 10E Electra—was ready. Earhart publicly professed her "profound gratitude and appreciation to Purdue University, its students and staff."

Technical difficulties ended her first attempt in March 1937, but Earhart and navigator Fred Noonan tried again that June. At first things seemed to be on track, but then tragic legend steps in: At precisely ten a.m. on July 2, 1937, Earhart and Noonan took off from New Guinea for Howland Island, a tiny atoll that would serve as a way station on their journey homeward. They would never be seen again. There are many theories as to what happened, and it's no surprise that ghostly legends have sprung up in at least one place where she spent her last days: Purdue University.

Many of the stories involve the haunting of hangar number 1 at the Purdue airport. Maintenance workers have reported seeing a figure matching the description of Earhart standing in the shadows—in fact, one army worker is said to have been so startled by the apparition that he fired shots at her!

The specter has also been encountered in the residence hall where Earhart lived while on campus. Marvis Boscher, who was manager at the hall for many years, said that girls living there felt cold drafts in the end room on the first floor (where Earhart once resided) and saw windows opening of their own volition. Former students tell of

occasionally glimpsing a shadowy figure of a short woman with close-cropped hair lurking in the hallway outside the room. Uniformly, the tales relate that when approached, the figure seems to dissolve into thin air. Other stories tell of hearing an old-fashioned typewriter clicking from the vacant room late at night, a time at which Earhart was known to do her writing.

In the end, one thing can be said for sure: This extraordinary woman, who dared to extend the limits of human endeavor, has become part of the history of Indiana. And if the stories told in the area of hangar number 1 at the Purdue airport are to be believed, perhaps a part of her presence lingers there still.

Just Outside Kokomo . . .

The following two stories involve locations just outside Kokomo. It seems that many ghosts—of the young, Native American, and even bovine variety—call this area home.

Jerome Haunts Jerome

I live in Kokomo. A few miles outside of town there is a small community named Jerome, which was supposedly named for the son of Chief Kokomoko. Jerome was said to have worshipped dark spirits and he was exiled from the tribe. He formed his own tribe a short way from his father's, taking many followers with him.

Jerome's body is buried in a small cemetery in Jerome. The cemetery is set a little way off the main road that runs through the town. If you follow the short gravel road that runs into the cemetery,

you'll realize it forms the shape of a six. It is said there are hounds of hell that protect the spirit of Jerome and his place of rest, and if you spend enough time in the cemetery, you'll start to see the shapes of Indiana warriors in the woods that surround it.

I used to party in this cemetery, and have been out there both at night and during the day. A few times me and my friends were frightened off by what we thought were people watching us from the woods. Once I also saw a child playing in a yard along the road that leads to the cemetery. I turned my head for only a second and when I turned back, he was gone. This was followed closely by a run-in with a large black dog at the entrance road. Needless to say, we didn't stay for long on that particular day.—*T.J. Hate*

Indiana's Haunted Heifers

I attended college in Kentucky and knew a few guys from Indiana. One guy told me a story of the famous "ghost cows" of Northern Indiana.

Late at night, cows could be heard lowing from a field where there were no cattle. I figured the guy was making it up until I met a couple of girls who attended IUPUI who confirmed the Ghost Cows story. If I recall correctly, these mysterious cows were just outside of Kokomo.—*Bird Waring*

World's Largest Ghost Hunt

Ghostly legends exist throughout the world, but a section of roadway between Valparaiso and Chesterton can claim a truly unique distinction: It is the site of what has been called the largest mass ghost hunt in world history.

The ghost in question has been known for many years as the Lady in White. Her name in life, according to the tale, was Annabel. She was a tall, willowy young woman with long auburn hair. Unfortunately, she married a man who abused her and their child. One cold January night after a particularly brutal beating, Annabel knew she had to leave. While her husband slept, she packed her few belongings, took her son from his crib, and left the house forever. But outside in the snowy woods, she became disoriented. She wandered deeper and deeper into the wilderness, desperately searching for a way out. Eventually, the numbing cold overtook her, and she and her baby perished. The next day, a search party found their bodies frozen to death in a snowdrift. Some days later they were lowered together into the frozen earth next to the home they had died trying to escape.

Annabel's spirit may live on, however. Over the years, there have been reports of the hazy form of a woman in white beckoning to passersby from a grove of trees in the area. When Campbell Street was laid close by the woods, more locals spoke of seeing the woman.

Of course, tales of Women in White are the bread and butter of folklore. What makes the story of Annabel unique is an event that sprang up from it. It is one that has gone down in the annals of ghost lore and garnered Annabel international attention.

It began innocently enough in late October 1965, with a tale spread by four students at Valparaiso High School. The previous Friday night they had been driving

GHOST HUNTERS IN YOUR BACKYARDS -
"LADY IN WHITE" FACT OR FICTION?

along Campbell Street when, glancing into the darkness, they were shocked to see the form of a woman in a long white dress standing in a grove of trees a few hundred feet from the road. The driver stopped his car, and he and his riders got out to see the figure gesture toward them, then disappear into the marshy woods. As they ran after her, they heard an eerie cry float through the evening stillness. It was a voice pleading, "Help me!" When the young people ran into the woods, however, the woman was gone.

For whatever reason, the teenagers' tale caught the imaginations of the local populace, spreading through Valparaiso High School and into the community. Before long, Valparaiso, Chesterton, and Porter were abuzz. Young people shared the story with their parents, who recalled other such sightings, and new reports began to surface daily. With Halloween fast approaching, the story of the Lady in White was reborn.

As October wore on, a steady stream of cars began patrolling Campbell Street, looking for the famed lady.

The stream soon turned to a flood as first hundreds—then thousands—of people came with hopes of seeing the ghost. A carnival-like atmosphere prevailed, with cars parked along both sides of the road as searchers of all ages combed the woods for some sign of the specter. Some came fortified with "liquid courage" (spirits to help one confront a spirit), and still others brought shotguns, determined to shoot the ghost if it appeared. Only luck prevented this dangerous combination from adding yet another tragic story to the area.

Not even the passing of Halloween put a damper on the mania, and by the first week in November, Indiana state police were called in. Stories about what was occurring in the area were picked up by regional, then national, then international news outlets. The Lady in White's fame was secured.

The one person who did not see fit to attend the festivities was the Lady in White herself. Whether shy by nature or simply unwilling to brave the onslaught of the curious, she was not seen during the several weeks of the melee.

Eventually, the police were able to disperse the crowds, and the Lady in White was largely forgotten. Yet she lived on in other circles. In 1978, a British Broadcasting Corporation film crew arrived in Chesterton to film a segment for a TV documentary on ghosts and ghost hunters. The crew stayed several days, filming the area and interviewing local witnesses. In the documentary, the segment was called "The World's Largest Ghost Hunt."

Today the area of Campbell Street that was once the scene of so much commotion is quiet once again. The story has mostly receded into the mists of time, and that's how many local residents like it. As one longtime neighbor put it, "I have lived here for many years and have never seen the ghost but, by God, those ghost hunters were a scary bunch."

Bull's-eye Lake Haunting

This story comes from a Northern Indiana town named Valparaiso. They have a small swampy lake of about fifty by fifty feet called Bull's-eye Lake. It is located on a road of the same name.

Many years ago, this swampy lake was part of a farmer's property. One day, as the story goes, the farmer loaded up his cart with the items he planned on selling in town. Not watching where he was going, however, the farmer caused himself, his cart, and his horse to fall into the tar-black water of Bull's-eye Lake. Over the years, people have tried to go into its murky waters, mostly to see how much of this story is true. Due to the depth and the blackness of the water, no one has ever reached the bottom. Yet, on dark nights if you go out to Bull's-eye Lake, witnesses say you can see the center of it glowing with a strange illumination that almost pulses. Some say you can hear the farmer calling for help. Others say you can hear a horse whinny from the swamp grass that surrounds the lake. —*Miss Brenda*

Spirits of Tippecanoe

The Battle of Tippecanoe in 1811 may be the most important battle ever fought in Indiana. It played a pivotal role in both the western expansion of America and the fate of midwestern Native American tribes. The pastoral serenity of the town of Battle Ground, in which the battleground lies, belies its bloodier history.

On one side of the battle was a militia formed by William Henry Harrison, governor of the Indiana Territories and future President of the United States. During Harrison's tenure as governor, he spent a great deal of his time signing treaties with Native American tribes that took away much of their land.

The other side consisted of a confederacy of Native American tribes, who established themselves in a village they called Prophetstown, and that the white settlers called Tippecanoe. The tribal leader was the Shawnee Indian chief Tecumseh, but the man behind the battle was his brother Lauliwasikau. It was Lauliwasikau who had visions of a great Indian victory and who on becoming a medicine man adopted a new name by which he would become famous: the Prophet.

In choosing to go to battle, however, the Prophet had defied Tecumseh, who was not in Prophetstown at the time. The Prophet told his men that his magic would make them impervious to the white man's bullets, and he stubbornly persisted in continuing the battle, even when it was clear that his people were overwhelmed. Many died, and the lost battle helped shatter the dream of a united Indian Nation. Lauliwasikau was taken prisoner and died in an Indian settlement in Kansas in 1837, despised and rejected by his people.

Harrison would use his success at Prophetstown in his presidential campaign slogan, Tippecanoe and Tyler Too. He'd win the presidency, but only weeks after his inauguration, in March 1841, he developed pneumonia and died. His one-month tenure as President is the shortest in American history, and some suspect "the curse of Tecumseh" caused his demise. But it is not the only odd event to indicate that battle repercussions continued.

One tale comes from Jerry Derrick, who grew up around Battle Ground. Derrick vividly remembers years when he and his friends would hang around in the battlefield, especially one ghostly encounter. It was in early November, and he and a couple of his buddies had driven over there on a Saturday night. The friends parked their car and then sat down on a hillside overlooking what had once been the field of combat. As Derrick recounts:

> We were laughing and cutting up and the talk turned to the battle. One of my friends said he wondered if there were any dead Indians buried in the field. I said that there probably was and then we just forgot about it. However, about a minute later I noticed that it suddenly had gotten considerably colder. There was a breeze that just came out of nowhere and it was stirring the trees around us. I remember that I . . . was just putting the hood of my jacket up when we heard chanting.
>
> At first, we did not know what was making the sound, but then it began to rise and fall with a regular cadence and as it got louder, we could hear a number of voices chanting almost like it was a song. Then it got a little clearer, as though it was getting closer and we could hear the tom-toms beating along with the rhythm of the chant.

The boys couldn't figure out what was making the sounds and decided to return to their car, but their progress was halted by a sound that stopped them in their tracks. Derrick remembers:

It was a war cry. It sounded right next to where we were standing. Not in front of us, or behind us, but it sounded like it came from exactly where we were standing. Yet the moon was out and we could see no one was around. Needless to say, we cut and ran like the devil back to my friend's car. Just before we jumped in, one of my friends looked back toward the field and swore that he saw a figure on horseback watching us from a distance. I did not see anything, but I was too busy nose diving into the back seat to look around.

Carl Lisek tells a still more extraordinary tale of the battlefield. It's one that his father, Bill, told him years ago. Carl stresses that his father was a "very truthful man" and was "not one prone to exaggerate anything."

Bill Lisek's job required him to be called to work at all hours, including during the middle of the night. While returning home from one of these late-night trips, on a road near the site of the famous battle Bill Lisek saw a scene out of time and reason.

Carl's father said it was a beautiful morning, and as he looked over at the field he saw that the fog was lying close to the ground, giving it an almost surreal look. He noticed at first one, and then many shapes moving through the fog that shrouded the field. "Dad said he looked, and he could see figures moving around in the mist, and then he saw the forms of riders on horseback," Carl says.

Lisek pulled his car over to the shoulder of the road and peered into the fog. A battle unfolded before his unbelieving eyes. Carl says his father "saw Indians swarming forward, some on horseback, with old-time rifles and tomahawks and soldiers in strange-looking uniforms shooting back at them. This was not some dream or vision—my dad said it looked very real except that there was no sound—it was like watching a silent movie, only in 3-D."

At first, Bill Lisek thought it might have been a historical reenactment, but this thought passed as he saw Indians shot from their horses, blood spraying from their wounds. Soldiers on the ground broke from their positions and ran, only to be clubbed to the ground by their pursuers. No historical reenactment could ever portray such appalling reality.

Then, abruptly, the vision passed. "My dad told us that he was not sure just how long the battle in front of him lasted," Carl says. "He said that it could have been a few seconds, or it could have been ten minutes—he could not tell—but then suddenly it was gone, and my dad was left sitting there in his car, unable to believe what he had seen."

Many years later, while reading a history of the Battle of Tippecanoe for the first time, Bill realized his vision, coming just after dawn, corresponded almost exactly with that of the actual battle.

Perhaps the most poignant stories revolving around Tippecanoe are the recurring tales of a solitary Indian apparition, said to be seen sitting on Prophet's Rock, the place where Lauliwasikau watched the ill-starred battle unfold before him. According to legend, it is the ghost of the Prophet himself, lamenting a fate decided so long ago. He may be mourning a nation and a way of life that was lost on the bloody battlefield or awaiting a chance to redeem himself from the dishonor that once engulfed him.

Perfect Attendance—Even in Death

Many devoted teachers have taught (and still do) at Kahler Middle School, in Dyer. None, however, are so noted as the school's namesake: Agnes Kahler, who devoted fifty-two years of her life to education. To those who were fortunate enough to have her as a teacher, she was both a friend and a role model. Such was her impact that the Lake Central School Corporation renamed the school after her in 1958, four years before she retired. When she died in 1983, she was buried in St. Joseph Cemetery, which overlooks the school she loved. Today a few people wonder if she's still being marked "present" there.

Jean Wease was principal of Kahler from 1978 to 1993, and in the course of her duties she heard a few odd stories involving the classroom in which Miss Kahler taught fifth grade for years. Mrs. Wease put a new teacher in the room and explained the room's history to her. She says the teacher was so impressed that "she put a special plaque with a tribute to Agnes Kahler in her room. She framed the obituary that the paper had run on Agnes and hung it over the door."

Eventually, with a shift in classrooms, a new teacher, Ms. Nikkie Whitcombe, moved into the classroom. "In the process," she says,

> I took the plaque down from where it hung over the door and put it on my desk, thinking that I would return it to the teacher who had left it there. After a while I left for lunch and locked the door behind me, but when I got back the picture was gone from my desk. The door had been locked the entire time, and there were no children there who might have taken it. We sent out notes asking if anyone had picked it up, but in all the years since then it has never been found.

Whitcombe also reports that one school day in 1999, her teaching was disrupted when five books launched themselves from a bookcase and landed several feet away. And one day a small slate board she keeps on a ledge under her blackboard "just flew off of the ledge and landed two feet away. Neither I nor any of my students were near it when it happened. It was just a little spooky."

Mary Tanis, who has worked at the school for twenty-seven years, recalls several eerie experiences. Her classroom was next to the one in which Agnes used to teach. Her door would open or shut by itself, despite its being, she says, "solid and very heavy." Sometimes the doorknob would turn, but once the door was open, nobody would be in the hallway.

She also had an odd episode involving a clock. She was teaching her class while a computer technician worked on the classroom computer. "Suddenly," Mrs. Tanis says, "the clock in the classroom flew off the wall and landed six feet away. It did not simply fall off the wall—it flew off with enough force to pull the wire out of the wall. The computer tech worker stopped what he was doing, and the kids looked at me wide-eyed. I just smiled and said, 'Don't worry, it's just Agnes.'"

The custodial staff has had even eerier experiences. One night a staff member waxed the floor in the hallway outside Miss Kahler's former classroom. A few hours later the worker was shocked to find a set of footprints in the fresh wax leading from Miss Kahler's classroom to the stairs. By all appearances, the person who had left them had made her way toward the stairs, but the footprints vanished before reaching them.

Garland Lauderdale was head custodian from 1988 to 1997 and remembers many inexplicable events. "I had staff tell me that they would not work alone in the building. One woman said that she was cleaning the floor once when all of a sudden a projector screen pulled itself out from the wall, and then folded up and flipped off the wall. She was really spooked." Another young woman told Mr. Lauderdale that she too refused to work alone. She heard footsteps and saw lights switch on and off. And once, he says, "Her vacuum cleaner turned itself on when she was several feet away from it."

Lauderdale himself encountered several odd incidents. "My wife and son and I were in the building, and as we walked through the halls, I could hear desks moving in one classroom. I was afraid that someone had broken into the school, but when we got there, the sounds had stopped and no one was in the room. However, several desks had been knocked over, and one was tilted sideways against the wall. There was no way anyone could have gotten in or out of that room without me knowing it."

One of the most evocative incidents happened one night when Mr. Lauderdale was home. A custodian called and asked if Garland could come over right away, saying he and another custodian had something to show him. Once he arrived at Kahler, his employees "took me through the hallway to the back of the school and unlocked the door. Then one of the custodians pushed the door open against the snow that had drifted against it, pointed to the parking lot, and asked, 'See the footprints?'"

In the new snow was a set of footprints that led across the parking lot to the door that had just been unlocked. If someone had tried to get into the school only to find himself locked out, he would have had to turn and retrace his steps. These footsteps led to the door and just stopped. Mr. Lauderdale's eyes traced their path to its origin. They led across the parking lot and into St. Joseph Cemetery, where Agnes Kahler had been laid to rest years before.

Cemetery Safari

The way we bury our dead says a lot about the way we live our lives. Every graveyard that we whistle past carries stories of the earthly triumphs and tragedies of those who now lie within it. Some memorials are heart wrenching—like the tiny furnished dollhouses constructed for girls who passed away at a tender young age. Other grave markers proudly honor someone's memory by eternally proclaiming their achievements in life—be they Indiana's famous Johnny Appleseed or merely the world's greatest horseshoer.

There are also darker and more macabre tales to be found in our burial grounds, gruesome sagas of grave robbers and stories of telephone calls from beyond the grave. Come with us now as we visit some of the more storied stones and mysterious memorials of our state. But just be sure to count your steps on your way into one particular final resting place, because if the number of steps you take going out differs even slightly, well, let's just say, that could be a very grave sign!

Legend of Stiffy Green

One of the most well-known and beloved ghostly denizens of the Hoosier State is not a human at all, but a small dog. His story has been told and retold around countless campfires and dinner tables, earning this ghostly canine an odd sort of fame throughout the state.

Stiffy Green's story begins in Terre Haute in the first years of the last century. At the time, Terre Haute was a small community surrounded by farm fields, but beginning to show signs of the great city it would become. Of all the community's residents, none was better regarded than John Heinl. He was a gregarious older gentleman who owned the only florist shop in town. Part of his outgoing nature might have been due to the fact that despite his wide circle of friends, Heinl was essentially alone. He was childless, and his wife had passed away a few years earlier, leaving him alone in his home except for his beloved dog, Stiffy Green.

According to the story, the dog's strange name came from a pair of characteristics. First, being a bulldog, Stiffy Green walked with a somewhat stilted gait, and second, it is said that the dog possessed the unusual feature of piercing green eyes.

John Heinl and Stiffy Green were inseparable companions. On warm summer evenings, they would stroll the town's sidewalks together, meeting and greeting their various friends. Few of those friends would come too close, however, for it was well known that Stiffy Green was very protective of his master. It was said that as John Heinl slept each night, Stiffy Green would sleep next to his bed, keeping vigil on his beloved master in his rest.

Stiffy Green was presumably at his post the night that John Heinl passed away peacefully in his sleep. According to newspaper accounts, a large part of the population of Terre Haute attended the funeral, but the chief mourner was Stiffy Green. Mr. Heinl's friends brought the dog to the funeral and even to the interment at Highland Lawn Cemetery, where the dog watched with everyone else as his master's casket was slid into place at the Heinl family mausoleum. This accomplished, the mausoleum gate was shut, apparently ending John Heinl's earthly history. Yet appearances can be deceiving.

After the graveside service, Heinl's friends discussed what to do with Stiffy Green. One of John's distant cousins agreed to adopt him, but when the dog was approached, he growled, unwilling to leave his master's side even in death. A rope was found and tied around the dog's collar, and he was led off to his new home.

Yet the next morning he was gone. During the night he had chewed through his rope and disappeared. A search was mounted throughout the town, and Stiffy Green was found at the cemetery, sitting stoically outside the gate of the Heinl mausoleum, patiently guarding the eternal rest of his master. The dog was transported home and tied more securely, but within a day or two he had escaped again, only to be found back at his post in front of the mausoleum. This occurred several more times. No matter how securely the dog was tied, he still managed to escape and find his way back to his master.

Eventually, it was decided to let the dog stay at the cemetery. Cemetery workers adopted him, put up a shelter for him behind the mausoleum, and fed him parts of their lunch or dinner. And Stiffy Green seemed content there for a year or two, until he too died of old age.

By now, Stiffy Green's story had leaked out into the community and the dog had become almost as famous as his master. After the dog's death, a group of John Heinl's friends met to discuss the disposition of the animal's body. While some suggested that it be buried or simply discarded, another friend came up with a different idea. The dog's body was taken to a local taxidermist, who

restored it to a startling likeness of life. Although this idea may seem macabre to modern sensibilities, it was not an uncommon practice in the early 1900s to preserve a favorite pet after its death.

Stiffy Green's preserved body was taken once more to Highland Lawn Cemetery, where it was lovingly placed next to John Heinl's casket in the family mausoleum. One of the friends present remarked that it was appropriate that the master and friend were now together again, and once again the gate was shut.

This was not to be the end of Stiffy Green's story, however. The first odd incident occurred a few months later when, late in the afternoon, a worker heard the sound of barking coming from somewhere in the cemetery. This was not an uncommon occurrence, and the worker went to find the dog and run it off. But as he walked toward the sound of the barking, he began to feel uneasy, for he realized it was leading him in the direction of the Heinl mausoleum.

Just as he arrived at the hedgerow that separates the mausoleum from the road, the barking abruptly ceased. The worker instinctively crouched down behind a bush, his heart beating hard. After a long, silent moment, he gathered enough nerve to peer through the bush to the mausoleum beyond and was relieved to find nothing unusual. He could not see a dog anywhere.

Thankful and a little abashed at his own fears, the worker rose. It was then that he saw something that took his breath away. Through the gathering twilight of late afternoon, along the fence that separates Highland Lawn Cemetery from the streets of Terre Haute, the worker swore he saw a pair of figures. One was the shadowy, indistinct form of an old man with a walking stick and a pipe; the other, the diminutive figure of a small dog padding contentedly by his side. Even from a distance, he would later say, he could see the dog's eyes glow green with peace and happiness now that he and his master were together forever.

Since that time, many claimed to see the two strolling the grounds of Highland Lawn Cemetery and many more have made the trek to the Heinl mausoleum, peering within to see the preserved body of a small dog that seems to guard against anyone who would disturb his master's sleep. Some years ago Stiffy Green's body was removed from the mausoleum, but perhaps more than his memory lingers. If one walks through the grounds of Highland Lawn in the evening, one might still catch a glimpse of a pair of shadowy figures walking contentedly in the gathering twilight.

Green Glowing Memories

I was a freshman at Indiana State when some girlfriends and I drove out to the cemetery one night in early October. Of course, we had all heard the story of the ghostly dog, and they said that you could see him in this mausoleum. Some upperclassmen said the dog's eyes glowed green when you hit them with a flashlight, so we brought a couple of flashlights along with us to try it out.

It was the perfect night for the trip—a little foggy and kind of desolate. When we got to the cemetery we drove around for probably half an hour before we found the right mausoleum, and then it took us another five minutes to get the courage to go up to it. Finally my roommate and I got out and walked up to the mausoleum and shone our flashlights into it. Sure enough, there was the dark figure of a dog sitting to one side. It was weird to see it look so lifelike, like it was going to wag its tail or something.

When I shone my flashlight on the dog's eyes, they reflected back a green light. Then I think one of us jostled the flashlight because for a second the dog seemed to move just a little. That made us both scream and we ran back to the car like our hair was on fire. Just as I was jumping in, I swear I heard the sound of a dog bark right close by. It totally freaked me out and I yelled at the girl driving to get us out of there.

We peeled rubber back to campus, where we told a bunch of the other girls in the dorm what happened. They wanted to go back, but I wouldn't go. My roommate went, and when she returned an hour or so later she was really scared. She swore they got out and went to the same mausoleum, but this time the dog wasn't there—it had vanished.

I am not sure just what we saw that night, but it was one creepy place and I can still vividly remember the green glow of those eyes.—*Nancy L.*

World's Greatest Horseshoer

In 1893, William Jennings Wedekind left his home in Hagerstown and headed to Chicago for the World's Fair. Inside the seven- by twelve-foot display case he brought with him were close to three hundred and fifty examples of Wedekind's handiwork as a horseshoer. An important event at the fair would be a horseshoeing competition, and Wedekind intended to enter and win. He took with him dozens upon dozens of horseshoes designed to do everything from helping a lame horse walk easier to adjusting the gait of a horse. He even had a pair of rubber horseshoes.

When the awards were announced, it was pretty much a clean sweep for Wedekind. He took home awards for, among other things, having the largest collection, the best workmanship, and even an award for "using gearings in nippers," which sounds impressive even though we have no idea what it means. Regardless, the 1893 World's Fair ended with officials declaring Wedekind the "world's greatest horseshoer."

Shortly after the fair closed, everyone was after Wedekind's display case and the wonders it held inside. Legend has it that he turned down a cash offer of $100,000 for the case, which was then valued at roughly $20,000. Wedekind was content to simply return to Hagerstown and continue his horseshoeing. But word of his showing at the World's Fair spread quickly, and soon people were coming from all across the United States to have the world's greatest horseshoer work on their horses.

Wedekind passed away in 1926, and his famous display case was willed to his wife. Despite many generous offers, she, like her husband, refused to sell it. When she died 1957, the case was donated to a local museum.

Wedekind's grave is located inside Hagerstown's West Lawn Cemetery. It's a rather large cemetery, but it's not hard to find the final resting place of the world's greatest horseshoer. Just look for the gravestone with an anvil on top of it.

Dollhouses of the Dead

People visiting graves of loved ones have been known to leave behind many strange objects. It's not uncommon to find graves adorned with trinkets, toys, and even stuffed animals and dolls. But if some of those dolls find their current living conditions getting a bit cramped, they might consider a move to Indiana, where they will have their choice of not one, but two dollhouses to choose from, each with its own full view of the cemetery.

The first dollhouse lies within the gates of City Cemetery in Connersville. In 1900, a year after the death of their daughter Vivian at the tender age of five, Horace and Carrie Allison placed the fully furnished house over her grave. They lovingly looked after the house until Horace died in 1946, after which Carrie continued to care for it until her death in 1969. After that, Vivian's sister, Lovell Allison Beeson, became the house's caretaker, even going so far as to replace it with her own personal dollhouse when the original one began to rot.

Around 1980, vandals nearly destroyed the dollhouse when they knocked it over one evening. Fearing further vandalism, a gentleman living near the cemetery, John Powell, watched over it until his death in 1990. Shortly after Powell's death, two local men—Louis Brockman, a retired carpenter, and Connorsville police officer Darrell Maines—decided they needed to do something to ensure that the dollhouse would remain intact forever.

Over the course of many weeks, Maines and Brockman gave the dollhouse a complete renovation inside and out. They added new furniture to the inside, including a miniature photograph of the *Mona Lisa*. They even poured a new concrete foundation and bolted the dollhouse to it so that it could not be knocked over by either the wind or vandals. Finally, new landscaping and shrubs were added to the grave site, completing the look that visitors to the cemetery can see today.

The second dollhouse is located only a short drive away at East Hill Cemetery in Arlington. This dollhouse marks the grave of Lova Cline, daughter of George and Mary Cline. Lova was born an invalid in 1902. The dollhouse, built by her father, a carpenter by trade, was one of the few toys she was able to enjoy. Sadly, she was not able to enjoy it for long, as she passed away in 1908. Grieving for his daughter, Cline moved the dollhouse to Lova's grave, where it has remained to this day. When he passed away, he left behind specific instructions in his will that a close family friend, Lova Ward-Wooten—who had been named after the young Lova Cline—be appointed the official caretaker of the dollhouse.

Unfortunately, Lova's dollhouse would run into trouble several times in the 1970s. Shortly after an article describing the antiques that were used to furnish it ran locally, vandals broke into it and made off with everything. Members of the Posey Township 4-H Girls Club replaced the furniture, but several years later, in 1979, the house was robbed a second time. In an attempt to curb further robberies, Lova Ward-Wooten and her daughter, Sheila Wooten-Hewitt, painstakingly created furnishings for the house that were made entirely out of "worthless" cardboard. To add a touch of realism to the furnishings, the women covered the cardboard with paint and an assortment of fabrics.

Ward-Wooten passed away in 1999, but her daughter continues to care for the dollhouse. In 2002, she even erected a sign comprised of several sheets of laminated paper in front of the dollhouse, chronicling its long history. In a somewhat macabre final touch, at the bottom of the sign is a faded, almost unrecognizable copy of a photo showing the young Lova Cline lying in her coffin.

Where Is Johnny Appleseed's Grave?

He was born John Chapman in September of 1774, but all the world would come to know him as Johnny Appleseed. He was the pioneering nurseryman who introduced the apple to large parts of the Midwest. Not much about his life is known, and even in death, Chapman is shrouded in mystery. Even his final resting place is debated. There is a rock on the property of the Canterbury Green Apartment Complex in Fort Wayne that claims to mark the spot where he was buried. At one time, a family named Worth had a small cabin here. When Chapman fell ill in March 1845 he was brought to the Worth cabin, where he passed away. According to legend, the family buried Chapman's body next to their cabin and placed the rock over his grave.

However, most people believe that after his death, Chapman's body was buried in a small family plot in Fort Wayne now known as Archer Cemetery. The grave was marked with the names John Chapman as well as his nickname, Johnny Appleseed. In 1916, as part of a celebration for Indiana's one hundredth anniversary, a small iron fence was placed around Chapman's grave, complete with a plaque.

Today visitors to the grave site in Archer Cemetery often pay their respects by leaving behind gifts of apples on Chapman's grave. Others simply stare at the headstone and wonder whether or not Johnny Appleseed is buried there.

A Really Long Distance Phone Call

Within the pastoral grounds of Highland Lawn Cemetery in Terre Haute stands the Sheets family mausoleum, eternal resting place for Martin Sheets, his wife, Susan, and their infant daughter, Ethel. While the mausoleum is an ornate structure, there is nothing truly unique about its appearance, particularly amid the many striking and beautiful monuments that grace the cemetery grounds. However, this impression is deceiving, since the mausoleum and at least one of its occupants have attained near legendary status in Terre Haute and across Indiana.

Martin Sheets—or Mort, as he was known—seems to have been larger than life, even in death. He was born September 11, 1853, near Terre Haute. Though historical records are sketchy, it is known that in the early 1900s Sheets moved to Texas, where he is said to have struck it rich in the oil fields. Several years later he sold his oil holdings and returned to Terre Haute a wealthy man. However, he never forgot his sojourn in the arid south. As a resident who had known Sheets at the time later described him: "He was a powerfully built man, with a full chest, massive shoulders, thick neck, exceptionally dark skin, a black Vandyke beard and eyes that you felt when he looked at you. He always wore cowboy boots, a Texas hat and a black shirt."

Given this description, it is not hard to imagine the swath that Mort Sheets cut on the streets of Terre Haute upon his return from Texas. Moreover, his behavior did little to diminish this striking impression. Indeed, Mr. Sheets seems to have become a local character in the city. At times, he could display a philanthropic bent. Among other things, he purchased a large home on Seventh Street in Terre Haute and presented it as a gift to the nearby Union Hospital as a home for single nurses. The gift was no doubt appreciated, even if Sheets insisted upon the installation in front of a large sign (that he had prepared) proclaiming the structure the MARTIN A. & SUSAN SHEETS NURSING HOME.

Many stories were told at the time of the eccentric Mort Sheets. He once threatened with a six gun a troublesome neighbor who kept parking cars in front of the Sheets property. Yet it is possible that his fame would have been lost to the mists of time except for one peculiar obsession that grew to haunt him toward the end of his life. For some reason, Mort Sheets began to have a morbid fear that he would one day be buried alive. Given the comparatively archaic state of medical science at the time, such occurrences had no doubt happened; however, they were extremely rare. But so strong was Mr. Sheets's apprehension that he began to prepare for that eventuality.

In the early 1900s, Sheets erected a striking mausoleum at Highland Lawn Cemetery. Sadly, the first occupant of the mausoleum would be his daughter, Ethel, who died at thirteen months of age. After her interment, Mort Sheets began to make plans for his eventual death and burial there.

The first indication of his bizarre designs came when Sheets appeared at the local Bell Telephone office and requested that a telephone be installed in the mausoleum. This, he explained, was to allow him access to the outside world in case he were to somehow revive in his coffin and need to call for help. As peculiar as this must have sounded, it seems that the telephone company took the request in stride. As the commercial superintendent of the Indiana Bell office later noted in a *Terre Haute Star* article, "At that time it was considered no big deal or oddity and no one thought anything unusual about it, because all who knew about the installation knew Mort Sheets."

Accordingly, the line was installed, complete with a working telephone in the mausoleum. While this no doubt might have caused some stir, until after his death in 1926, no one fully understood the depth of Mort Sheets's conviction that he would be buried alive. Codicils were found in his will that dictated not only that the phone line be kept active, but that a rocking chair and bottle of his favorite whiskey be interred in the crypt with him. One might surmise that it was his intention, should he wake up in his coffin, to somehow liberate himself, call for a taxi, and then sit down and have a drink while he waited for a ride home.

In the end, Mr. Sheets's wishes were honored, and he was buried with the items he desired. Unfortunately for Mort Sheets (but perhaps luckily for whatever cab driver he might have called), Mr. Sheets's first death was his last; after his burial, he seems not to have awakened.

However, some might wonder if he has been heard from. Some time after his interment at the mausoleum, a strange rumor began to circulate in Terre Haute. It centered on the death of his wife, Susan, a few years after him. According to the story, Mrs. Sheets passed away of a stroke in the middle of the night and her body was not discovered until the next day. When she was found, her lifeless hand was clutching the phone in her kitchen, which was off the hook. Of course, the conclusion made at the time was that Mrs. Sheets, perhaps feeling the first symptoms of the impending stroke, had gone to the kitchen to call for help, only to die before she was able to make the call.

However, according to this unsubstantiated rumor (still heard in the vicinity), after the woman's funeral, when the door to the Sheets mausoleum was unlocked to place her coffin next to that of her husband, a peculiar thing was noticed. The phone on the wall next to Martin Sheets's casket was off its hook, despite the fact that the doors had been locked since his interment some years earlier. Casting ominous looks among themselves, those present placed the phone back on its receiver and vacated the crypt without delay.

A few years ago Highland Lawn Cemetery landscaped the section around the Sheets mausoleum and the phone line leading to it was taken down. At this point, some eighty years after the death of Martin Sheets, it is conjectured that Mort has gone on to his eternal reward and will not be making any phone calls. A few in Terre Haute, however, still wonder if perhaps the phrase might well be any MORE phone calls.

Slow! Dead Body Ahead!

If you find yourself traveling the back roads of Amity, there are lots of things you'll need to watch out for in the road: deer, skunks—a grave. That's right, a grave. The grave of Nancy Barnett is sitting smack in the middle of CR 400.

Nancy and her husband, William, great-great-great-grandson of Pocahontas, settled in the area in the 1820s, right along Sugar Creek. When she died on December 1, 1831, she was buried close to the creek. Over the years, several other individuals were buried alongside Barnett and the area became something of a makeshift cemetery.

Around 1901, the county took a look at traffic in the vicinity and decided that a road needed to be built through the area of Amity. The chosen location meant that the road would go straight through the cemetery in which Nancy Barnett was buried, and shortly before construction began, the county announced its plans to dig up and relocate all the graves. This didn't sit well with Barnett's grandson, Daniel O. Doty. Doty voiced his disapproval to county officials and asked that his grandmother be allowed to rest in peace where she was. Officials said there was nothing they could do, and that Barnett's grave was going to be moved along with all the others. That's when Doty decided to take matters into his own hands.

When county workers arrived at the cemetery to start moving the graves, they found Daniel Doty sitting on top of his grandmother's grave with a loaded shotgun in his hands. Doty calmly stated that his grandmother wasn't going anywhere and that if the workers still wanted to move her, they were going to have to go through him. The workers wisely decided not to challenge Doty and instead set about digging up the other graves. When they were done, all that remained of the cemetery was a single grave with an armed man sitting on top of it.

And there he stayed. Legend has it that whenever county workers came out to work on the road, Doty was there with his shotgun. True or not, today when you travel down the two-lane CR 400 you'll come across a yellow diamond-shaped sign alerting you to the fact that the road ahead divides. Look closely at the sign and you'll notice a small white cross in the center of the divided section. That's because right up ahead the road divides in front of Nancy Barnett's grave and then joins back up on the other side.

DUKIE BABY BURNETTE
MY DARLING BABY
5-1970 — 6-1982

RALPHIE
MR. AND MRS. SAM SMULYAN
A LOVING FRIEND ALWAYS
JUNE 7, 1966 — SEPT. 17, 1983

DUSTY LARISON
BERT—MARTHA—YOLANDA
1967 — 1983
WITH LOVE

HAPPY BUTLER
WE LOVE YOU "RU RU"
1972 — 1983

IMPY HOPE
1965 — 1983

PIERRE ROWE de PAREE
AKC
ALWAYS LOVING YOU
1970 — 1982

TIFFANY BURK
7-14-1970 — 8-17-1983

TEAC BURK
12-25-60 — 8-20-84

PRINCESS SNOWVENGIE
CLAYTON
GOD BLESS HER
SHE WAS LIKE A BLOOMING ROSE
JUNE 2 1969 - MAR. 26. 1982

BRIDGET LAWSON
MOMMYS BABY
1967 — 1981

STAR SOWDERS
1973 — 1983

GEEJAY
MY FAITHFUL POODLE
1971 — 1982

SAM RITTMAN
1968 — 1982

BABY GIRL VICKIE
YOU GAVE US YOUR ALL
HARKER HUNLEY
MAY 31 1965 AUG 12 1981

SKEETER MESSER
OUR BUDDY
1971 — 1981

BRAHMS WILSON
1969 — 1981

HIM CLARK
LOVE YOU ALWAYS HIMBO
MAY 2 1968 - JUNE 17 1982

SUGAR BENNETT
MOMMYS GIRL
1974 — 1982

AMANDA LYNN PETTY
2-23-1971 — 8-24-1982
WE THANK GOD WE HAD HER AS LONG
AS WE DID. BUT OH HOW IT HURTS
NOW THAT SHE'S GONE
MOMMY AND DADDY

LASSIE BURGAN
1968 — 1982

MAX
1967

LITTLE DOGGIE MASHINO

FRITZ WELHELM SHELLEY
HE WAS LOVED BY ALL
OUR LITTLE BOY
JULY 11 1966 - JUNE 19 1982

HEMI CROQUART
1970 — 1983

HERBIE HYLTON
1975 — 1984

PEPPER KINDRED
OUR BOY
1977 — 1984

SAM MAY
OCT. 3 1968 — JAN. 3 1984

PENNY LUDT
JAN. 1 1974 — MAR. 27 1984

TRACY

Pets Rest in Memory Gardens

Some 50 years ago, after spending most of her adult life as the dog pound superintendent for the Indianapolis Police Department, Leona Frankfurt announced her retirement. Her co-workers thought Leona would find something to occupy her time that was about as far removed from dogs as she could get. Those who knew her well, though, knew that Leona was a true animal lover and would always need to be around them. So it wasn't much of a surprise when shortly after her retirement, Leona announced that she was opening up a dog kennel along Pendleton Pike in Indianapolis. What was a bit strange was that attached to the dog kennel was roughly 10 acres of open field, which seemed a lot of land for a kennel. Not too much if you were planning on creating a pet cemetery, though, which is exactly what Leona Frankfurt did.

In the 50+ years since it first officially opened, Memory Gardens has become the final resting place for over 5,000 beloved family pets.

Acre after acre of the cemetery is dotted with tombstones erected in memory of furry friends that were considered so much a member of the family that many stones bear a last name. There are even hundreds of above-ground burial vaults, some of which are inscribed with messages so touching that even a manly man will find he has "something in his eye" after reading them. Everywhere you look are tiny trinkets adorning the graves—a collar, a chew toy, a Frisbee.

Given the fact that I had more than a few nightmares after being exposed to Stephen King's *Pet Sematary,* I was a bit apprehensive about entering a real-life pet cemetery. I shouldn't have been because you won't find any zombie cats here, only peace and tranquility. For if anything, Memory Gardens stands simply as a touching memorial to all those who taught us the meaning of unconditional love, asking for nothing in return save that we never forget them.—*Jim Willis*

Missing Thirteenth Stone

Just outside Huntington lies a cemetery with the famous 13 Graves. It's where the remains of 12 murdered women lie, plus a man who resides in the 13th grave, who killed the women. The gravestones are all flush with the ground, and if you stand on the man's stone and walk to the end while counting the stones as you step on them, you will count all 13 stones. Turn around and walk back, counting the stones as you go and beginning with the one you are standing on. You'll count only 12 stones this time. Look down, and you are on the last female stone. The 13th stone cannot be found.—*Tony Vining*

Pollie Barnett, Wandering Soul

In Fairview Cemetery, near New Albany, lies the final resting place of a woman whose life was a long, sad journey. Few details are known about the early life of Pollie Barnett. It is said that she was born in Solsberry, on September 23, 1836, as Pollie Lay. She was married to George Barnett, a woodchopper, but that's all we know about him or his marriage to Pollie. What is known is that around 1858 she moved to the small community of Fairplay, south of Worthington, with her two daughters.

While poor, the mother and children seemed content, eking out a living from their garden and whatever odd jobs Barnett could find. However, her joy and perhaps her sanity were forever destroyed several years later when her older daughter, Sylvania, mysteriously disappeared. Historical details of the event are impossible to ascertain, but one local legend says the fifteen-year-old attended a local quilting bee one night, never to return home. Another tale says she vanished while gathering wood for a fire.

Perhaps the most evocative story of her disappearance, however, says that she and her mother had been arguing on the day she vanished. The cause of the argument, predictably, centered on a young man. Pollie, a protective mother, was known to keep a tight rein on her daughter, judging she was too young to "keep company" with

any of the local boys who came calling. That morning, however, Sylvania had revealed to her mother that she had been secretly seeing a local boy. Barnett, ever protective, laid down an edict that forbade her daughter from ever seeing the boy again.

The girl, however, refused to waver. Tempers flared, and harsh words were exchanged. Finally, in a fit of pique, the young girl stormed from the house. Barnett naturally assumed Sylvania would return that day, but when nightfall came and she had not come back, Barnett, by now regretting their quarrel, rode to several neighbors' homes to inquire if they had seen her. None had.

By the next morning, the local populace formed search teams and began to scour the area. No trace of the girl could be found. After several days of fruitless searching, the volunteers had to admit that Sylvania was gone forever, and they gave up their search. But Barnett did not.

Something in this tragedy must have wounded her irreparably. Neighbors noted that she became "odd." She began to carry her black cat in her arms everywhere she went, talking to the animal in low tones as though it were a child. She gave up sleeping in a bed, instead telling her neighbors that she would sleep on the floor until her daughter returned. While most of the neighbors looked at her with sad benevolence, understanding the infinite sadness in her soul, others were less charitable. Some began to whisper that she was a witch, and at least once, she was accused, without supporting evidence, of burning the barn of a neighbor.

However, it was her wandering that eventually garnered her the most attention. Soon after her daughter's alleged death, Barnett began to ramble the roads, calling for Sylvania. At first, it was assumed that she would eventually give up her search, yet the community would

soon learn the depth of her grief and her determination.

For the next thirty-two years, Barnett continued her wandering. It has been estimated that during that time she walked some 54,000 miles through five counties. Sometime she was joined on her rambles by her younger daughter, but most often her only companion was her black cat. She became a familiar, if heartbreaking figure in the area—an old woman solemnly trudging the dirt roads and rustic lanes of southern Indiana, plaintively calling for her lost daughter. Occasionally she would accept lodging from benevolent farmers in the area, but most often she slept in the open by the side of the road, ready to resume her search at the first light of dawn. Through rain and storm and snow, she maintained her journey in search of Sylvania and perhaps in search of forgiveness for their last, tragic words.

Like so much of Pollie Barnett's life, the details of her death are sketchy. Some say she was found along a dirt road in Owen County. Others say she died in her sleep at home, on the floor as was her custom. Whatever the circumstances of her death, the end of her road seems to have had an effect on the good citizens of nearby Linton. A fund was established to give Barnett a proper burial, and a headstone was erected in her memory. Atop the headstone was carved the figure of her cat, her companion on her long journeys. The inscription on the stone reads,

HERE POLLIE BARNETT IS AT REST,
FROM DEEPEST GRIEF AND TOILSOME QUEST,
HER CAT, HER ONLY FRIEND,
REMAINED WITH HER UNTIL LIFE'S END

One can only hope that the end of Barnett's journey brought the reunion with her daughter that she sought for so long.

A Truly Upright Hoosier

John Plesant Burton was truly an honorable, upright Hoosier pioneer. He was born July 8, 1758, in Richmond, Virginia, of a well-respected family and served as a private in the Revolutionary War. In 1826, at the age of sixty-eight, he came to Lawrence County with his wife, Susannah, and a large family — three children of their own, plus six orphans. Here he was given a land grant in recognition of his service in achieving American independence. With such a large clan and substantial holdings, the Burtons would soon become one of the founding families of Lawrence County.

Indeed, the *History of Lawrence County*, written in 1854, notes of the Burtons:

> The family is represented in all the professions from the pulpit to the school room; in civil offices from Road Supervisor to Governor; in the military from private to Major-General. In religion they are principally Baptists, and are honorably represented in all the benevolent institutions. A majority of them are members of the Masonic Order. Most of them vote Democrat. They are remarkable as a sociable, peaceable and respectable family, and the ladies are especially noted for their beauty and social and moral attainments.

John Plesant Burton deserves much of the credit for developing Lawrence County. He came to the area when it was largely unsettled, and he was responsible for much of its growth and prosperity. However, it is one odd anecdote of Burton's death that has reserved his place in Hoosier history.

Shortly before Burton's seventy-ninth birthday, he became gravely ill. Calling his children to his bedside, he gave specific instructions regarding his funeral. He was to be buried with the full rites of the Masonic order, of which he was a long-time member. Further he would not be buried in the family plot at the Burton Family Cemetery but three quarters of a mile away near the grave of his daughter-in-law. And finally, it was his adamant wish to be buried standing up, in a grave eleven feet deep.

To modern sensibilities such a request probably seems bizarre. Yet throughout the nineteenth century several people of note were buried in an upright position. Revolutionary War hero George Hancock, an aide-de-camp to George Washington and a member of Congress, was buried standing up in Ellison, Virginia. The famous English poet Ben Jonson is buried in Westminster Abbey standing up — in order, in his words, to save space. A more evocative reason for being buried upright was given by Texas pioneer Britt Bailey, who reputedly stated in his will, "I will be buried standing upright facing west. I have never lied to man in this life and I'll be damned if anyone can come by and say 'there lies Britt Bailey.'"

John Burton's reason for his unusual entombment is unknown. However, it is known that his wish was honored. Newspaper accounts of the time indicate that as many as five thousand people attended the funeral, some coming by wagon from fifty miles away. The large group followed the black-draped wagon bearing Burton's mortal remains to the grave site, where his coffin was slid into its extraordinary grave. The marker placed over the grave states only the name of the deceased, the dates of his birth and death, and the fact that it was his request to be buried standing up.

Over the years, the area of the grave has become a bit of a tourist attraction, with families coming to stand by the only known grave of a Hoosier buried in an upright position.

One Hundred Steps of Doom

Some people have this weird fascination about wanting to know how they are going to die. If you're one of those people, you might want to schedule a trip to a cemetery on the outskirts of Brazil—the one in Indiana—where, according to legend, you'll receive a vision of your death. But before you go, just make sure you're good at simple addition, otherwise you might not make it through the night!

Built into the side of a hill on the back roads outside Brazil is Carpenter's Cemetery, which locals have renamed the 100 Steps Cemetery. The "steps" part of the name is obvious because while there are graves all along the side of the hill, the main portion of the cemetery sits at the end of a long stone staircase. It's the "100" that's open to debate, due mainly to the fact that many of the steps are cracked, broken, or missing. So it's next to impossible to get an exact count of just how many steps there are. Of course, that's where the spooky part of the legend comes from.

If you're dying to catch a glimpse of how you'll die, here's what you do: First, you'll need to go to the cemetery at midnight. Once you get there, you need to climb the staircase, counting each and every step as you go. When you reach the top, turn and look over the tombstones out into the open field. If you do, the ghost of the man whom many claim is the original caretaker of the cemetery will suddenly appear before you and magically show you a vision of your death. Then he will vanish right before your eyes. Pretty creepy, huh? But wait, there's more.

As soon as the vision fades, you'll need to climb back down the stairs and count them once again. If you get the same number as when you climbed up, you're okay. But if you get a different number, the vision the caretaker showed you will come true, possibly even that very night.

Oh, and if after seeing a vision of your death you decide you'll try skirting all this stair-counting business by avoiding the steps and simply climbing down the hill, you're in for a surprise. Legend states that if you bypass the stairs and descend the hill, about halfway along you will be pushed down the hill by an invisible, evil force. The shove will be so intense it will leave red handprints on your back that will remain visible for several days. Just something to consider before you take that first step up to the top of 100 Steps Cemetery.

Elephant Hill

In Connersville, anybody living there can tell you the story of Elephant Hill. Long ago, in the early 20th century, a circus came to the town. In that circus were, of course, some elephants that were a part of the show. One of them started to get ill, and it eventually died and was buried in the town. Nobody knows for sure where the elephant is buried, but they now have streets and hills named after this legendary elephant, and if you grow up there, it is one of the first things you learn about the history of the town.—*Sarah Gibbons*

Lobby and Office, Mudlavia Hotel, Kramer, Indiana

Abandoned
in Indiana

here is no feeling as unsettling as being alone in an abandoned place. Wandering through an old building—a home, a grand hotel, even an amusement park, you sense the emptiness quite acutely. These locations, which once bustled with activity, are now quiet and desolate.

Why were these places left to deteriorate? Were they struck by some disaster or tragedy, or were they merely forgotten by time? In some cases we will never know the secret stories of why they were left to fall into ruin. But that kind of mystery makes the site only more enticing. The broken windows, crumbling staircases, and darkened corridors beckon us inside. We go in search of something intangible, clues to the past or answers to mysteries that we can never solve.

Indiana is so full of abandoned weirdness that there's an entire Web site devoted to it! That's thanks to John McDonald, the publisher of www.LostIndiana.net, who was generous enough to contribute some of the following stories. John and the *Weird Indiana* team have sought out all things creepy and abandoned in the Hoosier State so you don't have to. As you know, these places might not only be unsafe, but can also be on private property, and investigating them would be trespassing. So in the pages ahead, let *Weird Indiana* take you to these sites where time has left behind mystery and forgotten dark places.

Central State Hospital

The story of Indianapolis's Central State Hospital is one of hope and despair, tolerance and cruelty. It is a story of a place that was once praised for its treatment of mental illness but was eventually closed down because of rumors of horrific abuse.

The Indiana Hospital for the Insane, as it was called at the time, opened its doors in 1848. It consisted of one brick building on one hundred wooded acres. Over the next half century, many more buildings were added to the site as more and more demands were placed on the facility and its staff. Eventually, a huge Gothic building called Seven Steeples was erected for the housing of female patients and another dormitory was constructed for the men. A chapel, a hospital that treated physical ailments, a cafeteria, and several other structures were added to the grounds.

The asylum treated thousands of patients over the years, from those suffering from emotional stress to the dangerously deranged. In those days, the term "insane" had a much broader definition, and those coming through the doors of Central State Hospital (as it was renamed) ran the gamut of mental issues.

Perhaps the most feared of the patients were those judged to be "criminally insane." These people, too prone to violence to be housed in other facilities, were kept here under tight security and sometimes, in the early history of the hospital, in a state of constant restraint. Stories say that in the 1950s, while renovating more than five miles of tunnels under the hospital, workers found dark rooms in the underground corridors where chains and shackles were still bolted to the stone walls.

It was not uncommon for even less severely ill patients to be forced to sleep on straw mattresses, under leaking roofs, in cold cells with little ventilation or fresh water. Treatment often consisted of cold-water baths, straitjackets, and even confinement in cages and crates.

Not surprisingly, such techniques brought little success and patients rarely improved. In the days before medication, most mental patients spent their entire lives locked up inside an asylum.

Over the years, in part because of the public awareness about the abuse, conditions improved somewhat at Central State. The use of restraints was diminished, and more attention was paid to treating the inmates rather than just confining them. A new pathology laboratory was constructed, and hundreds of autopsies were performed there. It was hoped that by studying the remains of the mentally ill a physical cause could be found for the ailments that plagued them. But despite these improvements, allegations of patient neglect and worse still filtered out from behind the hospital walls.

In the late 1970s, most of the hospital's ornate Victorian-era buildings were declared unsafe and were torn down to make way for institutional brick dormitories. Even this was not enough to save the place. Amid continuing rumors of patient mistreatment, combined with funding shortages, the state of Indiana closed down Central State Hospital in 1994. Luckily, the state chose to preserve at least some of the buildings on the grounds, including the old pathology building, which was converted for use as the Indiana Medical History Museum. The rest of the facility remains abandoned, although it is heavily guarded by the Capital Police, the branch of the Indiana State Police that is responsible for guarding state-owned properties in and around Indianapolis.

Even though Central State has been closed for years now, there are some who maintain that it is not empty. According to some visitors, staff members, and even police officers, many of those who died during the time the hospital was in operation are still here, searching for a release from suffering that they never found in life. Their cries are sometimes heard within the walls of the buildings, and their apparitions have been seen wandering the grounds.

Of course, the official word from the Indiana Board of Health, which currently owns Central State, is that the place

is not haunted. But if one asks some of the current and former employees of the facility, they just may tell you differently. There are spirits here, they say, lurking in the darkness.

Cold Spots and the Smell of Death

There is an abandoned mental hospital near downtown Indianapolis that is said to be the most haunted site in Indiana. There are many stories of ghosts that represent the old inhabitants of the area. One is of an inmate that beat another inmate to death with rocks, and the wooded site reportedly is the home of a shrieking ghost. The old boiler room is haunted by ghosts who turn the boilers on and off.

The Indiana National Guard (of which I am a part) has used this facility as an anti-terror training facility and on one of these exercises I volunteered to work the night shift and the place felt weird. In the early morning we had to check all of the central administration buildings rooms to make sure nothing was left behind and check the downstairs rooms, little more than just cells.

The most remarkable experience that I had first hand was on a warm night when I had to walk from the administration building to the north gate. It happened as I walked through the central tree grove where an inmate was once stoned to death. At one point I noticed a severe drop in temperature (my job in the USAF is a combat meteorologist) of at least 15–20 degrees and my breath actually fogged suddenly as it came out of my mouth. About thirty feet later the temp returned to normal and my breath stopped fogging.
—*Eric Lawrence*

Lost Mudlavia Spa

It's not surprising that a place with a name like Mudlavia is no longer found on modern maps of Indiana. When the spa that bore this exotic-sounding moniker opened its doors in 1890, though, there was nowhere else like it in the state. It went on to host the rich and famous from around the world and spawned scores of legends, from tales of gangster hangouts to wandering ghosts.

The site began as a simple farm in 1884. The owner of the land, Samuel Story, suffered from severe rheumatism and discovered the healing powers of the local water as he worked his land. As he trudged painfully through the fields behind his plow each day, he drank the water from a spring on his property, only to discover that the pain in his legs slowly went away. Word quickly spread about these miraculous "healing waters" and eventually caught the attention of H. L. Kramer, who

was in the springwater business. It was Kramer who developed Mudlavia.

In order to attract people to the mineral springs, Kramer built the Hotel Mudlavia, a grand spa of almost epic proportions. The entrepreneur spared no expense, knowing that only amazing surroundings would bring in the kind of clientele he envisioned. Workers filled the hotel with marble and onyx, silver fixtures, and Tiffany glass. The lobby boasted imported tile floors, a grand staircase, and a golden fountain with water pumped in directly from the fabled springs. The sprawling white building, with its red tile roof, towered four stories above the surrounding countryside and offered an impressive view in every direction.

The "Hotel Home of Health" at Mudlavia Health Resort, Kramer, Ind.

of the first structure. Eventually, three fires would finally destroy the structure, which was rebuilt after each fire occurred.

Along with its curative powers, Mudlavia also gained a reputation as a hangout for gangsters and bank robbers like Al Capone and John Dillinger. How many of these stories were actually true will never be known, but they do add other threads to the rich tapestry of the local history.

Today the ruins of Mudlavia can be found at what was once the small town of Kramer. This wide spot in the road is near Carbondale, which is close to Attica. All that remains today are a few charred and crumbling buildings, an

Noted celebrities like poet James Whitcomb Riley and boxing champ John L. Sullivan were lured to Mudlavia for both the five-star hotel accommodations and the lithium- and magnesium-rich waters. The water and even the mud were packaged and sold all over the country.

For years, Mudlavia was a great success. Trains brought passengers from distant places, and were met at the station by horse-drawn coaches that brought the visitors to their palatial guest rooms. Once registered, the guests were enrolled in complete health programs involving mud baths, special diets, exercise for the body and spirit, and, of course, large quantities of the healing water.

Sadly, though, this small piece of Indiana heaven was fated not to last. A disastrous fire destroyed the original resort, and the rebuilt version never achieved the luster

original smokestack, and, if the legends are true, a few ghosts of the past. Stories abound of eerie apparitions, footsteps on old stairways, and the voices of hotel guests who vanished decades ago.

The only thing at Mudlavia that manages to hold on to the luster of the past is the water. The springs still run and are still bottled today. Until recently, the water was bottled under the name Cameron Springs, then Perrier. The present owner sells the water to bottlers who market it under a variety of names. He believes the water still holds special qualities, although claims of rheumatism cures can no longer be printed on the package.

The days of "healing cures" may be long gone at Mudlavia, but traces of those times still remain. Although the grand hotel is only a memory, there is still a bit of magic here, even among the ruins.

Last Train to Gary

Railroads first came to the Midwest in the middle part of the 1800s, literally creating cities where none stood before. Frontier settlements, like Chicago and Detroit, became booming metropolises almost overnight and were soon thriving centers for commerce and manufacturing. In those heady days, Gary was born.

To support the thousands of workers moving in from around the country, Gary almost immediately needed a new passenger and freight station. In 1910, the tracks of both the Lake Shore & Michigan Southern and the Baltimore & Ohio rail lines through the city were elevated, and Union Station was built into a hill between them.

The station was constructed in a beaux arts style, using a technique called steel-reinforced poured concrete. This sturdy method, revolutionary at the time, is widely used today and likely explains why the building remains standing, even though it has been abandoned for years. The outside is in good condition, but the interior is another matter.

Because of its location between the elevated tracks, the station is nearly hidden until a visitor is almost right

next to it. The entrance to the building faces west toward Broadway and looks out on the street with empty eyes. Not a single window remains intact; all were broken out decades ago. The only sign of the old station that is still visible is a painted notice on a pillar outside the entrance that states no parking—cabs only.

The main interior of the building is a large, open room that rises two stories to the roof, which was constructed from something less durable than the exterior walls. The steel supports have rusted away and portions have collapsed to the floor below. A dangerous-looking steel staircase at the rear of the room climbs up to a loading platform. Because the station was built into a hill, the front is two stories high, but the rear exits only from the second level. Other than this staircase, there is really not much left inside to suggest this was ever a train station—no signs, no ticket windows, no waiting benches, merely rotting debris. Aside from the ruined building and some ghost staircases to the tracks, there is not much else to see here. This is simply a memory of days long past, like old photographs that show large crowds purchasing tickets in the great room.

There are a number of plans in the works to try to put the station back into service in some way. One of the tracks near the building is designated for an ambitious project called the Midwest Rail Initiative, which would create high-speed rail service between Detroit, St. Louis, Chicago, and Indianapolis. If that works out, the station might come to life again. But plans to put the station back into operation have been floating about since it closed in the 1950s. Meanwhile, the cruel hand of time presses on, and each year a little more of the sparkle fades from what was once a grand jewel of Gary.

Union Depot, Gary, Ind.

There is just something about an empty, abandoned hotel that gives even the most hardened weird traveler a good case of the heebie-jeebies. Is it the empty rooms, sometimes still filled with dusty furniture as if waiting for their next occupant, that creep us out? Or is it the unmanned front desk, intact but eerily lacking someone on duty, that raises the hair on the back of our necks?

There is no clear answer to these questions, but one thing is certain: Indiana has more than its share of empty hotels, motels, and motor lodges. What follows is two of our favorites.

Dunes Highway Holiday Inn

Hotels were part of the childhood of many of us weird travelers. Back in the days when gas was actually affordable, many families spent two or three weeks of their summer on the American highway. We let the interstates and back roads take us to the country's national parks, amusement centers, and the offbeat and weird spots that could be found only in the United States. These family trips may be what got us hooked on weird travel in the first place.

We remember the excitement of arriving at a hotel for the night after a long day on the road. We'd get a chance to swim in the pool, eat bad burgers from the adjacent restaurant, and, if we were really lucky, talk our parents into a few quarters to use in the game room. Many traveling families spent more than their share of nights in questionable motor lodges if nothing else was available, but there was always one hotel chain that you could count on to be top-notch—Holiday Inn. The sight of that sparkling green-and-yellow sign was like spotting an oasis in the desert. You could always be sure of clean rooms, comfortable beds, and fully stocked ice machines.

In 1951, a man named Kemmons Wilson traveled from Memphis, Tennessee, to Washington, D.C. He was appalled by the conditions at many of the motor courts—parks where travelers camped overnight

in out-of-the-way places—in which he stayed, and when he arrived home, he was determined to create lodging that was simple, clean, and affordable. As Americans began their love affair with their cars, Wilson knew that standardized rooms—with a quality and layout a family could count on—were the wave of the future. A draftsman by trade, he sketched out plans for a prototype hotel and, having just watched the classic Bing Crosby movie, dubbed it Holiday Inn. An American icon was born. By 1970, there were more than 175,000 Holiday Inn rooms available throughout the land.

The motel on the east side of Gary was identical to hundreds of others in the chain. It had a large lobby

with a restaurant, scores of rooms that opened to the outside, and, of course, an outdoor swimming pool. During its heyday, this Holiday Inn was located on a busy stretch of road called the Dunes Highway, which is also U.S. Highway 12 and 30 between Gary and Portage. This was once a major road around the southern tip of Lake Michigan, but much of the traffic later switched to Interstate 65. No convenient exit from the new interstate led to the doors of the Dunes Highway Holiday Inn, and it was forced to close in the mid-1970s. It reopened as an independent motel called the Interstate Motor Inn, a place Kemmons Wilson would not have recognized. The once family-friendly haven for motorists became a seedy fleabag and was frequently visited by the local police. At least one murder occurred here, and on one occasion a teenaged girl was kidnapped. This motel also closed down, and the site was put up for auction in 1997—apparently with little success.

Today the old hotel is nearly in ruins, and portions of it have been demolished. The lobby building's front door and windows are boarded over, but most of the rest of the doors and windows are missing. The awning out front is still painted "Holiday Inn green," a fading reminder of times past.

To the right of the front doors, the boards that once covered the windows into the lounge are missing, so it's possible to see the typical interior of dark wood, tacky carpet, and overstuffed chairs moldering in the back. The liquor is long gone, but one can still picture ghostly patrons of days gone by sitting at the bar. It's not hard to imagine these same guests, perhaps coming from a wedding reception or family reunion, walking down the hallways in search of a drink or a bite to eat. The red carpeting is still on the restaurant's floor, but it is stained by rain and weather and by pieces of the ceiling that have collapsed onto it. This must have been a nice place to eat at one time—with views of the neatly trimmed courtyard and the swimming pool—but those days are long gone.

Perhaps the saddest reminders of the past are the motel rooms that can be seen through panes of missing glass and broken doors. For the most part, only the harshly colored wallpaper of the 1970s remains in the rooms. The carpets have been stripped away, and the fixtures have long since been destroyed, ravaged by time and vandals, both of which are heartless enemies.

Gary's Sheraton Hotel

The city of Gary has earned a tarnished reputation over the last few decades for its down-trodden business district, abandoned steel mills, and vanishing population. The decline began at some point in the 1960s and, on many fronts, continues today. The Sheraton Hotel on Broadway was one of the many casualties of the city's decline.

It was with high hopes that the hotel opened on December 18, 1978. It came complete with two luxury suites, a lounge, a restaurant, and meeting rooms for up to three hundred and fifty people. It was attached to a new three-hundred-car parking deck and became the centerpiece of an urban redevelopment effort that was started by Mayor Richard G. Hatcher.

Mayor Hatcher had big plans for Gary's future. Seeking to revive the city's downtown, he started a massive public building campaign, which was assisted by the federal government. The plans called for a new convention center, sports complex, and a new downtown hotel.

The grand opening of the hotel was an exciting event. A live band called the Independent Movement was the first entertainment in the Visions Lounge, a disco lounge typical of the era, with mirrors, colored lights, and a throbbing sound system. The hotel hosted the Twelve Days of Sheraton, during which the Gazebo Restaurant added a new entrée to the menu each day. The staff cleaned and prepared for the throngs of guests who never seemed to arrive.

With little to do in downtown Gary, few tourists checked in. The new Genesis Convention Center, which was intended to be connected directly to the hotel, was delayed and then drastically reduced in size.

And most of the locals couldn't afford to put up their visiting relatives in a fancy hotel. Even traffic from the expressways didn't help. The Indiana Toll Road that passed on the north side of the hotel was lightly traveled compared to the Borman Expressway, with no tollbooths, that ran miles away to the south.

Without any sort of economic base to support it, the hotel was plunged into bankruptcy. The city took over the Sheraton's utility bills to keep it open for a few more years, but by 1983 Gary could no longer pay its own bills and had to lay off four hundred city workers. There is no record of when the Sheraton finally closed down. Most accounts say 1984 or 1985, but it's possible that it was months before that, when the city stopped paying the hotel's bills. The Sheraton Hotel was left standing—silent and eerily empty.

A briefly hopeful moment occurred when Donald Trump brought the Miss USA pageant to Gary's Genesis Convention Center for three years, but that went nowhere. Guests of the pageant, including host William Shatner, stayed at Trump's new casino hotel on Lake Michigan's shoreline, not at the Sheraton. And so the old place was forgotten once again. Over the years, rumors have circulated about its reopening as part of some chain or another, but for now its fate remains to be seen.

Madison's Forgotten Army Airfield

There is nothing quite like stumbling onto an abandoned site that, under past circumstances, you would never have been allowed to enter. The old army airfield near Madison is just such a place.

This abandoned military airfield is located on the land that was once part of the Jefferson Proving Ground, 55,000 acres devoted to the testing of bombs and munitions. The land was acquired in 1940, just before World War II, and the manner in which it was obtained was quite controversial at the time. Taken from sections of Jefferson, Ripley, and Jennings counties, it was land used mostly for small family farms, with a few woodlands dotted around it. When the government showed up and claimed the area, the families were forced to move. Several small communities were condemned, and about five hundred families were relocated to other areas. Many of them protested, but in the end the government got its way, leading to some very hard feelings.

Once the proving ground was in operation, the military tested all manner of bombs, bullets, and explosives there. It was set up with a firing line that ran east–west across the entire property near the southern end of the facility. Constructed along this line were permanent positions for firing ordnance to the northern sector, which was the impact area and was fitted out with various targets and ranges. Support buildings were located to the south of the firing line. The army also tested chemical weapons at the Jefferson Proving Ground, and a five-

thousand-foot-long runway was constructed so that large bombers could test airborne bombs and ordnance.

In 1988, the Base Realignment and Closure Commission recommended that this site be closed. Testing of munitions continued through the Gulf War in 1991, but eventually the death knell sounded for the proving ground. The last rounds were fired in September 1994, and the Jefferson Proving Ground was closed down one year later. Since that time, it has sat abandoned in the landscape of southern Indiana.

Today the proving ground and the abandoned army airfield are being offered for redevelopment. Still scattered about the base are pieces of forgotten aircraft, tank turrets that were used as targets, and old buildings, including a dilapidated hangar that bears the ghostly lettering MADISON FLYING SERVICE. This is a fascinating place, albeit a spooky one.

Lights Out: The Marble Hill Nuclear Power Plant

It was one of the greatest fiascoes in Indiana's business history—more than $2 billion spent on a project that never made it more than one quarter of the way to completion. Thanks to skyrocketing costs and tremendous waste, the Marble Hill Nuclear Power Plant is now a rusting hulk that nearly sent Public Service Indiana into bankruptcy. Somehow, this "vision of tomorrow" turned into a disaster of epic proportions.

The early 1970s marked the beginning of the nuclear power movement in America. This clean, wonderful power was supposed to save the environment from the pollution caused by the coal-burning power plants of the past. True, it had some dangers, including the waste material that it created. In spite of this, new plants began to be proposed around the country, including in Indiana.

In 1973, Public Service Indiana, which is now owned by Cinergy, planned a nuclear power generating plant at Marble Hill. Located in the southeastern part of the state, the $700 million plant was to be the largest capital project in Indiana history. The plant's design was to include twin Westinghouse reactors, which were supposed to be environmentally friendly, creating no hazardous emissions.

No matter what the claims of the company, though, there were numerous opponents to the project. Their complaints grew louder when the estimated construction costs rose to $1.4 billion in September 1977. Despite the controversy, construction on the plant began in the

fall of 1977, with an estimated completion date of 1982. The work was already under way when the disaster at the Three Mile Island nuclear power plant in Pennsylvania occurred in March 1979. The incident created even more opposition to nuclear plants as critics learned that entire systems could fail and create immense pressure inside the containment structures. After three days, the danger at Three Mile Island passed, but only after contaminating the nearby land and waterways.

Nevertheless, construction continued at Marble Hill, but only for a time. In May 1979, work ground to a halt when some alarming reports came from the project. Charles Cutshall, a former employee of Marble Hill's general contractor, Gust K. Newburg, filed an affidavit that stated that he and other Newburg employees were told to cover up construction defects before inspectors saw them. The defects were mainly in the concrete walls. Later inspection revealed honeycombs in the walls that were the result of shoddy work. It was later stated that if radioactive gas had breached the containment structure, as at Three Mile Island, residents within a thirty-mile radius of the Marble Hill plant would have been affected. Work was shut down on three separate occasions during the summer of 1979 to correct the growing number of conditions reported about poor construction.

In addition to the defects, costs had risen so drastically that the companies in charge of the project could not find the funds to continue the work. The Marble Hill plant was officially shut down in 1984 when Governor Robert Orr stated that its completion would bankrupt Public Service Indiana and cause huge increases in its customers' rates. Though over $2.8 billion had been spent, only a fraction of the plant had been completed when it was abandoned.

Most of the components, like the reactors and generators, were salvaged and sold to other companies for discounted prices, and in 2005 the turbine building was demolished. It took two blasts to bring the massive structure down. Perhaps because of the cost involved in demolition, the rest of the plant was left standing. Today two containment buildings remain at the overgrown site, telling a strange story of the nuclear plant that never happened.

Last Days of the Y&W Drive-In—Merrillville

The 1930s saw the development of a brand-new form of moviegoing, the drive-in theater. At first, the experience was purely a novelty, fueled not only by a love for the movies but also by the budding American romance with the automobile. After World War II, that romance really flowered, and by 1950 more than 1,700 drive-in screens could be found alongside America's streets and roadways.

In an environment where almost every town had at least one drive-in theater, competition was fierce and the operators vied to one-up their rivals. Concession stands gave way to roving bands of carhops, who sold hot dogs, popcorn, and drinks. Playgrounds opened for the kids, which led to miniature golf courses and carnival rides, turning many drive-ins into entertainment complexes. In Indiana, the

number of drive-in theaters swelled to more than 120 by 1958, more than one for every county.

But the drive-in theater experience had a relatively short life span. By the mid-1970s, America's fascination with watching movies under the stars began to fade. Families started to stay home and watch television in comfort rather than in the confines of their cars, and teenagers found other places to park and pet. The drive-in theaters began to vanish, although a few of them hung around for many years.

The Y&W Drive-In was one of the hangers-on. The now abandoned site rests on a busy stretch of South Broadway in the middle of Merrillville. This city, along with its next-door neighbor of Hobart, became a destination spot for those fleeing Gary in the middle 1960s and grew into a sprawling and prosperous suburb. The Y&W Drive-In became a nice place for northwest Indiana families to spend a summer evening.

The theater stayed popular for longer than most

drive-ins, not closing until 1998. It remains in fairly good shape today and is not secured in any way, meaning that someone can drive right off Broadway, past the vintage ticket booth, and into one of the three screen areas.

Theater 1, or Y&W 1 as it was known, was the largest of the venues. It had the concession stand and a playground area, of which there are a few remnants. Theater 3 is in the worst state of disrepair. The weeds here are higher, and most of the white paint has peeled away from the screen, indicating that the owners probably shuttered it first and continued to use only the other two screens.

Perhaps the greatest piece of roadside culture connected to the Y&W was its sign. There was no way that you could miss this monster when it was lit up at night. For years after the drive-in closed, it seemed to defy both time and the elements, remaining in great condition. It was finally sold and taken down in 2002, bringing an end to the era of the Y&W Drive-In.

Pendleton Pike Drive-In

Another Indiana drive-in that now sits as a lonely, silent testament to the grand days of cheap family entertainment is the Pendleton Pike Drive-In. It was known simply as the Drive-In Theatre when it opened in the 1940s, and advertisements proudly announced that patrons would have the unique opportunity to "see and hear movies while sitting in your car!"

Over time, as more people began flocking to the drive-in, the property expanded. At its height, the theater, which had since been renamed Pendleton Pike Drive-In Land, could fit close to one thousand cars full of film-loving families in its lot. But that's not all. With ninety-three acres of property, there was room for all sorts of other fun stuff, including a kiddie park, rides and attractions, and even a mini roller coaster. During the 1960s, a local AM radio station hosted Battle of the Bands contests at the drive-in all summer long.

As the theater entered the 1970s, its very existence was threatened by something that experts say happens only every five hundred years. The event, known as the Super Outbreak, stands as the largest tornado activity on record. During a twenty-four-hour period from April 3 through April 4, 1974, there was a grand total of 148 confirmed tornados across thirteen American states and one Canadian province. Indiana was one of the states hit hardest, with massive damage reported all around the Pendleton Pike area. Miraculously, the drive-in escaped with only minor damage and was up and running almost as soon as the storms passed.

But while the Pendleton could withstand Mother Nature, the one thing it couldn't compete with was progress. Try as it might, the Pendleton couldn't keep up with such things as television and multiplexes, and the giant screen went dark for good in 1993.

Today all the rides and attractions that once brought people by the hundreds to the drive-in every night are gone. The only thing remaining is the crumbling screen. The property is for sale, but there's not much interest in it. Back in 2000, developer Paul Estridge submitted a proposal to build a $25 million "Indianapolis Downs" racetrack there. However, that proposal was rejected by the Indiana Horse Racing Commission, and no new plans are in the works. Meanwhile, the Pendleton Pike Drive-In screen stands, keeping a silent watch over a weed-choked field while it waits to hear its fate.

Miniature Town of Littleville

If there is one word that describes the experiences of those lucky enough to have visited the former town of Littleville, it would have to be "magical." Today almost nothing remains of the little town within Chesterton that William Murray created in the 1930s, but there is no forgetting the wonderful qualities of the place. During Littleville's heyday, there was nothing else like it in Indiana — or the rest of the country, for that matter.

These days Littleville exists only in the Chesterton historic records, in the memories of some of the locals, and in hard-to-find film and magazine archives. Years ago, however, it attracted well over 100,000 visitors from all over America and from as far away as Japan.

William Murray's backyard city stretched across four twenty-five-yard lots and contained more than 125 electrically wired miniature structures. Murray started building the eccentric site to occupy his time during the Great Depression, when work was slow in coming. He

placed some of his little buildings in his garden, and others he sold to make a bit of extra money. A local businessman asked him to build a few houses as an attraction at his inn and service station, and when Murray saw how entranced people were, he decided to build his own little city.

Murray framed his buildings with wood that he took from orange crates and apple boxes, then mortared the frames with small stones. He made his own bricks and used linoleum to fashion shingles for the roofs. The houses stood from twelve to eighteen inches high, and by 1937 he had completed 80 of them. Two years later Littleville had grown to 125 tiny structures, including Littleville Bay (with a lighthouse, yacht club, and Coast Guard building), Littleville Airport, farms, an industrial area, a downtown business section with window displays, an amusement park, a stone castle, the Littleville & Southern Railway, and even a sewage treatment plant.

Murray's son-in-law Harry Koch pitched in to help with the construction and spent more than three hundred hours building a replica of Chesterton's Bethlehem Lutheran Church, which came complete with a tower that played music twice a day. He also helped to wire Littleville with electricity so that lights twinkled on street corners and could be seen shining in the barbershop, post office, grocery store, hardware store, paint shop, movie theater, and in the many homes that lined the streets.

Murray charged a nickel admission to see his tiny town and operated a gift shop on the

LITTLEVILLE, A MINIATURE TOWN, CHESTERTON, IND.

premises where visitors could buy postcards, calendars, and miniature houses. But he never planned to get rich from his hobby. Instead, he used the money to build and expand.

Littleville closed when America entered World War II, because emergencies created by the war, especially the rubber shortage, made it impossible to keep up. It became a miniature ghost town; the buildings were either destroyed or ended up in private homes. Murray eventually moved away, and the land where the town had rested was sold off and divided up to make room for normal-sized homes. Although he continued his hobby for many years in his new home, the houses that he built were never really put on display. He later passed away during a visit to Iowa, bringing a very special era in Indiana history to an end.

Needmore Pyramid

Over the years, some of the most famous buildings in the United States were built of Indiana limestone, including the Pentagon, the Empire State Building, and even thirty-five of the United States capitol buildings. A lot of that limestone came from Lawrence County, and by the time the 1970s rolled around, the county wanted some acknowledgment of that achievement. It regarded itself as the limestone capital of the world and wanted the world to know it.

Merle Edington, then president of the Bedford Chamber of Commerce, had just the way to publicize Lawrence County's limestone. His idea: create a limestone-themed amusement park. But this was to be no ordinary limestone-themed amusement park. Initial plans called for the creation of a one-fifth-scale replica of the Great Pyramid of Cheops and a 650-foot-long version of the Great Wall of China, both made of limestone.

So who do you turn to when you're strapped for cash but you want to build a limestone pyramid? Well, you could ask for donations. But if you really want to get your hands on some cash, you ask your rich uncle: Sam.

Edington wrote a letter to the U.S. government and was rewarded with somewhere in the neighborhood of $200,000 in federal funding to begin the project.

After scouting out several locations, a large section of land in Needmore was chosen, since the property conveniently backed up to a limestone quarry. First in line to be created was the replica of the Great Pyramid. A limestone foundation was laid, and while that was taking place, work began on designing the Great Wall of China. Also planned were restrooms, a souvenir shop, and several other buildings. The entranceway to the park would be flanked with pillars, topped with mini limestone pyramids, and a large welcome sign in limestone was built at the entrance to the park from which a NOW OPEN message was to be hung . . . but it never happened.

Why? Well, if there was one thing that could get Wisconsin Senator William Proxmire up in arms it was to see taxpayers' money being wasted. So in 1975, the Senator created his Golden Fleece award—one nobody wanted to receive. That's because Proxmire bestowed his monthly award to people whose practices represented, in his words, a "wasteful, ridiculous or ironic use of the taxpayers' money."

By the summer 1981, things were still moving slowly at the theme park. While some of the outbuildings, such as the restrooms and exhibit building, had been completed, only the base of the Great Pyramid had been built. It was right around this time that Senator Proxmire was made aware of the federal funding that had been provided to the park. And he wasn't happy about it.

So in September of 1981, Proxmire officially awarded the Economic Development Administration of the Commerce Department his Golden Fleece award for "spending $200,000 to build an 800-foot limestone replica of the Great Wall of China." The story went on the newswires and spread like wildfire across the country. Taxpayers everywhere were outraged. Needless to say, it wasn't long before the federal funding, and all funding for that matter, stopped. Shortly after that, construction stopped altogether and the project was abandoned.

It's interesting to note that Senator Proxmire issued a Golden Fleece Award every month between March 1975 and December 1988. Of the more than one hundred and sixty recipients of the award, the limestone venture ranks as number two on his all-time list, second only to millions of dollars being spent in 1975 on a study to determine, among other things, if drunken fish are more aggressive than sober fish.

Even though it's been over twenty years, there is a lot of the park left. The entrance is still flanked by two pillars topped with pyramids, although the pyramids themselves have seen better days. To the right of the main entrance, the limestone welcome sign still stands, its blank face staring back at you.

If you continue up the path beyond the entrance, eventually you will come to the remains of the base of the Great Pyramid of Cheops, slowly being enveloped by weeds. Behind the pyramid base are the restrooms and several other buildings, all of which have long since been gutted. All along the path are piles of limestone blocks. Whether or not these blocks were for building the Great Wall or something else is unclear. But one thing is certain: They aren't going anywhere soon.

As you head back down the path and leave the park, you'll notice there is a cemetery on your right. Inside the gate are hundreds of limestone gravestones, all for families who lived and died in the area. At that point, it might occur to you that you've just visited another cemetery, filled with the fading memories of one local man's dream.

INDEX

Page numbers in **bold** refer to photos and illustrations.

PICTURE CREDITS

All photos by the authors or public domain except as listed below:

Page 2 top right and lower right, **3** top left © Ryan Doan, lower left *Chicago Daily News* negatives collection, Chicago Historical Society (Library of Congress, Prints and Photographs Division); **7** © Dan Walworth; **8** © Abigail Wilkins; **9** left © Stephanie Willis, right © Haven Taylor; **10** left © John Springer Collection/CORBIS, right © Bettmann/CORBIS; **11** top and bottom © Ryan Doan, middle *Chicago Daily News* negatives collection, Chicago Historical Society (Library of Congress, Prints and Photographs Division); **12** © Timothy A. DeVore; **15** © Ryan Doan; **17** © iStockphoto.com/Katherine Garrenson; **19** © *Journal and Courier*/courtesy of Kris Baker, **20** © Ryan Doan; **22** left © Swim Ink 2, LLC/CORBIS; **24** *Chicago Daily News* negatives collection, Chicago Historical Society (Library of Congress, Prints and Photographs Division); **25** © Ryan Doan; **27** top © John Springer Collection/CORBIS, bottom © Bettmann/CORBIS; **28** © John Springer Collection/CORBIS; **31** © iStockphoto.com/Tim Fast; **33** © Ryan Doan; **34, 35** © Kimberly Patterson; **36–37**, **39, 45, 47** © Ryan Doan; **51** top © Craig Mayes; **52** © Ryan Doan; **54** © iStockphoto.com/Stefan Hermans; **55** right, **56** © CORBIS; **57, 61** © Craig Mayes; **62** © Rebeka Pavlovic; **63, 65** © Bettmann/CORBIS; **66** courtesy Holiday World; **68** © Franck Fotos/Alamy; **70, 71, 72–73** © Ryan Doan; **76** © Robert F. Kuhn/Museum of American Illustration at the Society of Illustrators; **78, 80, 82, 85, 86, 89** © Ryan Doan; **90** top © Roger Ressmeyer/CORBIS, bottom gettyimages/David Hume Kennerly; **91** bottom left © Bettmann/CORBIS; bottom right © *LaGrange News;* **101** © Bettmann/CORBIS; **102** left *Chicago Daily News* negatives collection, Chicago Historical Society (Library of Congress, Prints and Photographs Division), background © iStockphoto.com/Brian Morrison; **107** © Roger Ressmeyer/CORBIS; **108, 110** © Bettmann/CORBIS; **132** © NYPL Digital Gallery; **142, 146** © Debra Jane Seltzer; **147** left © Stephanie Willis; **148** © Bettmann/CORBIS; **152** © Beth Carey; **158, 159, 161** © Ryan Doan; **163** © Shaun Burris; **164–165, 166, 168** © Ryan Doan; **170** © CORBIS; **172, 175, 176, 178–179, 180, 181** top © Ryan Doan; **181** bottom © Bettmann/CORBIS; **182** © Ryan Doan; **185** © Abigail Wilkins; **186** © Ryan Doan; **187** courtesy donnysmith/findagrave.com; **188, 190** © Ryan Doan; **191** © Abigail Wilkins; **192** © CORBIS; **193** bottom © Bettmann/CORBIS, top © Abigail Wilkins; **194, 196, 197** © Ryan Doan; **198** © Bettmann/CORBIS; **200** © iStockphoto.com/Hulton Archive; **201** © Jef Jarecki; **202** © Ryan Doan; **207, 214** © Abigail Wilkins; **218** © Larry Fulford and Jacob Landis; **221** © Abigail Wilkins; **224** top right © Lou Thole, *Forgotten Fields of America*, courtesy Paul Freeman/www.airfields-freeman.com; **225** © John McDonald/www.LostIndiana.net; **226–227** © Mike Griggs; **228** © Eric Lawrence; **230, 231** © Xander Cook; **233** top left © John McDonald/www.LostIndiana.net, top right, bottom left and right © Kim Miklusak; **234–237** © John McDonald/www.LostIndiana.net; © Lou Thole, *Forgotten Fields of America*, courtesy Paul Freeman/www.airfields-freeman.com; **239** © Sherman Cahal; **240–242** © John McDonald/www.LostIndiana.net; **245** © Charles W. Cushman Collection: Indiana University Archives; **246–247** background © NYPL Digital Gallery.

EDITORIAL CREDITS

The following stories are reprinted from the Haunted Indiana Series of books by Mark Marimen, published by Thunder Bay Press and used with permission: *The Legend of Stiffy Green, Legend of Gypsies Graveyard, Gray Lady of Willard Library, Bridge to the Hereafter, Ghostly Mother of Stepp Cemetery, Wistful Spirits of Tuckaway, Return of the Black Widow, World's Largest Ghost Hunt, Spirits of Wyandotte Cave, The Odon Fires, Gentle Spirit of Kahler School.*

WEIRD INDIANA

By

MARK MARIMEN, JAMES A. WILLIS, and TROY TAYLOR

Executive Editors
Mark Sceurman and Mark Moran

ACKNOWLEDGMENTS

MARK MARIMEN

Once again I have so many people to thank for this book. First of all, thanks to Mark Moran for offering me this great opportunity and to my friend Troy Taylor for helping set it up. Thanks to Thunder Bay Press (especially my dear little sister Julie) for allowing me to rework some of the stories from my previous books in this one. Thanks to Dr. Doug Zale, who believed I could write even before I did. Thanks to my wife, Jane, for putting up with a crazy schedule, and a special thanks to my daughter, Abigail, for accompanying me on our photo expedition and for taking most of the pictures for my section of this book. Thanks also to my evil twin, Jef Jarceki, for helping with the photography, as well as to all who gave of their advice and time. You are all such an incredible blessing!

Dedication

This book is dedicated, once again, to Jane and Abby, who make my life fulfilled. I love you more than I can ever say. It is also dedicated to my mom, Patty, for her constant support, and in memory of Wilfred Wilkins, the greatest man I have ever known. Finally, this book is dedicated to a close circle of friends who have so irrationally loved me and to the family of DUMC for all you have meant to me.

JAMES A. WILLIS

Mark and Mark, for once again letting me get in touch with my weird side; my family, for making me the odd little man that I am today; Steve and Carol, for trusting me with their daughter; Julie, who's always willing to travel anywhere with me, provided I give her regular smoke breaks; Janine, Sam, Wendy, Mark, and Roger for joining me on my weird journeys; everyone at The Ghosts of Ohio; my friends, who knew I was weird from the beginning and hung out with me simply for that reason; Big Joe Palermo, for teaching me that life is short, so I had better enjoy every tomato; Ernie, Maddy, Bailey, and Khashoggi, for never letting me forget who's really in charge; Kris and Mike Baker, for guillotine pictures and for forming the James A. Willis Fan Club; Cocomo D. Squirrel, for being one of the best shotgun riders around; and last but not least, a special thank-you to all my fans who have used their smiles, handshakes, and encouraging words to let me know that I'm doing something right. You guys mean more to me than you'll ever know.

Dedication

This book is dedicated to Stephanie, without whose unending love and support these pages, and my life, would be empty.

TROY TAYLOR

This is never a solitary journey, and there are many for me to thank along the way for providing information, stories, and reports. These individuals, writers, researchers, storytellers, and general weirdos include Mark and Mark from *Weird N.J.*; my friends and fellow writers Mark Marimen and Jim Willis; Paula McHugh; Dick Wolfsie; Michael Newton; Wanda Lou Willis; Fred Cavinder; Jerome Pohlen; John McDonald; my wife, Haven; and of course, the dozens of people who provided the great information, weird sites, strange stories, and local legends. It's been another weird trip and one that never seems to end!

MARK MORAN

graduated from Parsons School of Design in New York City, where he studied fine art, illustration, and photography. It was a boring and misspent suburban New Jersey childhood that first led him to his lifelong fascination with seeking out and exploring the lost history and forgotten landmarks of his surroundings. Eventually he would endeavor to share what he had found with others through his pictures and stories.

These days he lives with his wife, Barbara, and their two daughters in a boring suburban New Jersey neighborhood (when he is not out tracking down satanic albino cannibals).

MARK SCEURMAN

is known as a graphic artist, publisher, and all-around nice guy. His journey to discover the weirder aspects of local history and legends began many years ago when his brother told him tales of Albino Village, where "they come out at night to get you!" Since then the roads less traveled have been the only paths he chooses to take.

He has an affection for rock and roll, draft beer, and collecting odd stories from newspapers. He resides in New Jersey (which he calls the weirdest state) with his wife, Shirley, and their daughter.

SHOW US YOUR WEIRD!

Do you know of a weird site found somewhere in the United States, or can you tell us about a strange experience you've had? If so, we'd like to hear about it! We believe that every town has at least one great tale to tell, and we're listening. It could be a cursed road, haunted abandoned site, odd local character, or bizarre historic event. In most cases these tales are told only in the towns in which they originated. But why keep them to yourself when you could share them with all of America? So come on and fill us in on all the weirdness that's lurking in your backyard!

You can e-mail us at: Editor@WeirdUS.com,
or write to us at:
Weird U.S., P.O. Box 1346, Bloomfield, NJ 07003.

www.weirdus.com